Elephants and donkeys grow big ears

THE
GUITAR
CHORD
BOOK

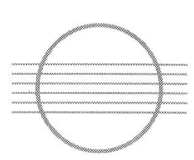

PAURIC MATHER

First Edition - 2016

Revised Editions - 2018 - 2020

Copyright © Pauric Mather - All Rights Reserved.

No part of this publication may be reproduced in any form or by any means graphic, electronic, or mechanical, including photocopying, recording, taping, or information storage and retrieval systems - without the prior written permission of the author.

ISBN-13: 978-1546637295

ISBN-10: 154663729X

Layout & Design

Hammad Khalid - Malaysia - HMDGFX.COM

Photography

Emma Curtin - Ireland

Translation

Florica Dohan - Ireland

Marco Chu - Australia

Carlos Reyes - Mexico

Andrea Santucci - Italy

Michel Schneider - Germany

Jean-Michel GEORGE - France

Joana Peixoto Meneses - Portugal

THE ONLY CHORD BOOK YOU NEED

YOU WILL LEARN

- HOW TO READ CHORD BOXES
- HOW TO POSITION YOUR CHORD HAND
- OPEN CHORDS
- BARRE CHORDS
- COLOUR CHORDS

AND MUCH MORE!

CONTENTS

How To Read Chord Boxes   6

How To Position Your Chord Hand   8

100 Most Played Guitar Chords   11

A

A	12 - 13
Am	14
A/E	15
Asus2	16 - 17
Asus4	18
A9sus4	19
A7	20
A7sus4	21 - 23
Amaj7	24 - 25
Am7	26
Am7/G	27

B

Bb	28
Bbm	29
Bb5	30
B5	31
B	32 - 33
Bm	34 - 35
Bsus2	36
Bsus4	37
B7	38 - 39
Bm7	40
Bmaj7	41
Bm11	42
B/E	43

C

C	44 - 45
Csus4	46
C5	47
C7	48
Cm7	49
Cmaj7	50 - 51
Cadd9	52 - 53
C/B	54
C/G	55
C/E	56 - 57
C#m	58 - 59
C#5	60
C#m7	61

D

D	(62)
Dm	63
D/B	64
D/C	65
Dsus2	66 - 67
Dsus4	68
D5	69
D6	70
D6/9	71
D7	72 - 73
Dm7	74 - 75
Dmaj7	76
Dmaj9	77
D/E	78

E

E	(79)
Em	80 - 81
Esus4	82
E7sus4	83
E5	84
Emaj7	85
E7	86 - 87
Em7	88 - 89
Em/G	90
Em11	91

F

F	(92 - 94)
Fm	95
Fsus2	96
F5	97
F6	98
Fm7	99
Fmaj7	100 - 102
F#	103
F#m	104 - 105
F#m7	106 - 107
F#7	108

G

G	(109 - 111)
Gm	112
G/F#	113
G/B	114
G/C	115
Gsus4	116
G5	117
G6	118
G7	119
Gmaj7	120 - 122
Gm7	123
G/D7	124
G/A	125
Gadd9	126
G#	127

HOW TO READ CHORD BOXES

Chord boxes are hugely helpful if you're an experienced guitarist. But because they only show you the front of the guitar neck, They do not work for most beginners.

However, if you're a beginner the secret is to combine *"The 3 Step Approach"* (Page 9) with the chord box.

Now they're much easier to follow - and save you time.

- **T** — Thumb
- **1** — 1st Finger
- **2** — 2nd Finger
- **3** — 3rd Finger
- **4** — 4th Finger

THE GUITAR CHORD BOOK | 7

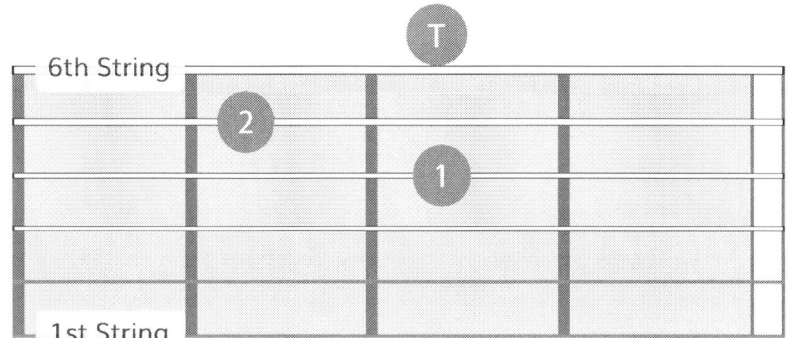

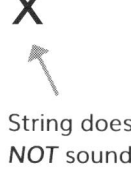

String does *NOT* sound

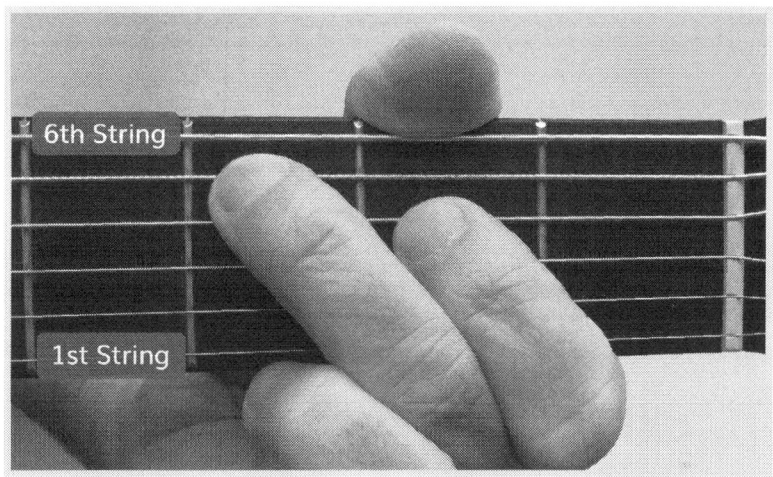

OR

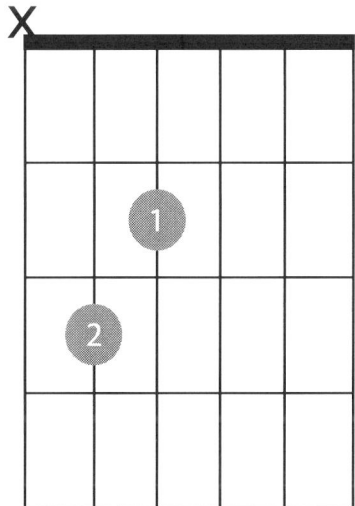
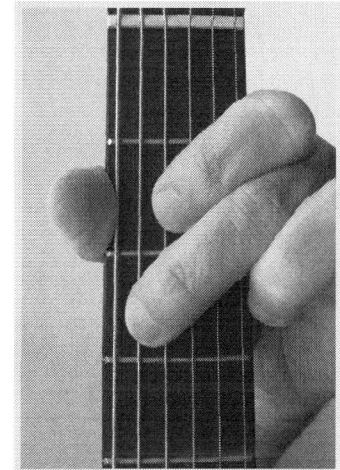

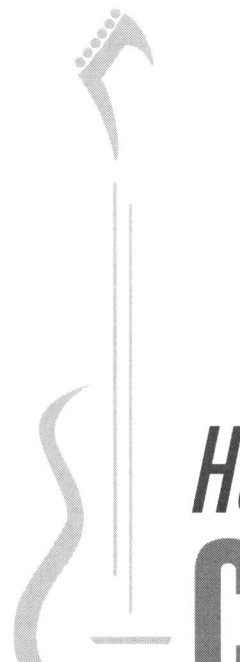

HOW TO POSITION YOUR CHORD HAND

Here is the simplest and best way to position your chord hand every time:

1 Tilt your guitar

2 Position your thumb

3 Then position your fingers

This simple approach makes it much easier to learn guitar chords.

And it's easier to speed up your chord changing too, which is the great secret of playing guitar.

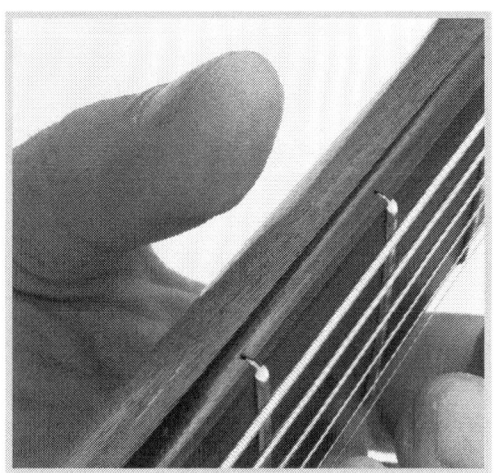

Thumb first - Then fingers

TILT YOUR GUITAR

Tilting makes learning chords so much easier. The guitar is now doing some of the work for you. It also helps to produce a good sound.

POSITION YOUR THUMB

1. Thumb on top for open chords
2. Thumb low and centred for barre chords

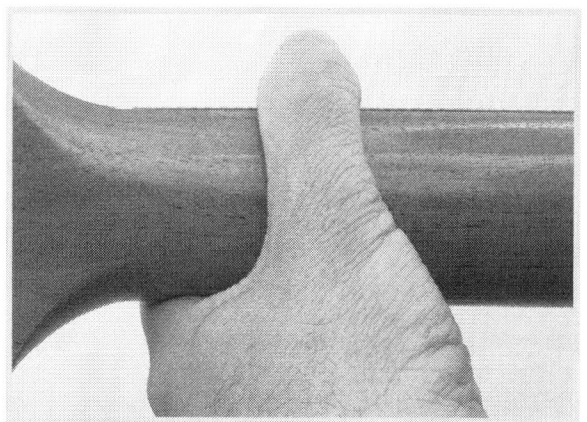

POSITION YOUR FINGERS

The simple 3 step approach here is technically perfect and exactly as played by top guitarists.

It can help you achieve in weeks, what many people took years to learn.

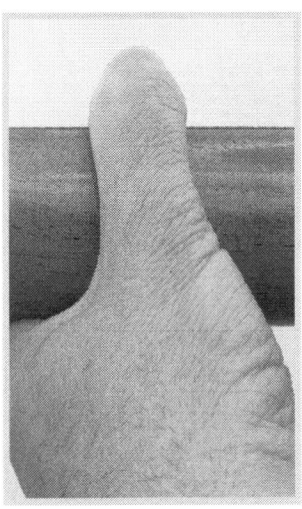 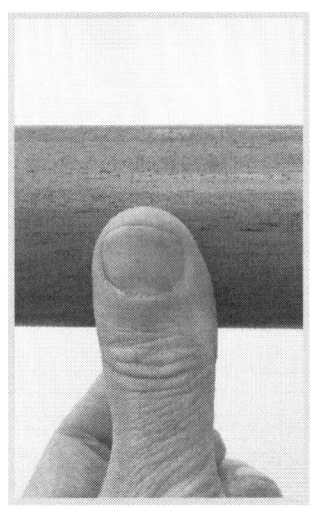 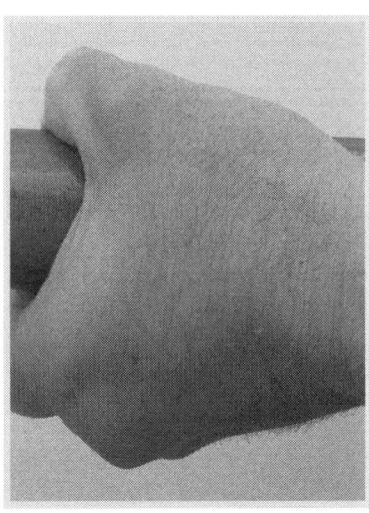

Open chords
Thumb on top

Barre chords
Thumb low and centred

Other chords
Grab the guitar neck

THE SECRET

Here is one of the great secrets of playing guitar. In fact without it, nothing is possible.

If you watch any great guitarist, in any style of music, anywhere in the world you'll see *"The Guitar Triangle"*.

- Makes room for fingers to move
- Lets you play with your fingertips
- Prevents knuckles from collapsing
- Makes chord changing easier

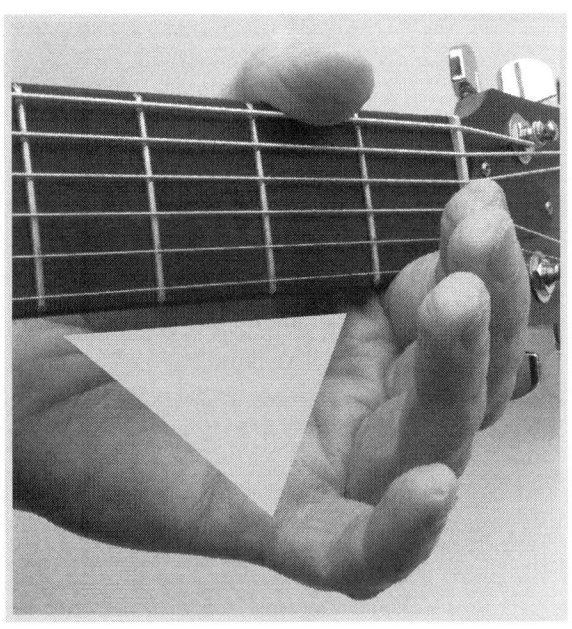

Open chords

100 MOST PLAYED

GUITAR CHORDS

A

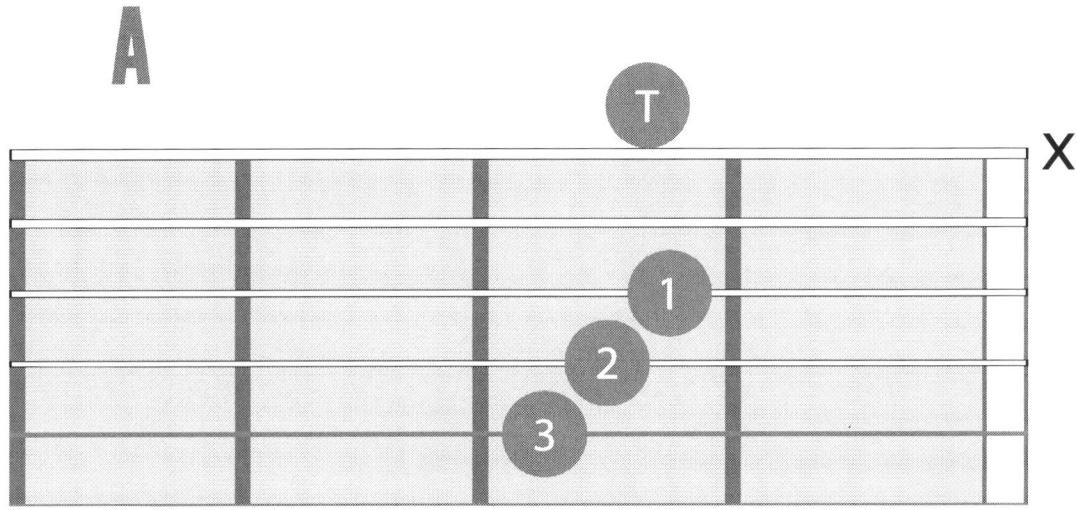

- Thumb touches 6th string
- Squeeze 3 fingers together
- Strum 6 strings - Only 5 sound

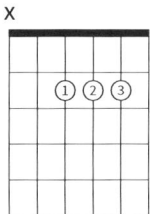

A ANOTHER WAY

4TH FRET

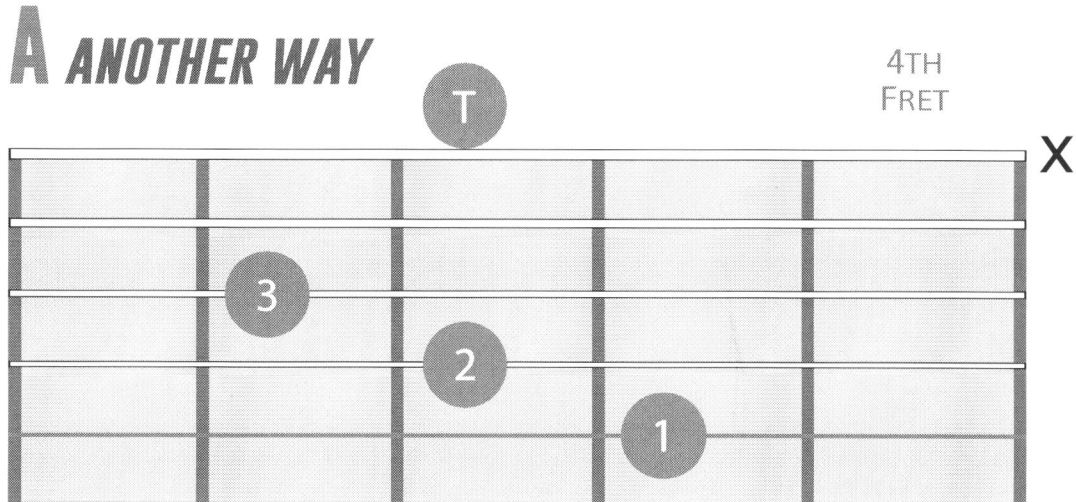

- Thumb touches 6th string
- 1st finger in corner of fret
- Strum 6 strings - Only 5 sound

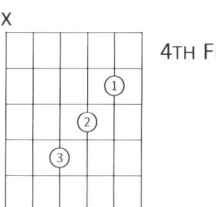

4TH FRET

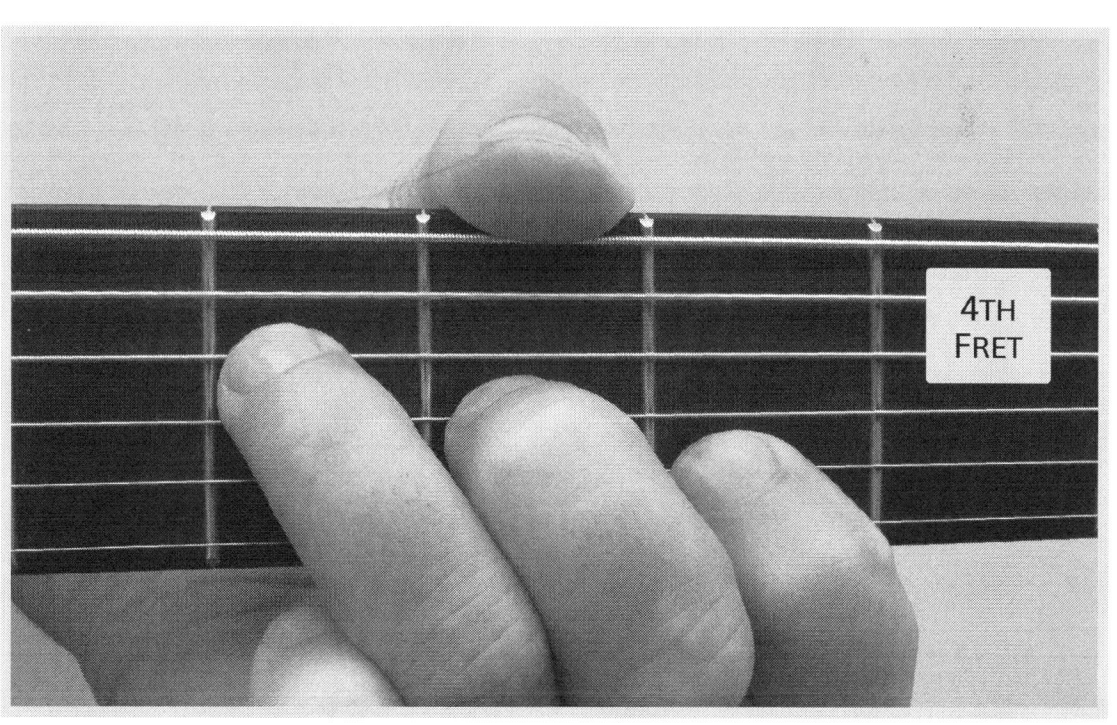

A_M

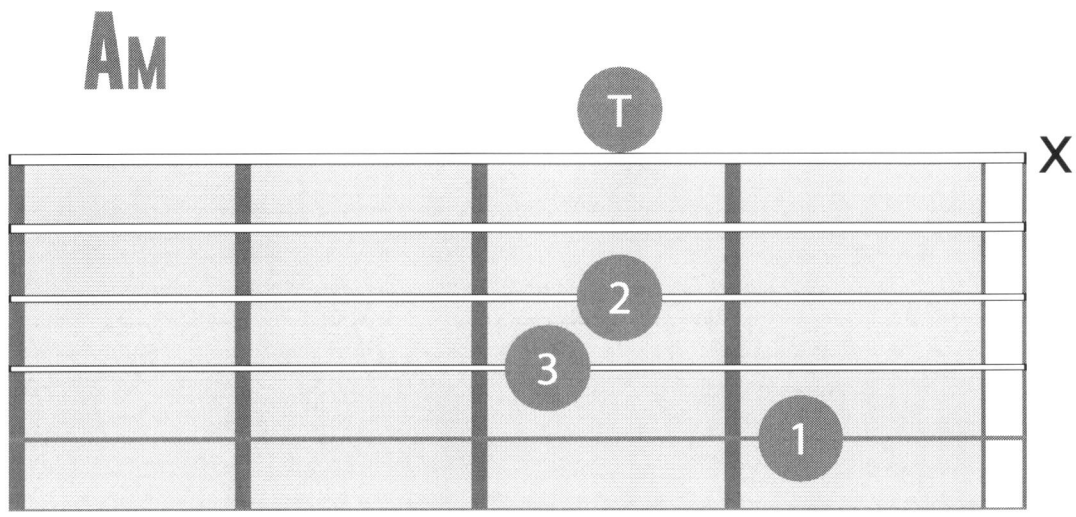

- Thumb touching 6th string
- 1st finger in corner of fret
- Strum 6 strings - Only 5 sound

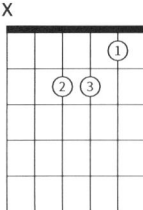

A/E

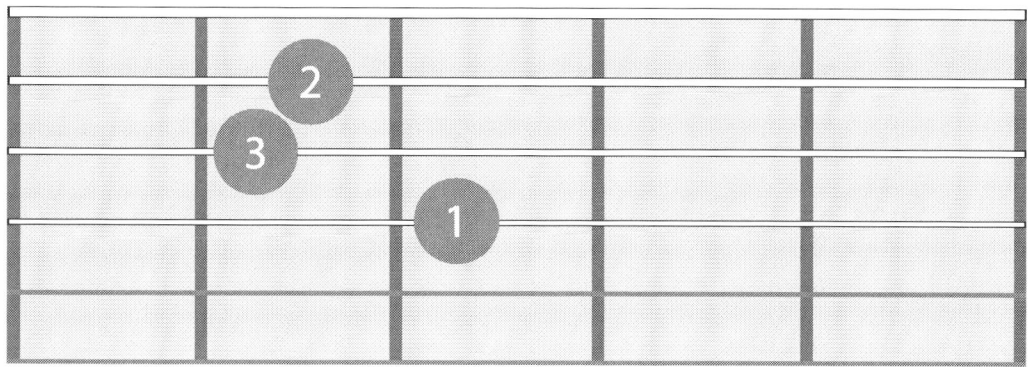

5TH FRET

- Sometimes played instead of A
- Thumb not touching 6th string
- All 6 strings sound

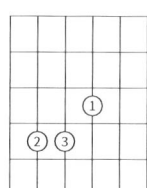

5TH FRET

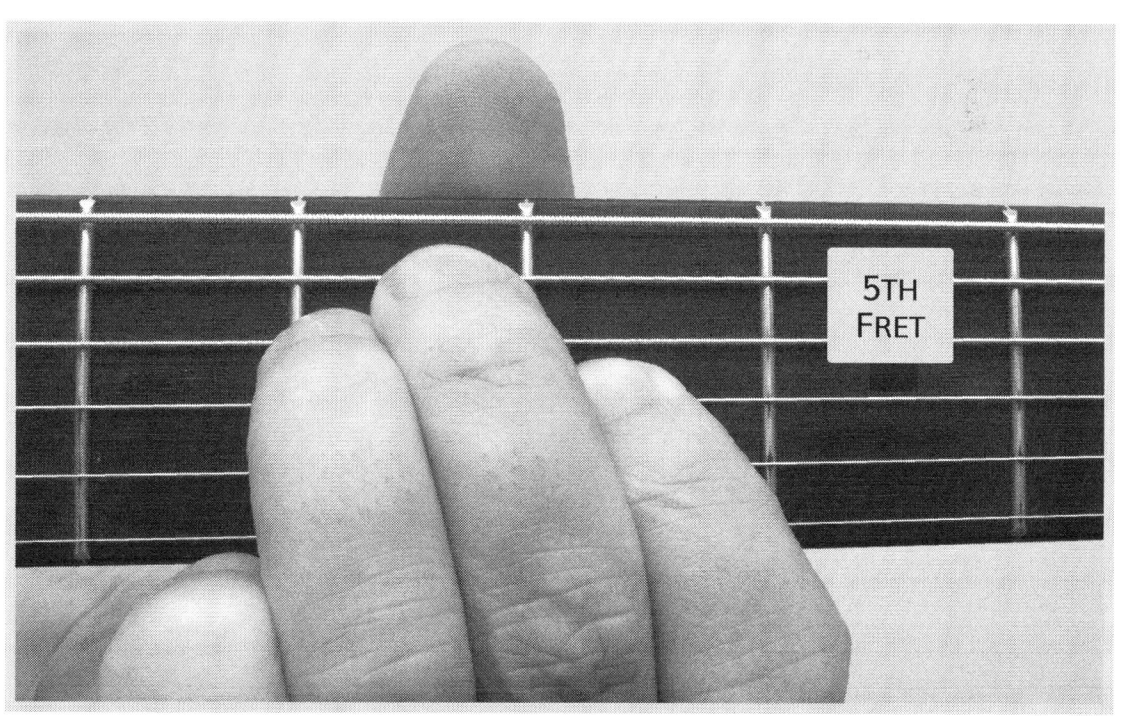

Asus2

- Thumb touching 6th string
- Can also played with 2nd & 3rd finger
- Strum 6 strings - Only 5 sound

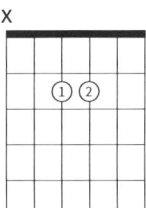

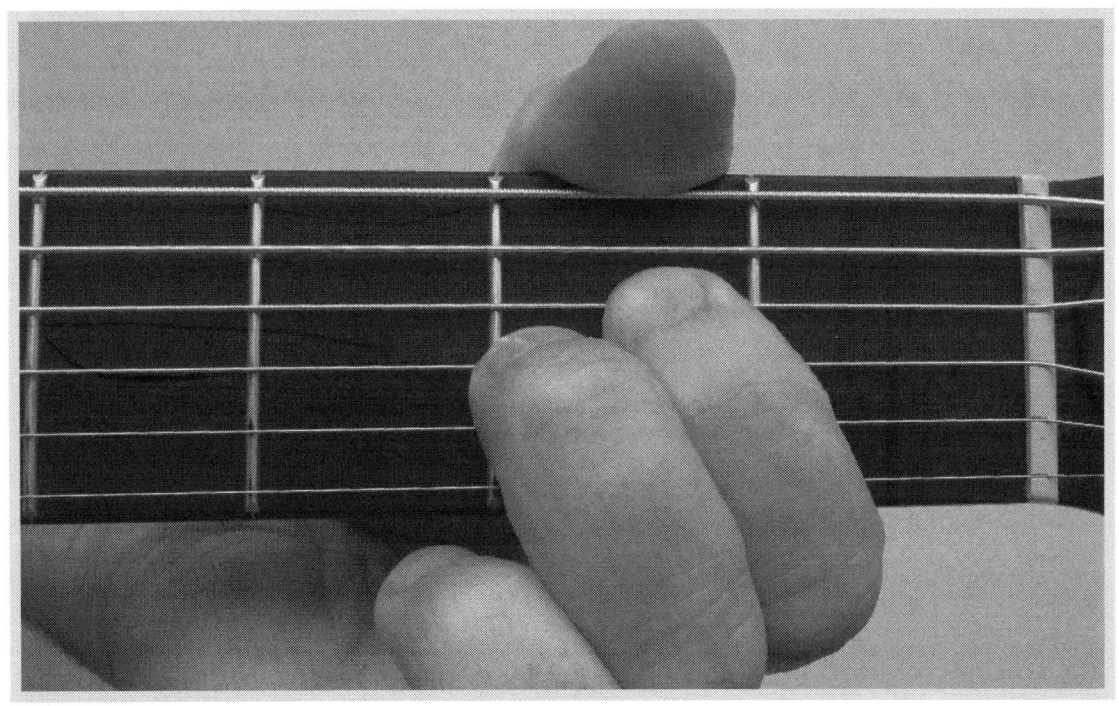

Asus2 ANOTHER WAY

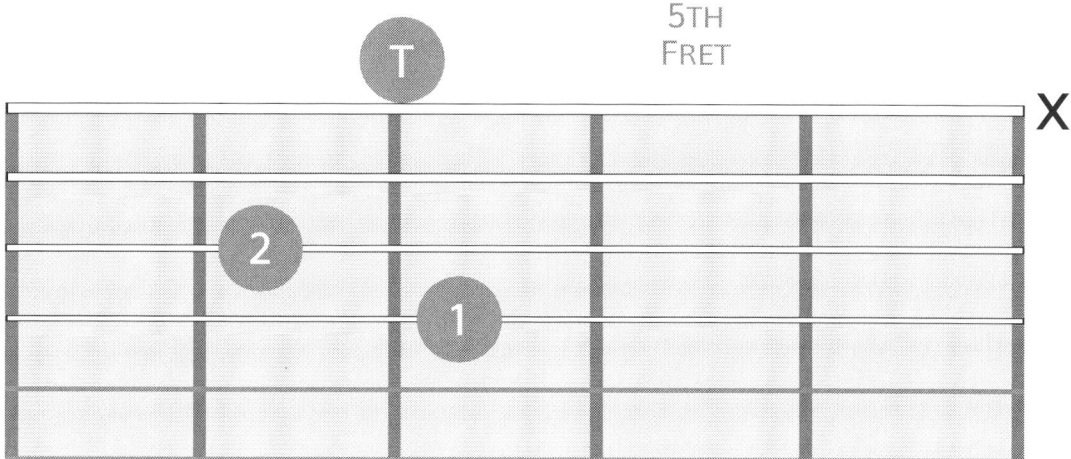

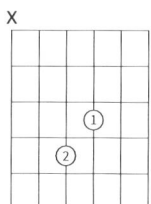

- Sometimes played instead of A
- Can also be played with 2nd and 3rd finger
- Strum 6 strings - Only 5 sound

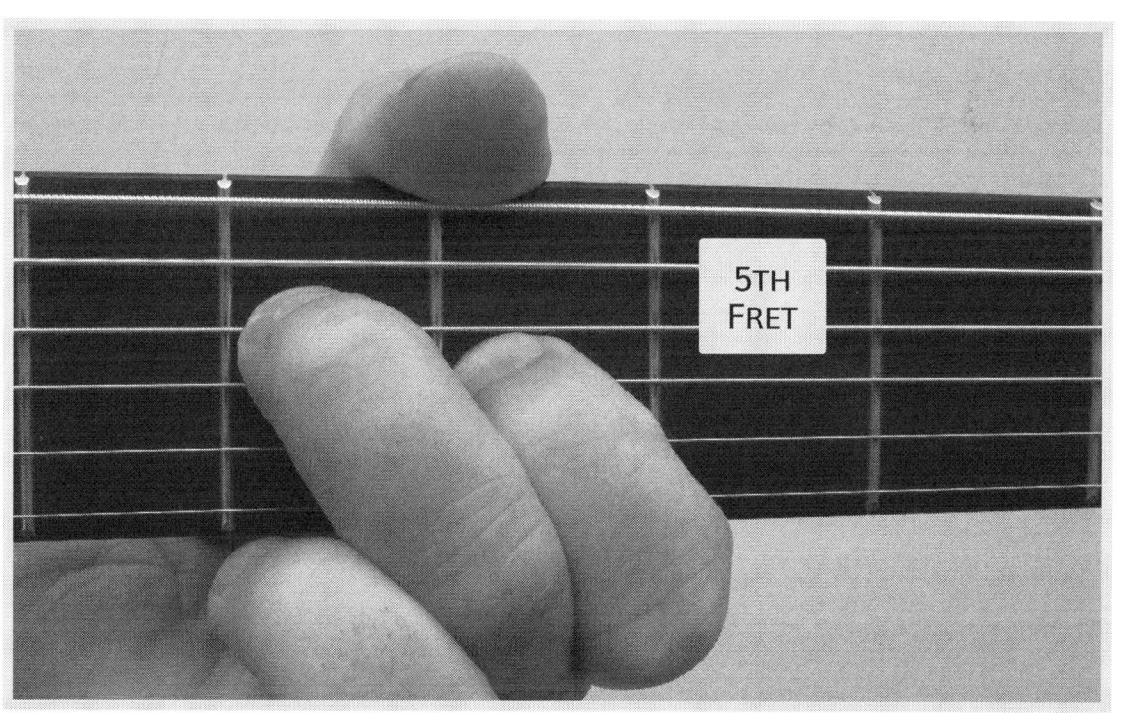

Asus4

- Thumb touching 6th string
- 3rd finger in middle of fret
- Strum 6 strings - Only 5 sound

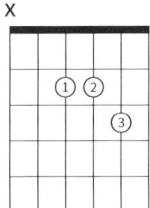

A9 sus4

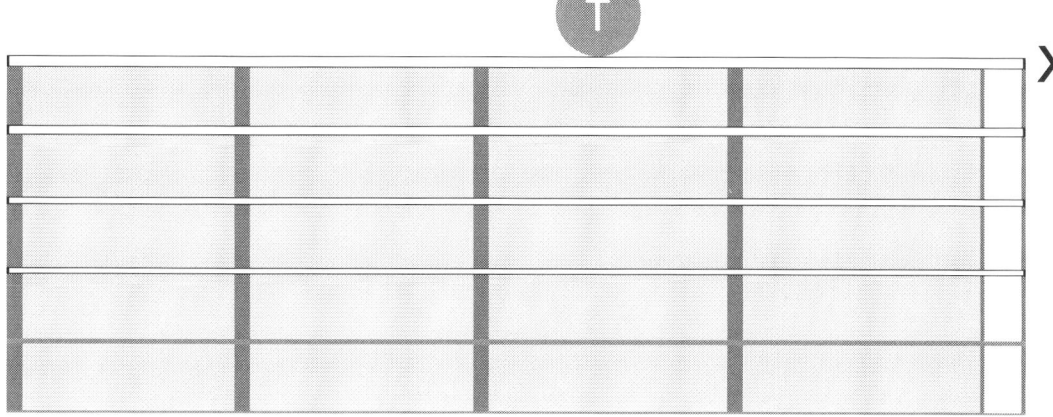

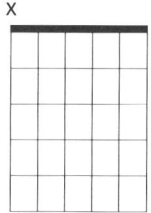

- Thumb touching 6th string
- Strum 6 strings
- Only 5 sound

A7

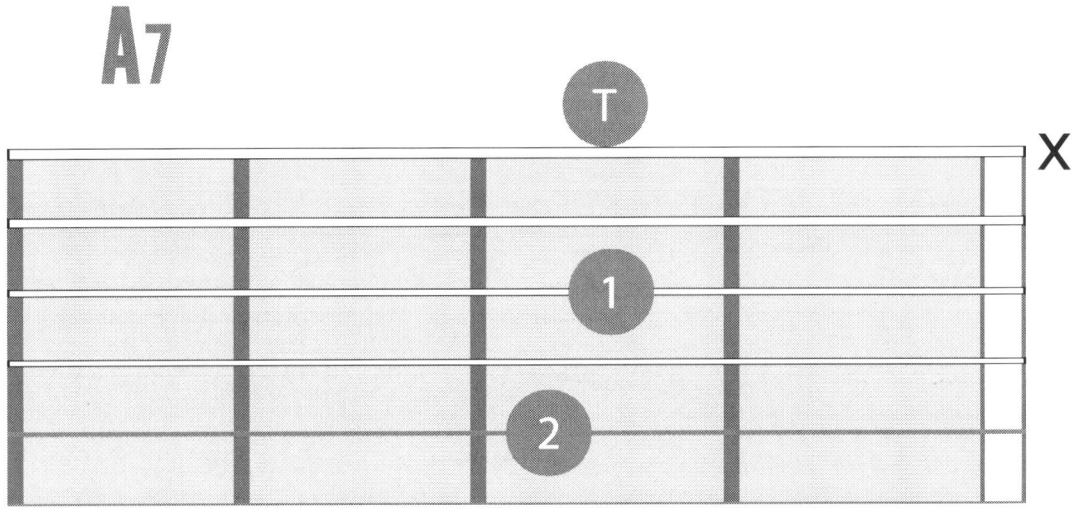

- Thumb touching 6th string
- Can also be played with 1st & 3rd finger
- Strum 6 strings - Only 5 sound

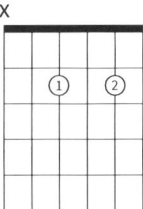

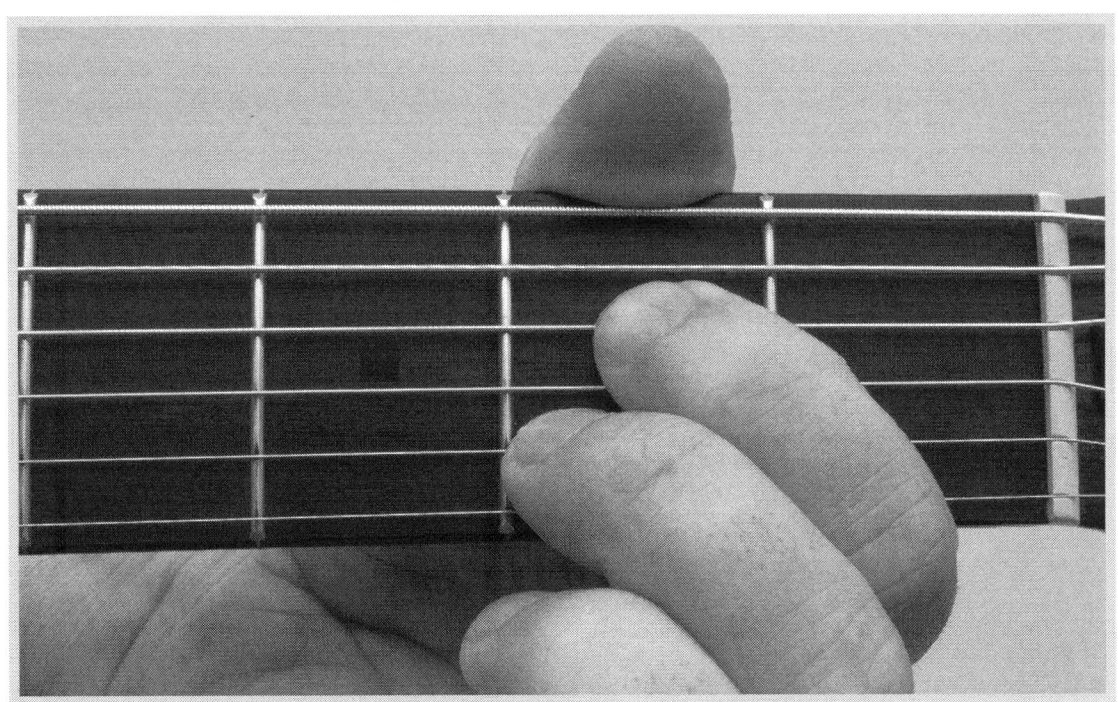

A7sus4

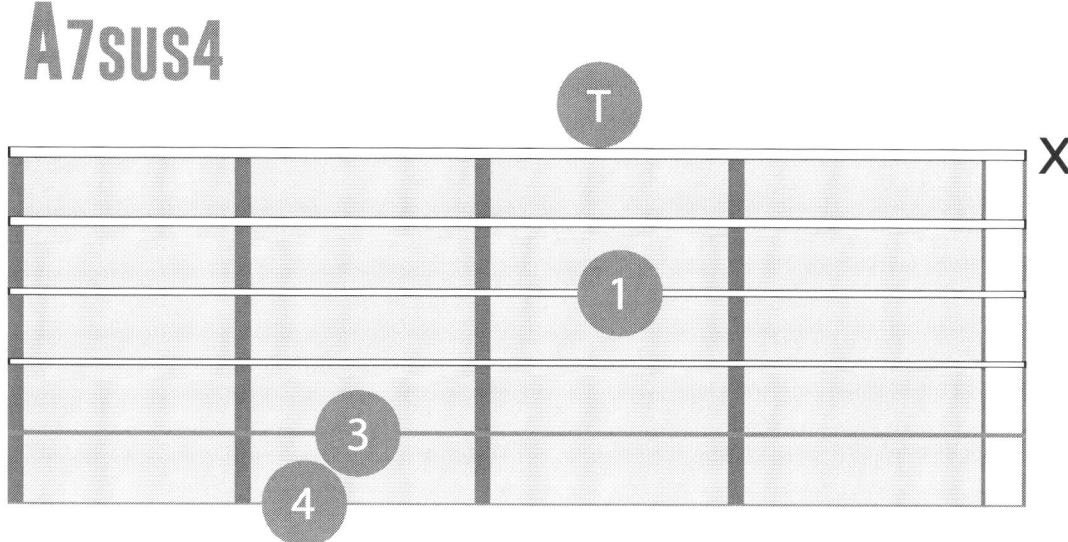

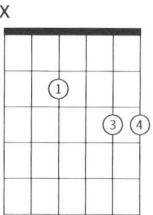

- Thumb touching 6th string
- 3rd finger in middle of fret
- Strum 6 strings - Only 5 sound

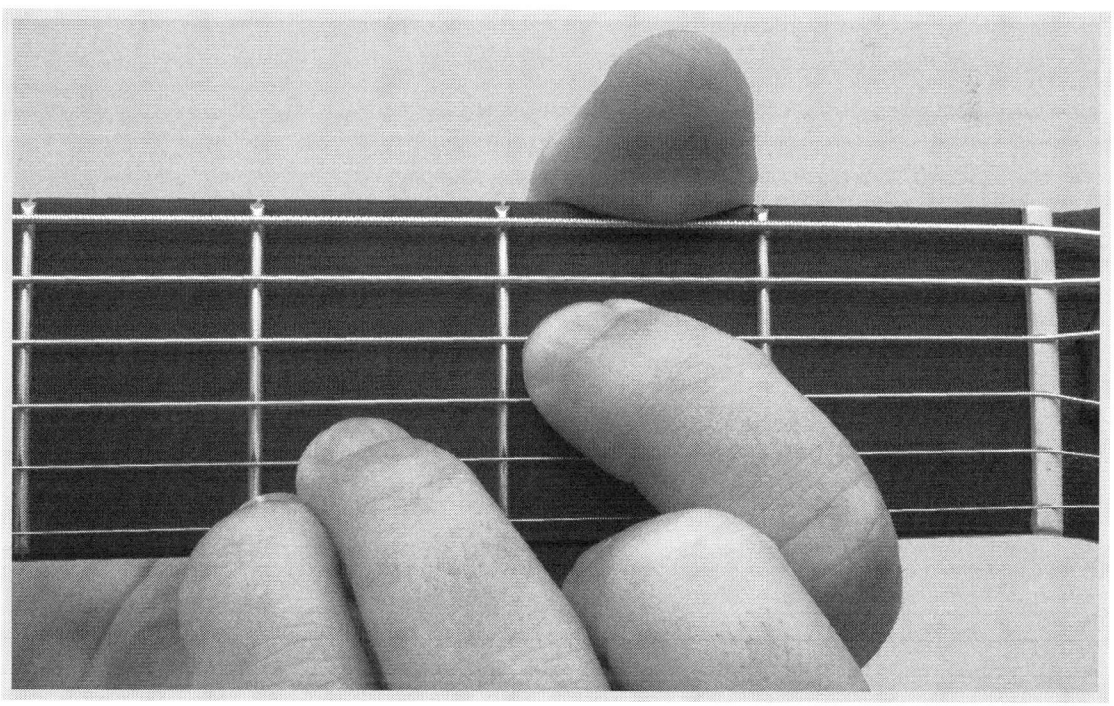

A7SUS4 *EASIER*

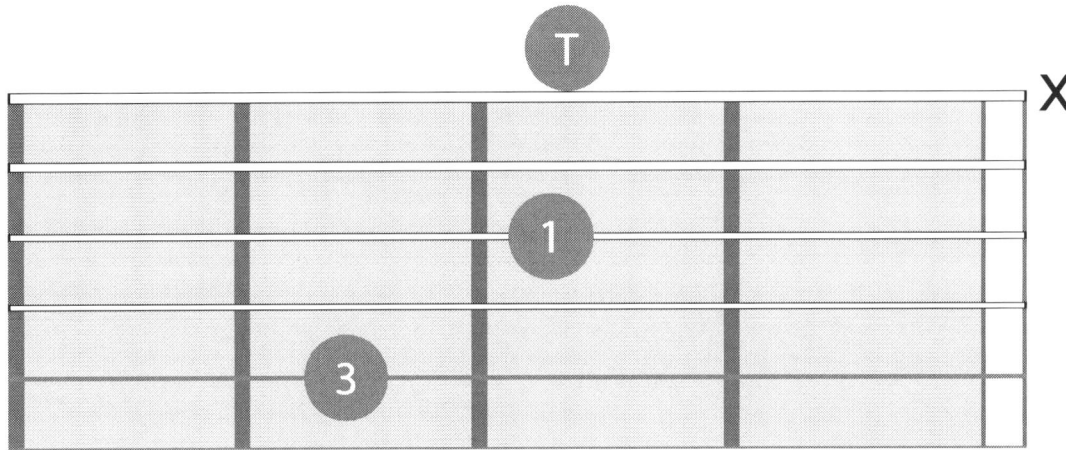

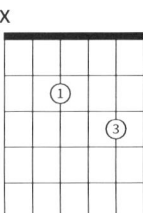

- Thumb touching 6th string
- 3rd finger in middle of fret
- Strum 6 strings - Only 5 sound

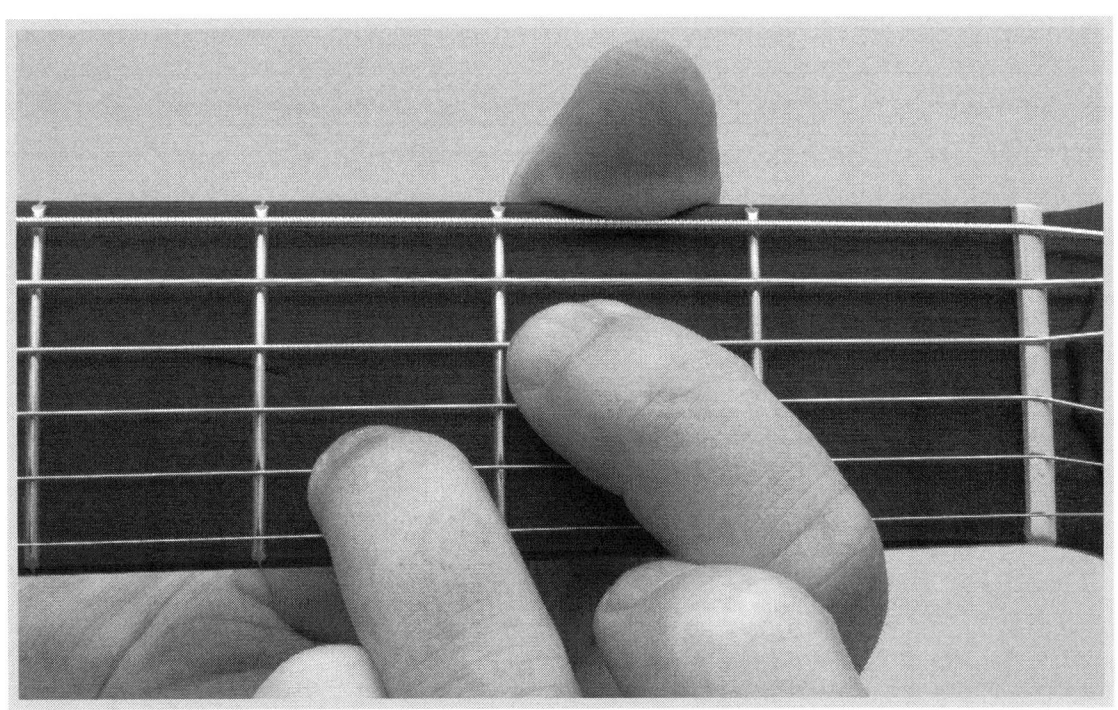

A7SUS4 *ANOTHER WAY*

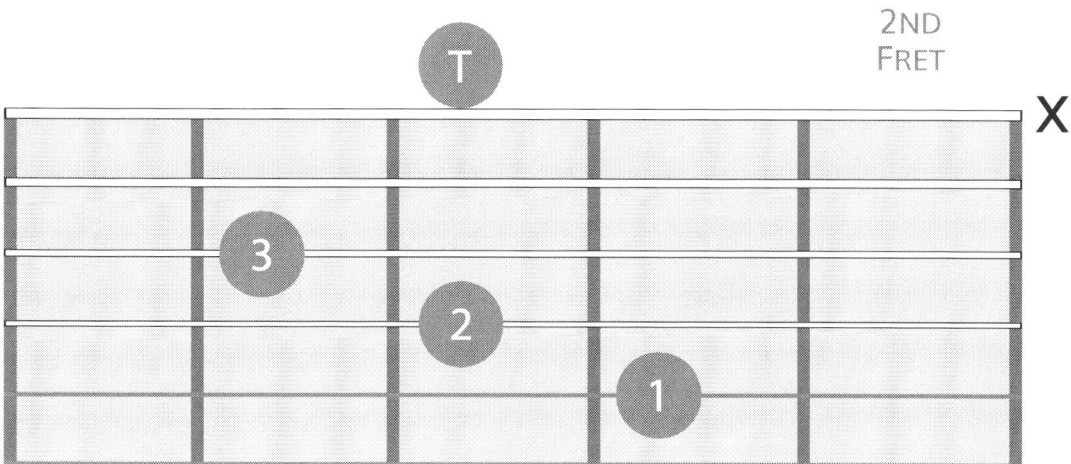

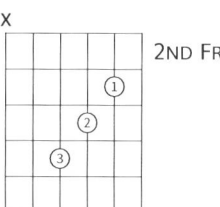

- Sometimes played instead of G
- Thumb touching 6th string
- Strum 6 strings - Only 5 sound

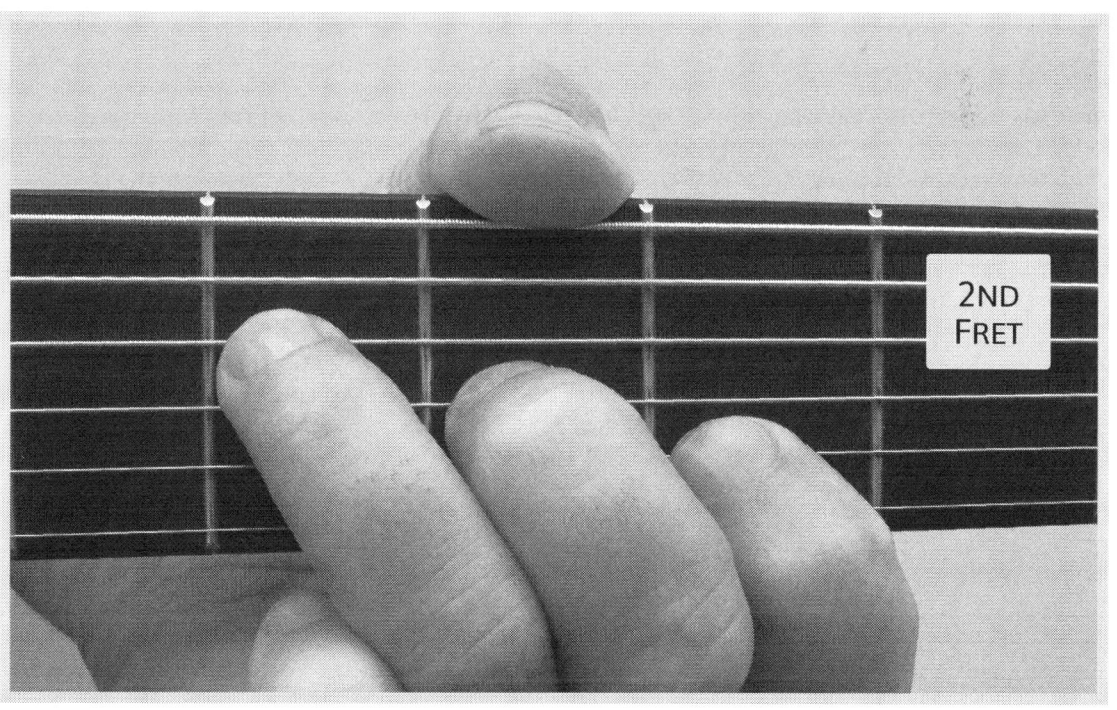

AMAJ7

4TH FRET

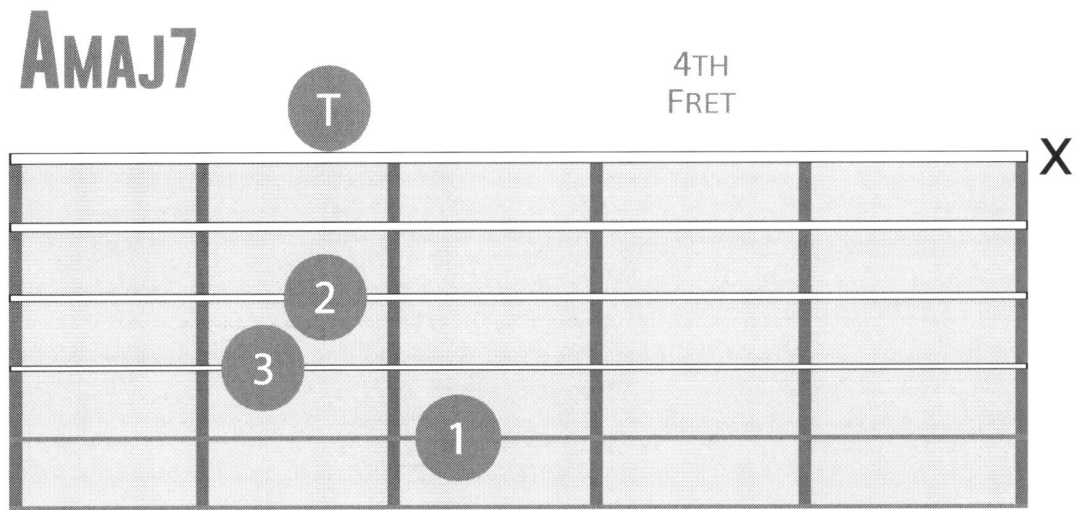

- Sometimes played instead of A
- Thumb touching 6th string
- Strum 6 strings - Only 5 sound

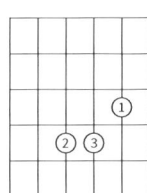

4TH FRET

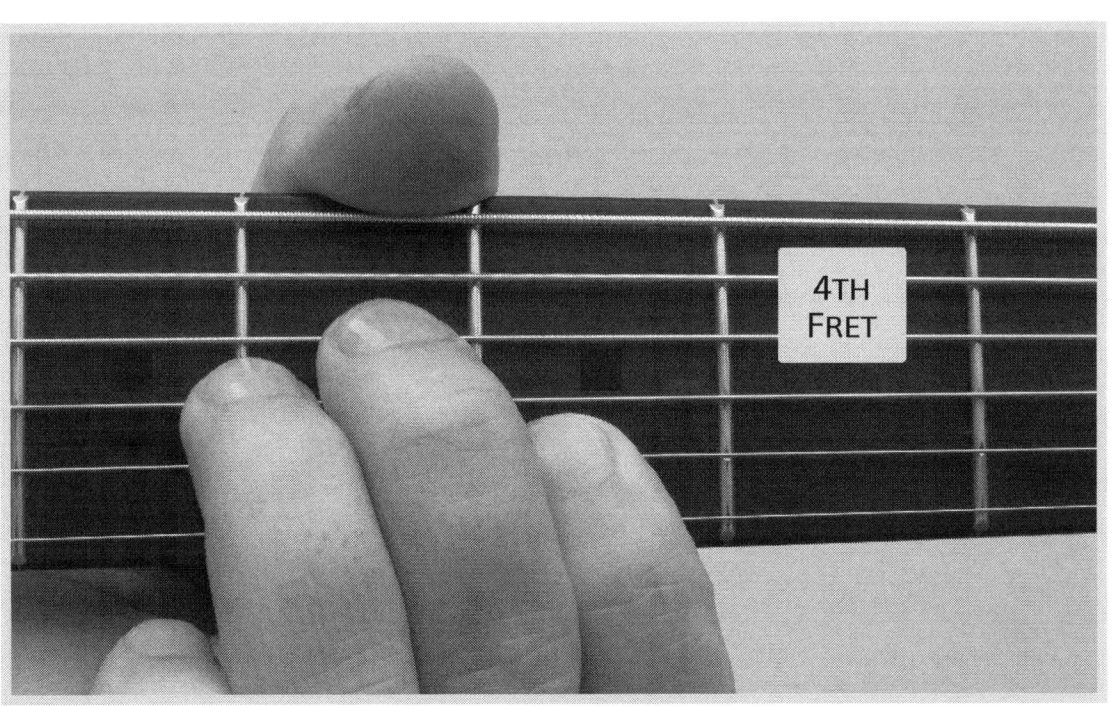

Amaj7 another way

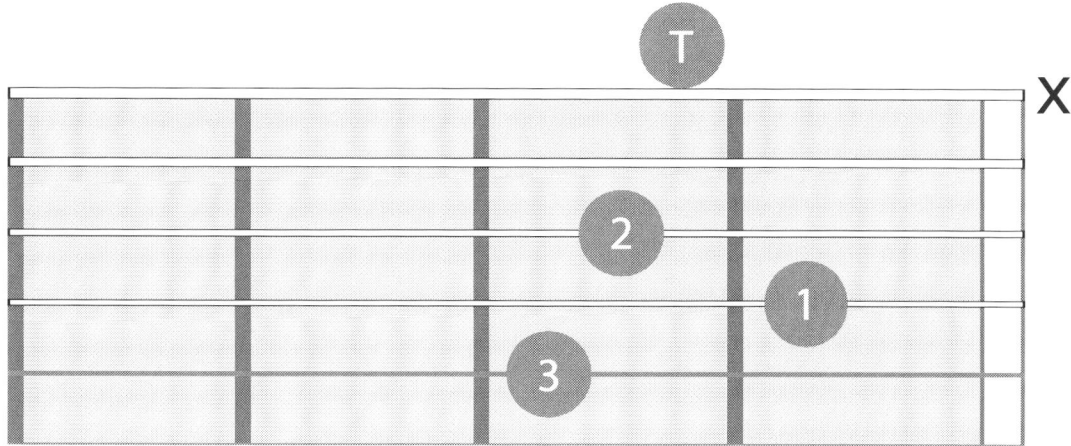

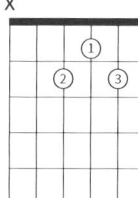

- Thumb touching 6th string
- 1st finger in corner of fret
- Strum 6 strings - Only 5 sound

Am7

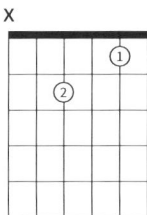

- Thumb touching 6th string
- 1st finger in corner of fret
- Strum 6 strings - Only 5 sound

Am7/G

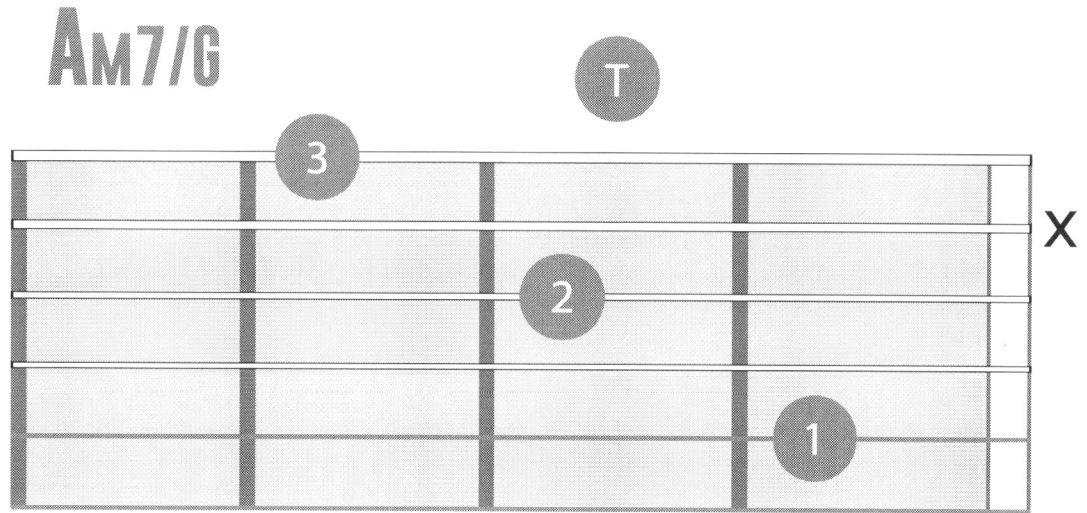

- Thumb not touching 6th string
- 5th string muted by inside of 3rd finger
- Strum 6 strings - Only 5 sound

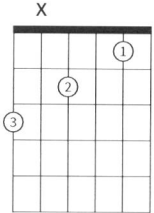

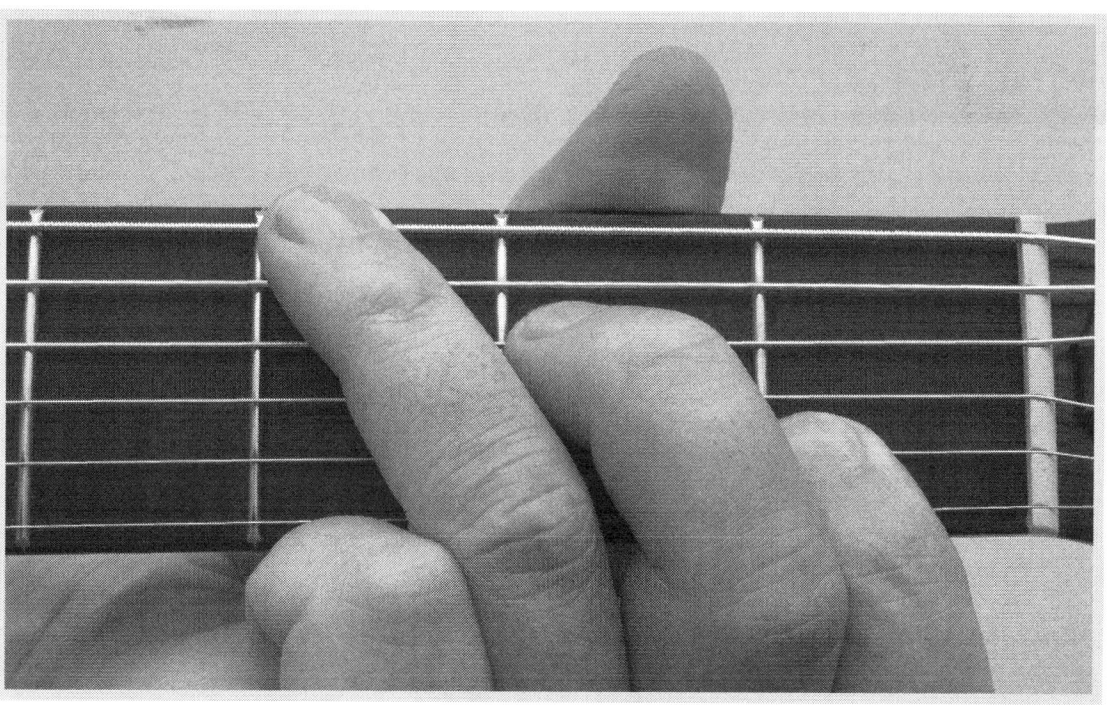

Bb

5TH FRET

- Stretch your hand
- Thumb low and centred
- All 6 strings sound

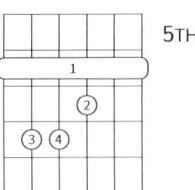
5TH FRET

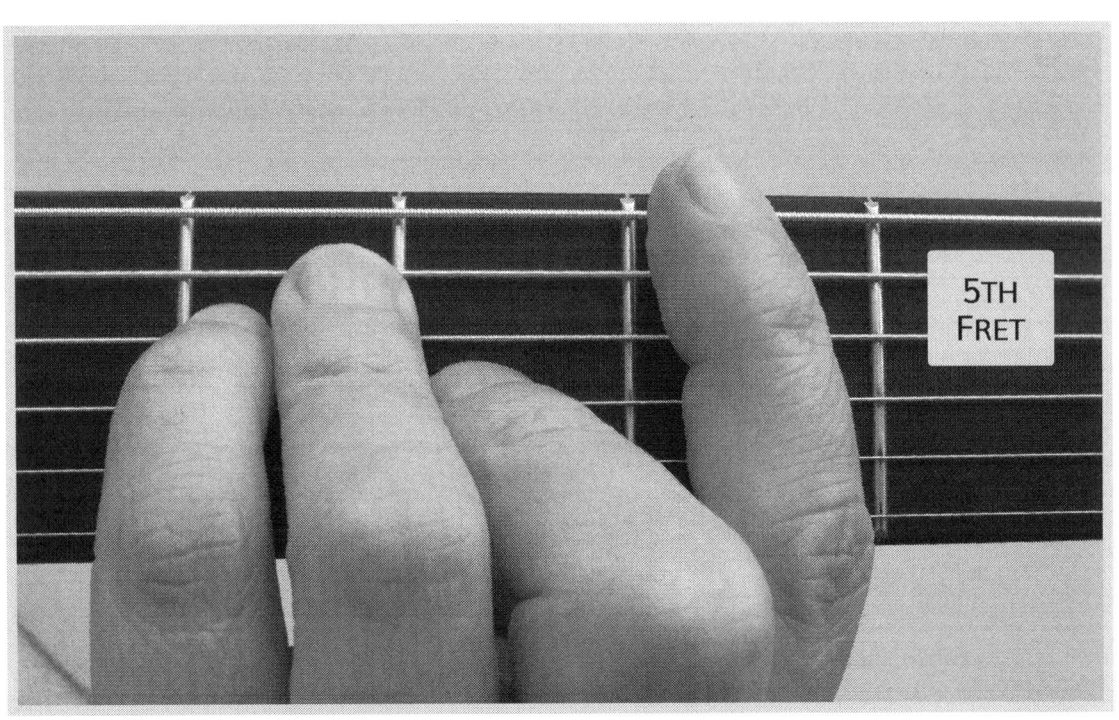

B♭M

5TH FRET

- Stretch your hand
- Thumb low and centred
- All 6 strings sound

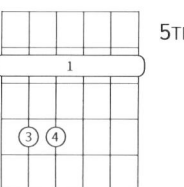

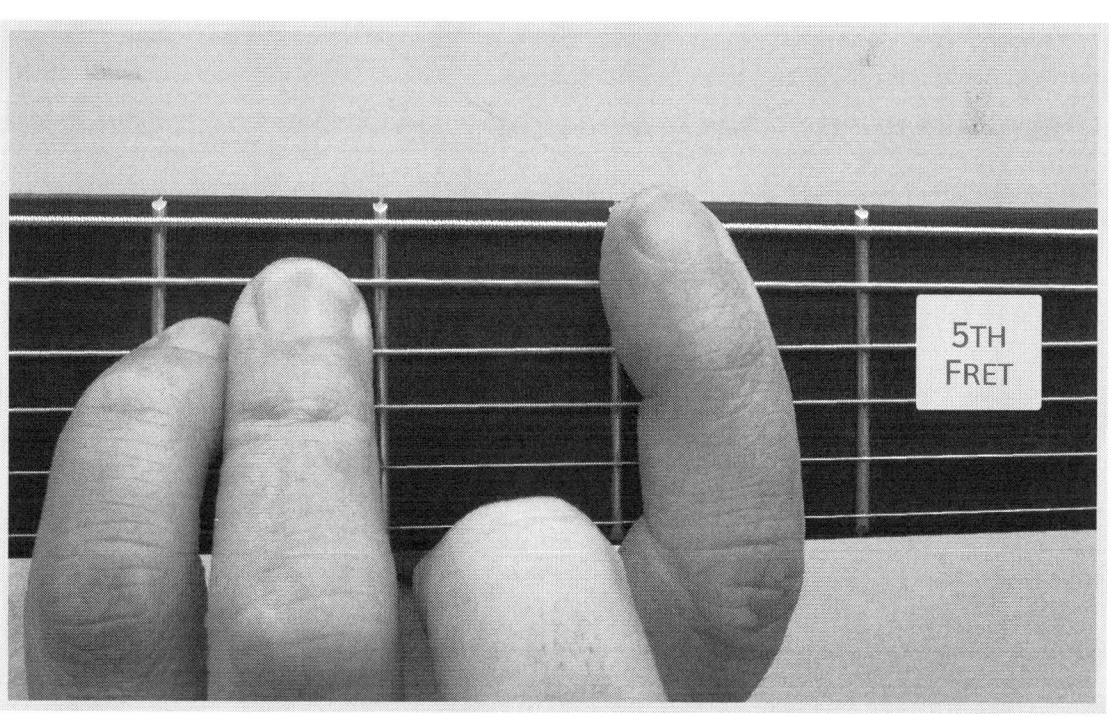

Bb5

5TH FRET

- Stretch your hand
- Thumb low and centred
- Strum 6th 5th and 4th strings

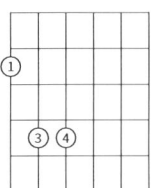

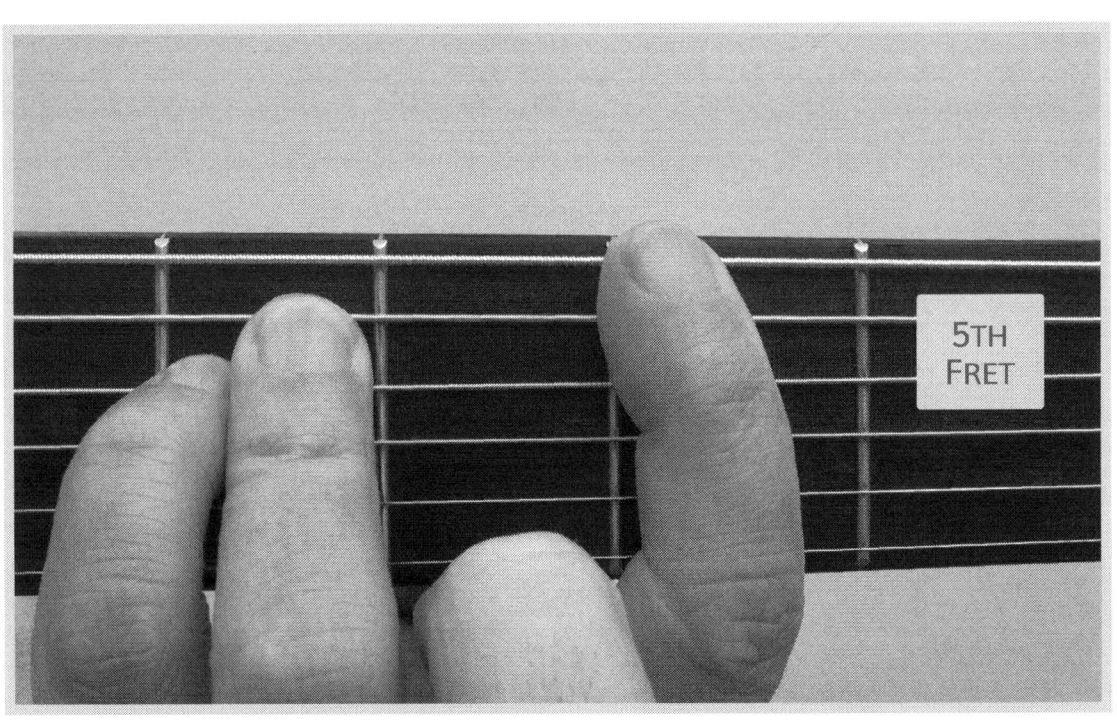

B5

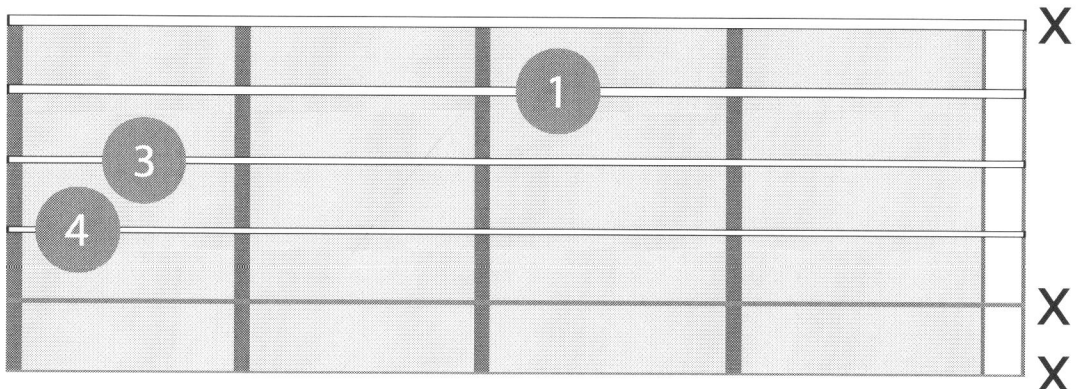

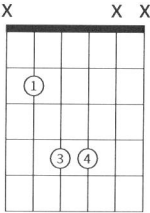

- Thumb low and centred
- 1st finger touching 6th string
- Strum 4 strings - Only 3 sound

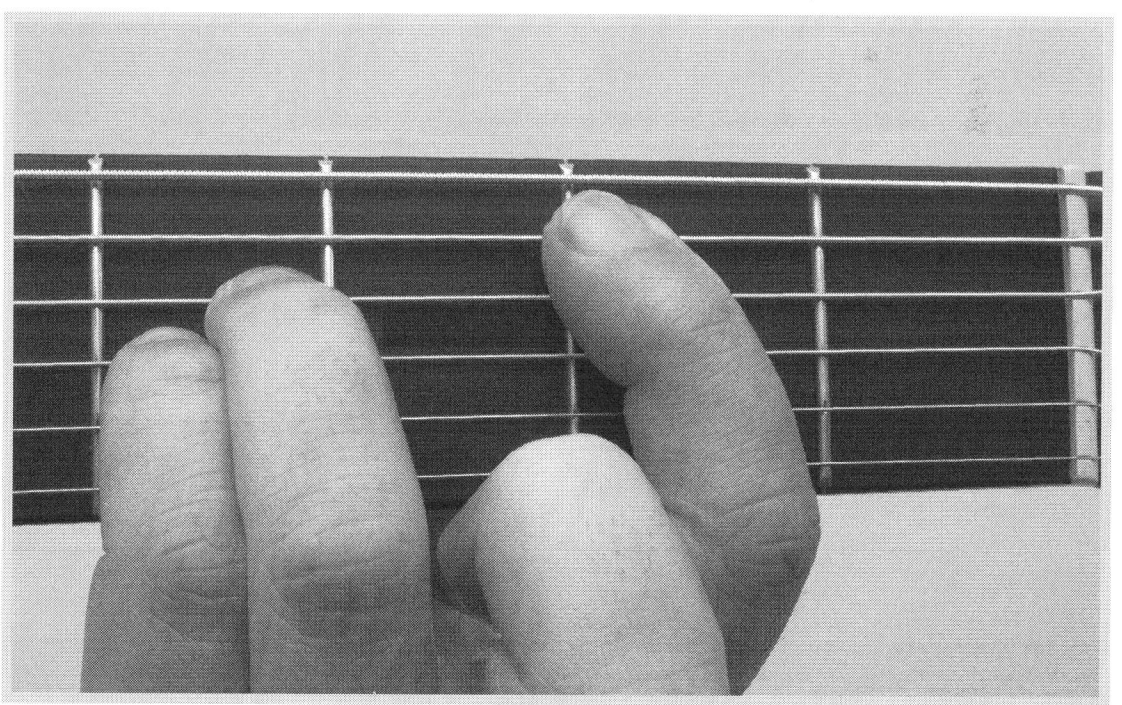

B

6TH FRET

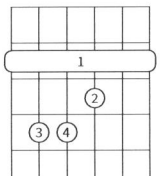

6TH FRET

- Stretch your hand
- Thumb low and centred
- All 6 strings sound

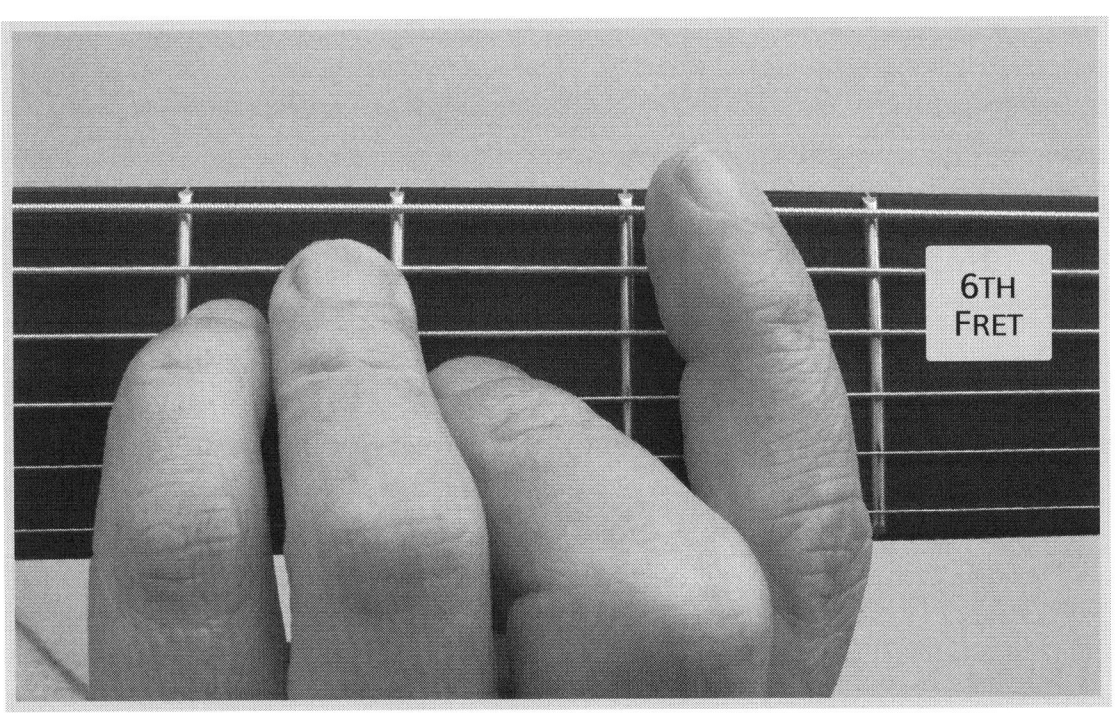

B EASIER

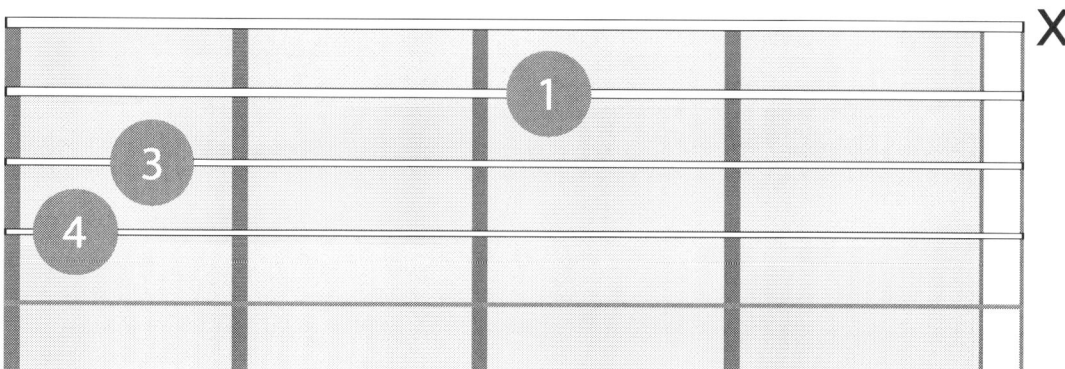

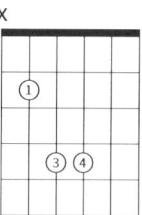

- Thumb low and centred
- 1st finger touching 6th string
- Strum 6 strings - Only 5 sound

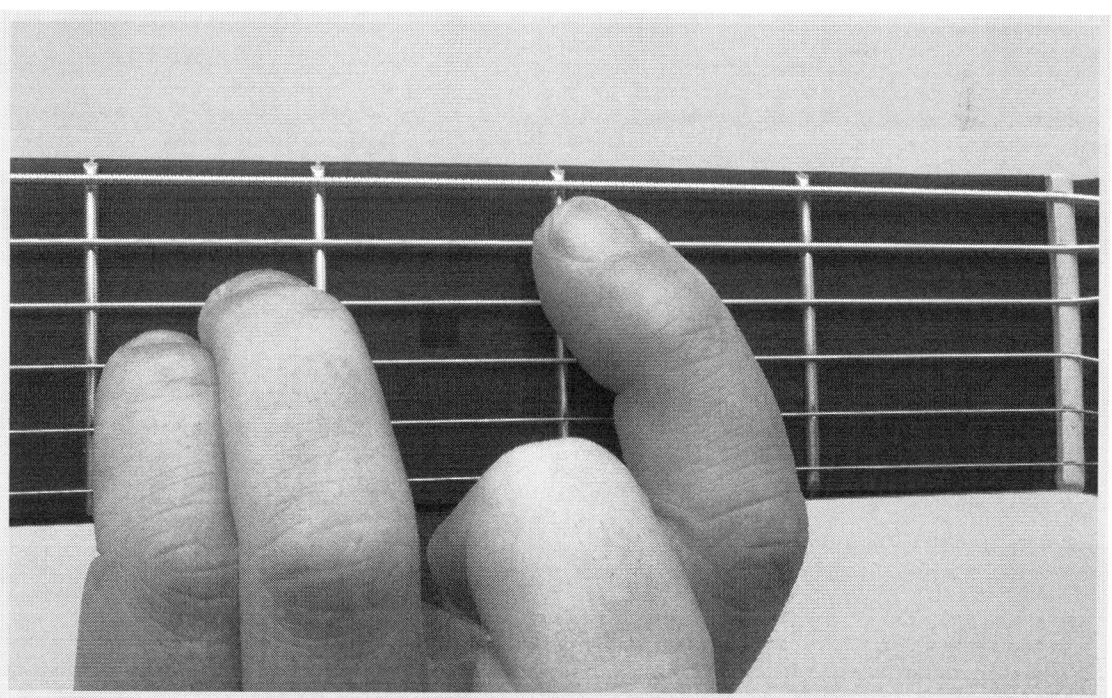

Bm

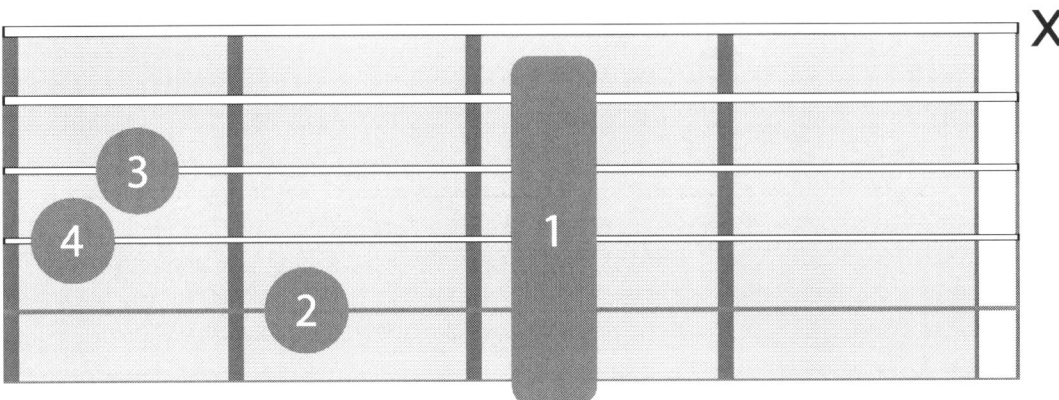

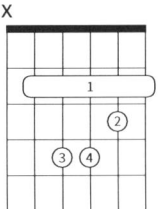

- 1st finger touching 6th string
- Thumb low and centred
- Strum 6 strings - Only 5 sound

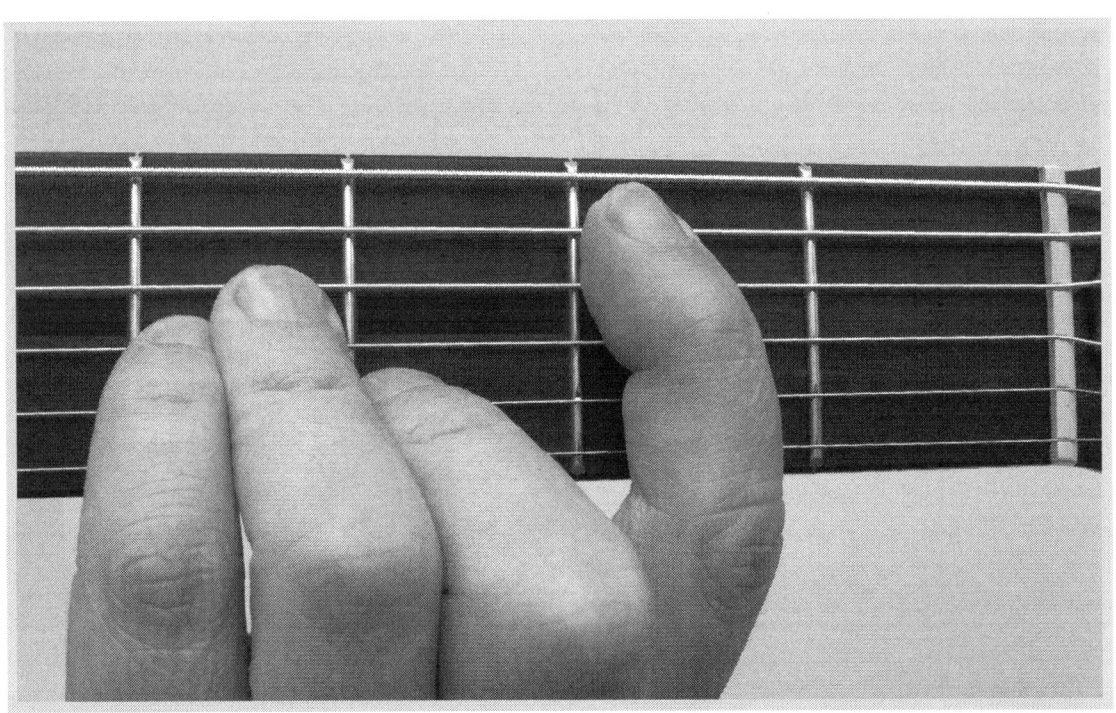

BM *EASIER*

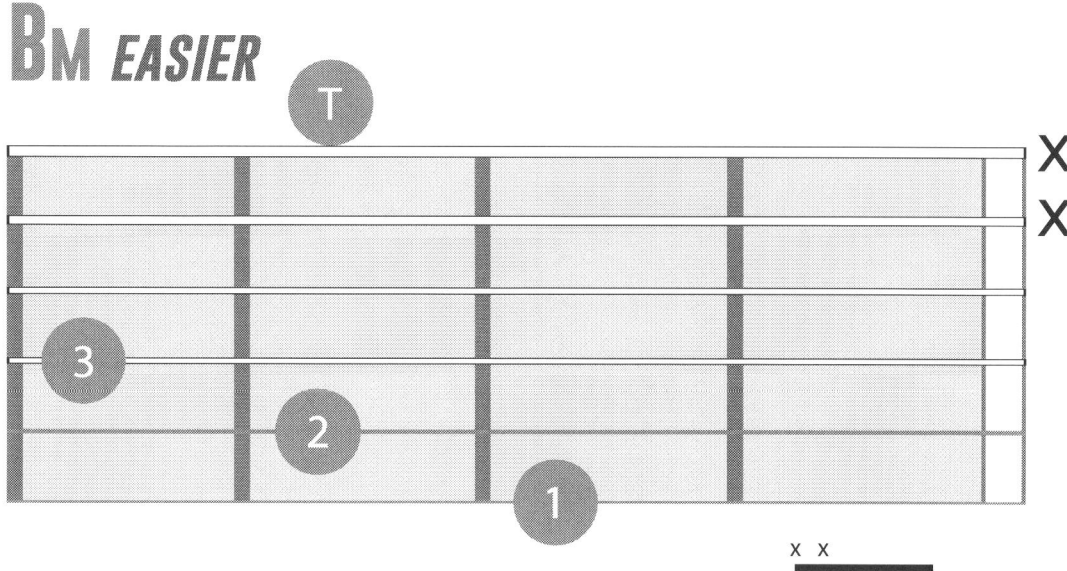

- Thumb touching 6th string
- 1st finger in corner of fret
- Strum bottom 4 strings

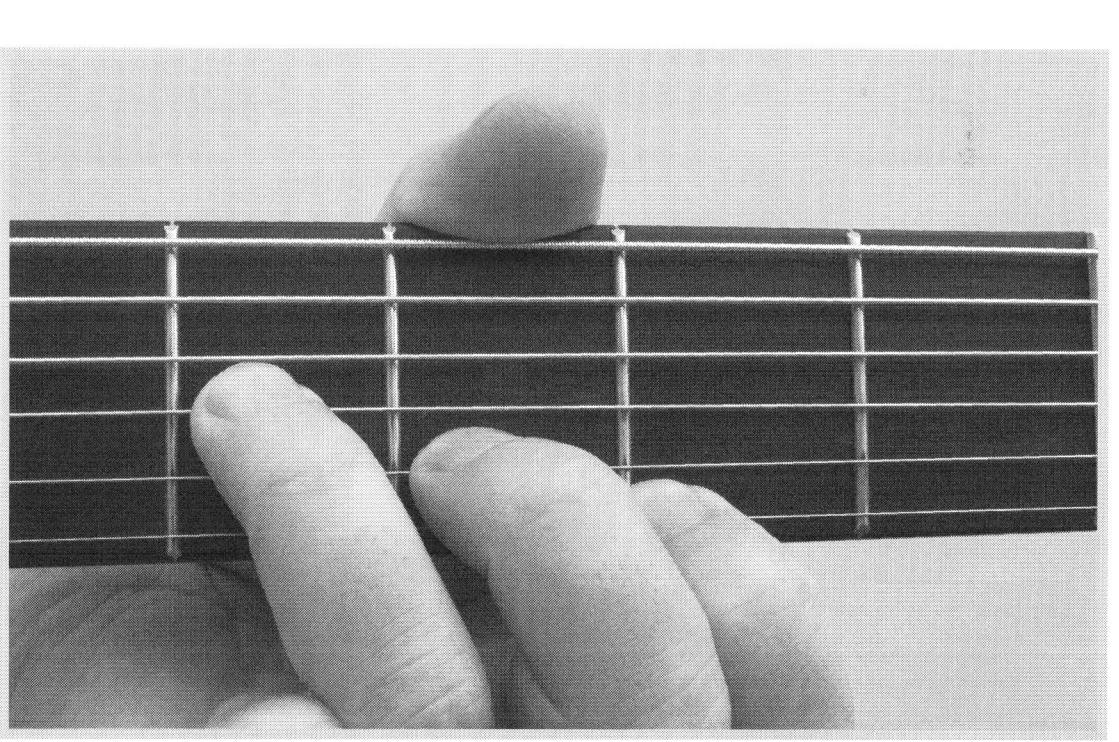

Bsus2

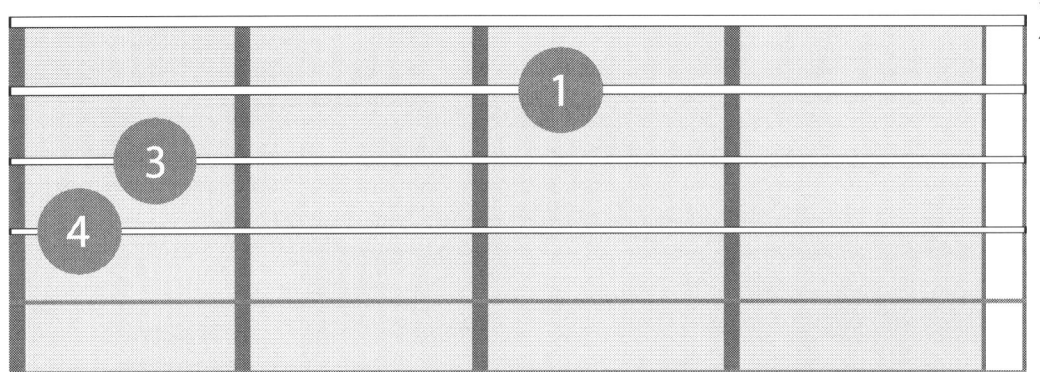

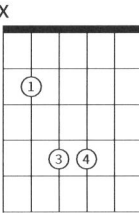

- Sometimes played instead of B
- Thumb low and centred
- Strum 6 strings - Only 5 sound

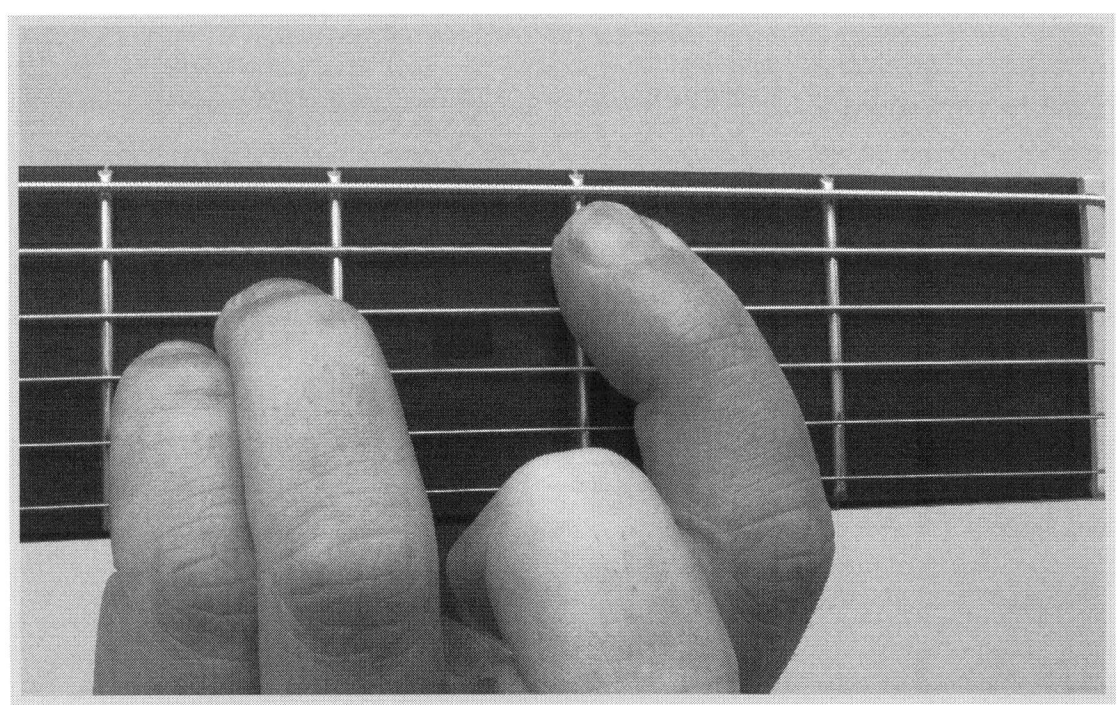

Bsus4

6TH FRET

- Sometimes played instead of B
- Thumb low and centred
- All 6 strings sound

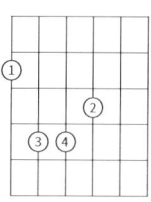

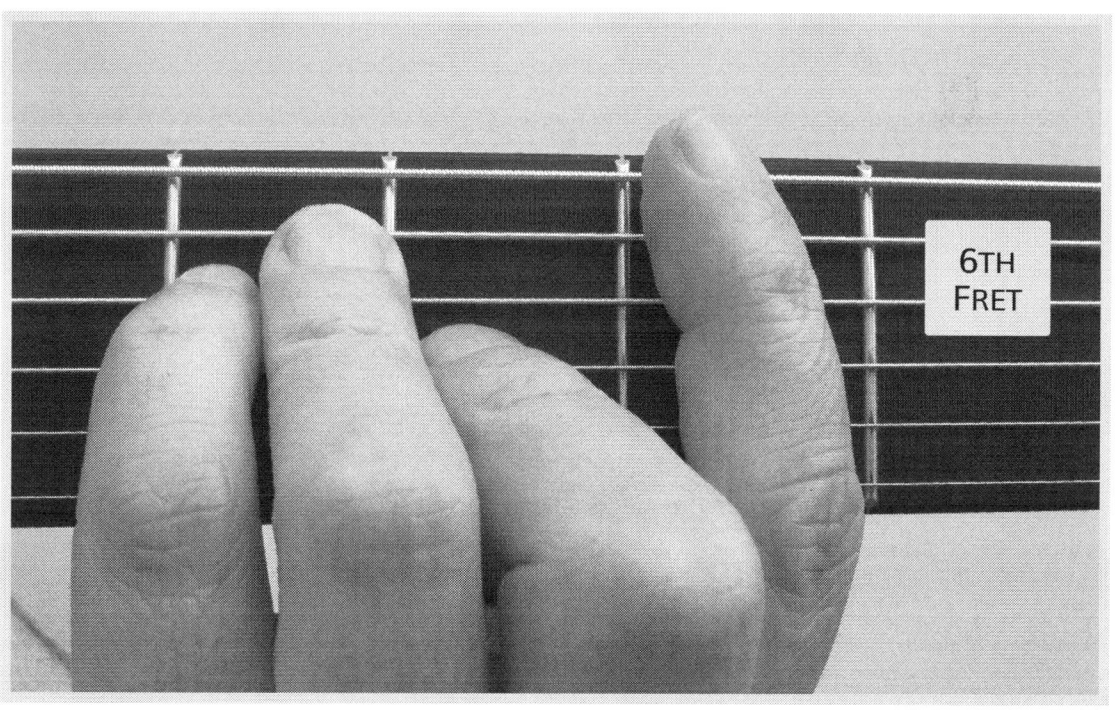

B7

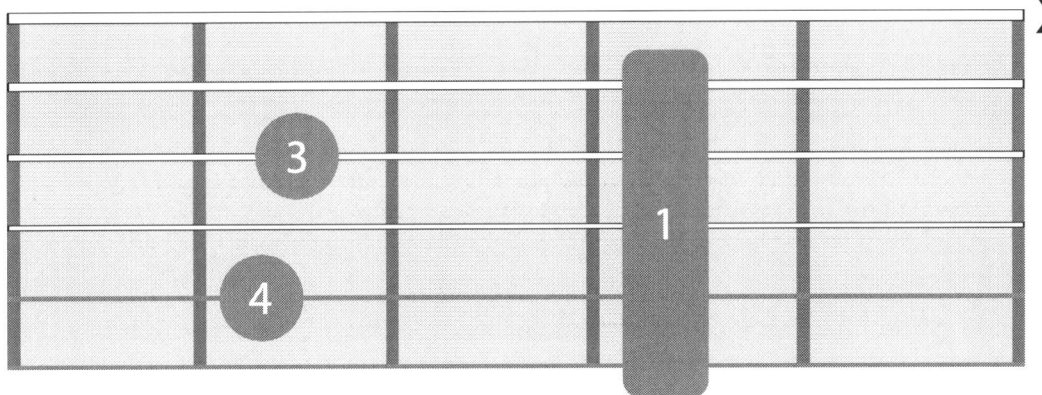

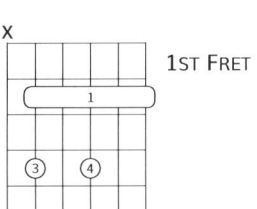

- Thumb low and centred
- 1st finger touching 6th string
- Strum 6 strings - Only 5 sound

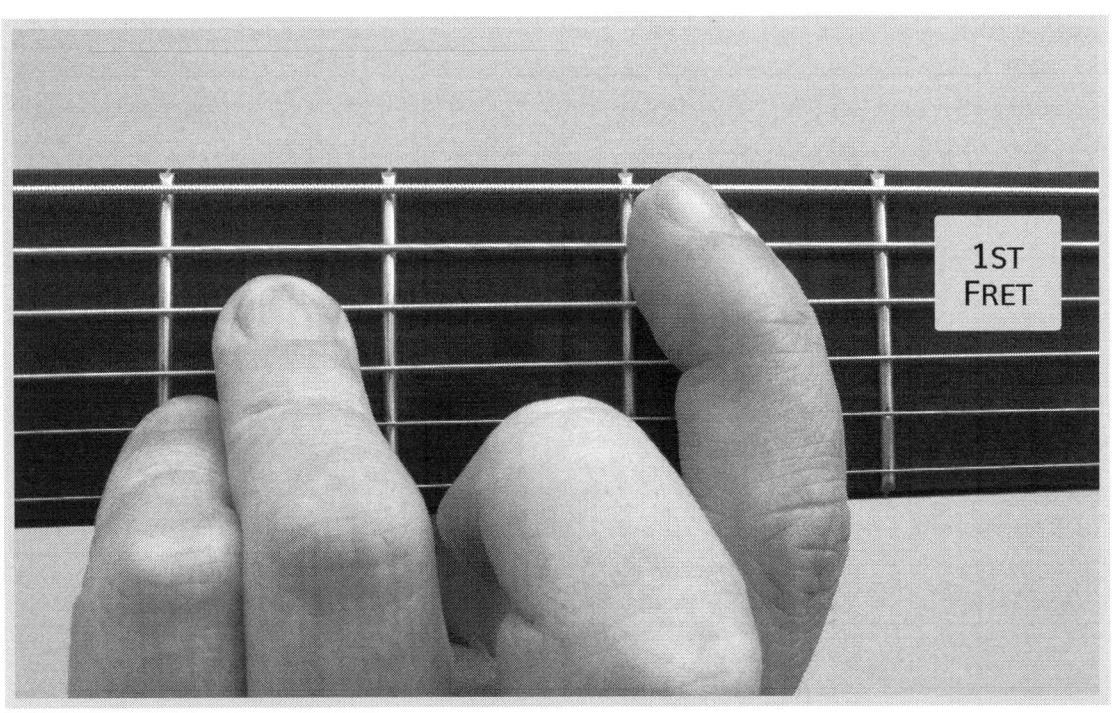

B7 *EASIER*

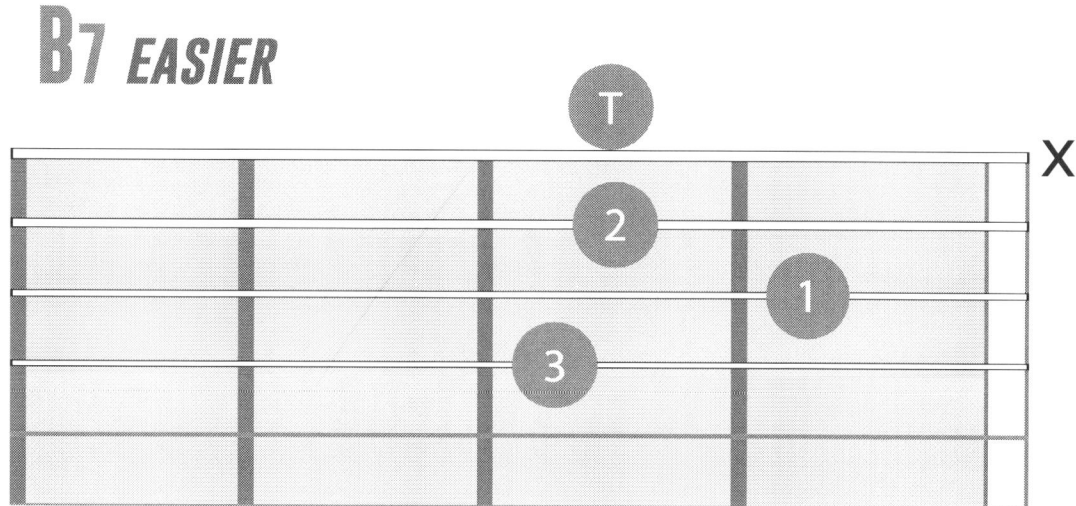

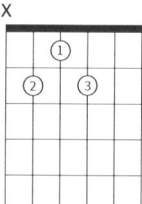

- Thumb touching 6th string
- 1st finger in corner of fret
- Strum 6 strings - Only 5 sound

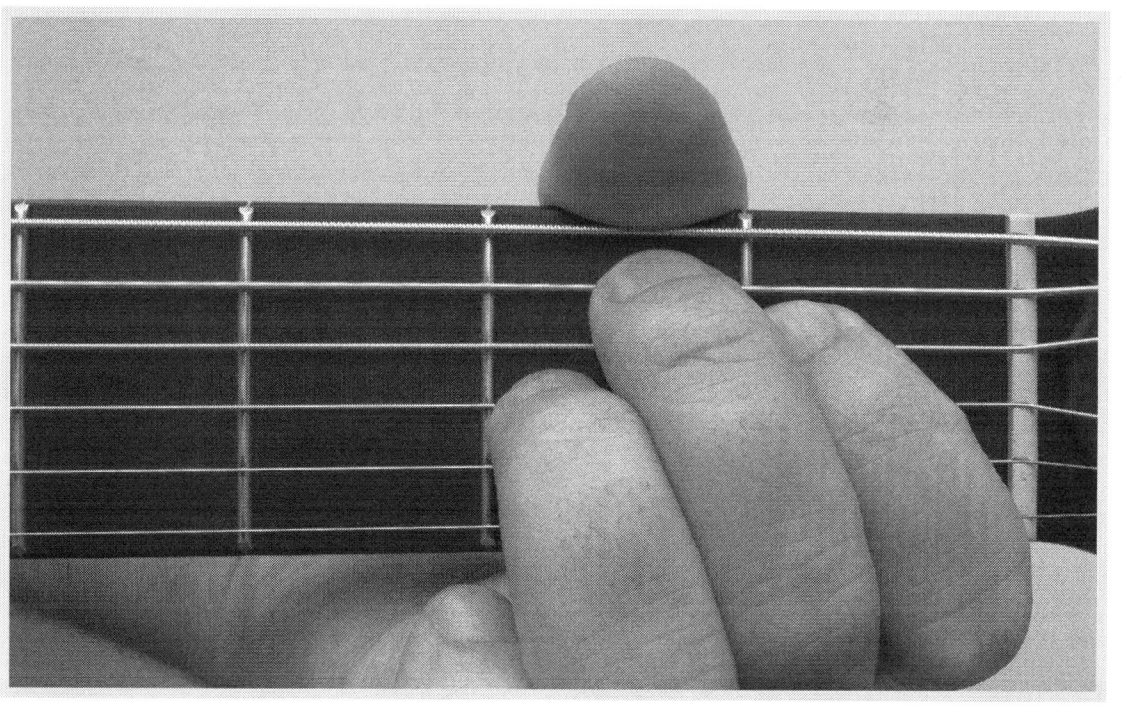

B M7

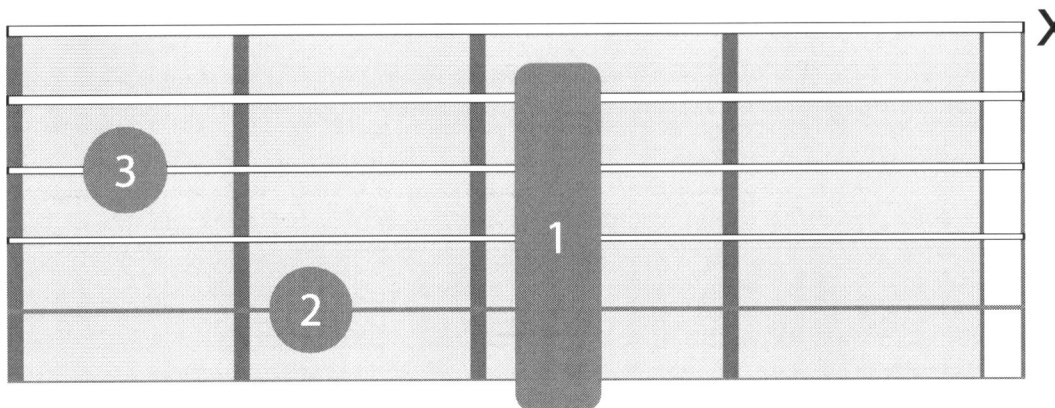

- 1st finger touching 6th string
- Thumb low and centred
- Strum 6 strings - Only 5 sound

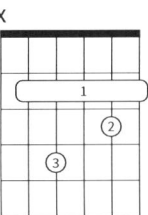

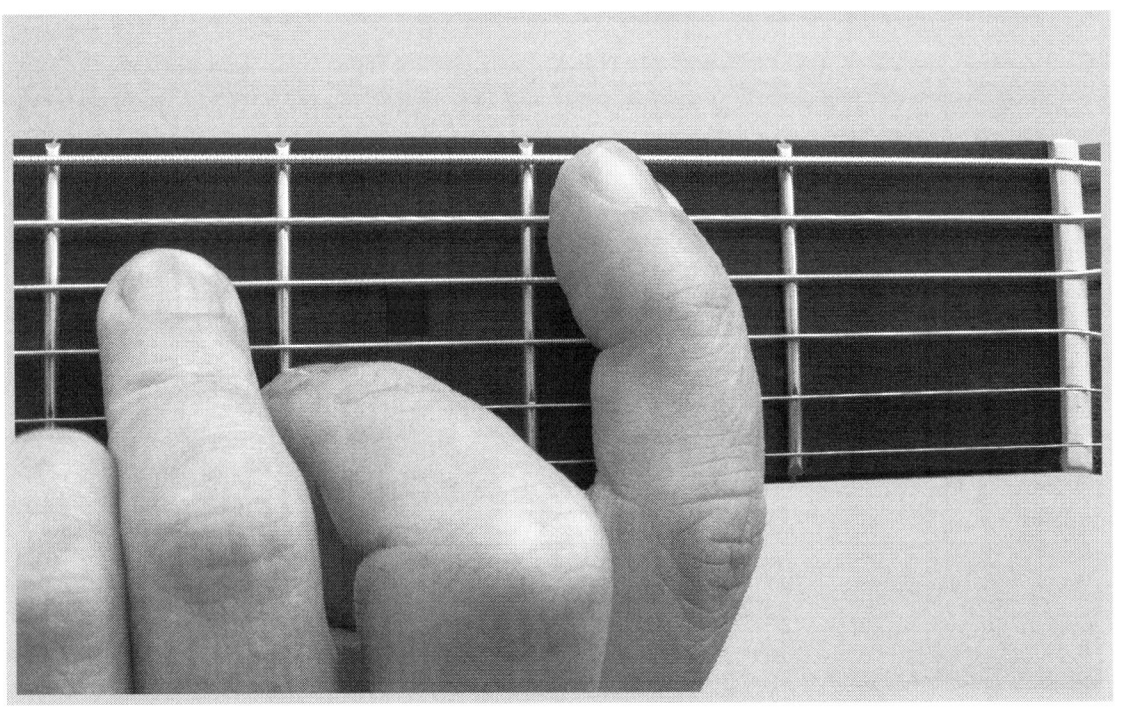

Bmaj7

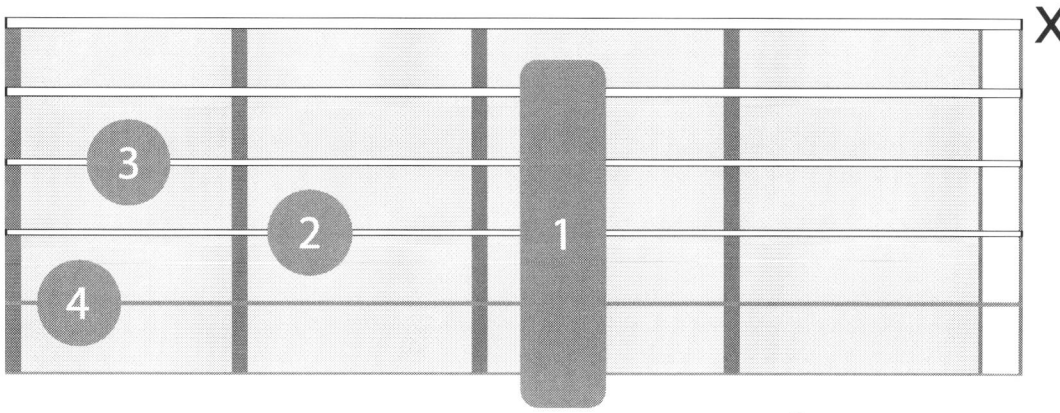

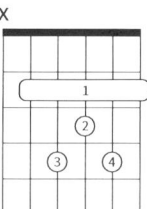

- Thumb low and centred
- 1st finger touching 6th string
- Strum 6 strings - Only 5 sound

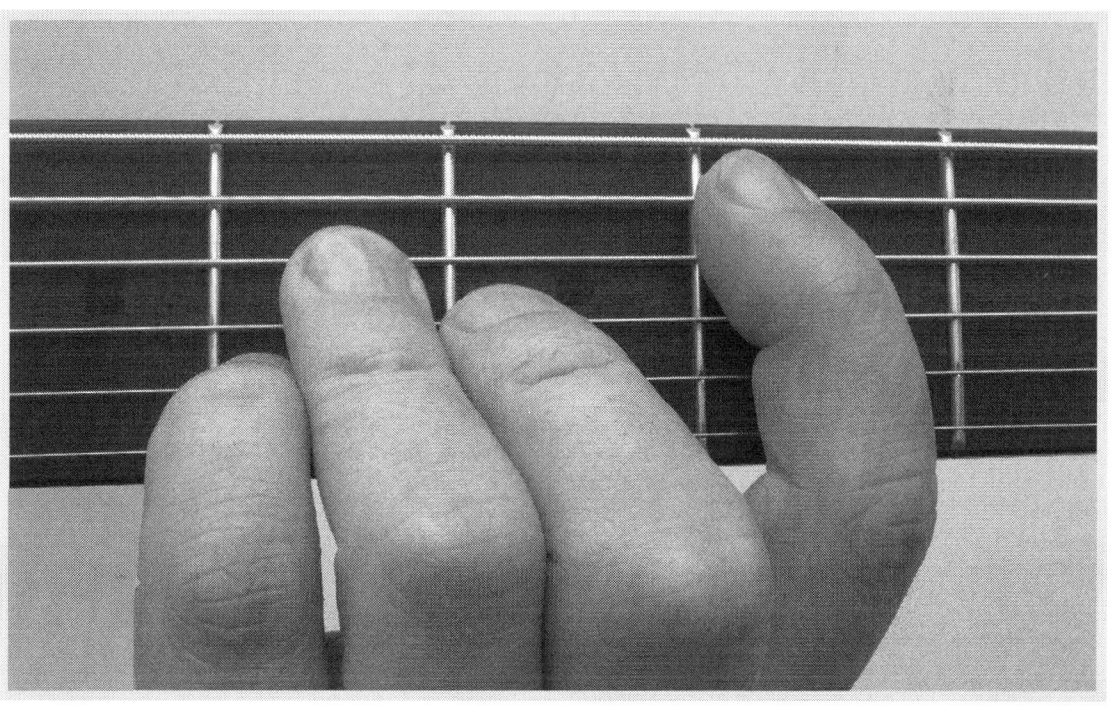

Bm11

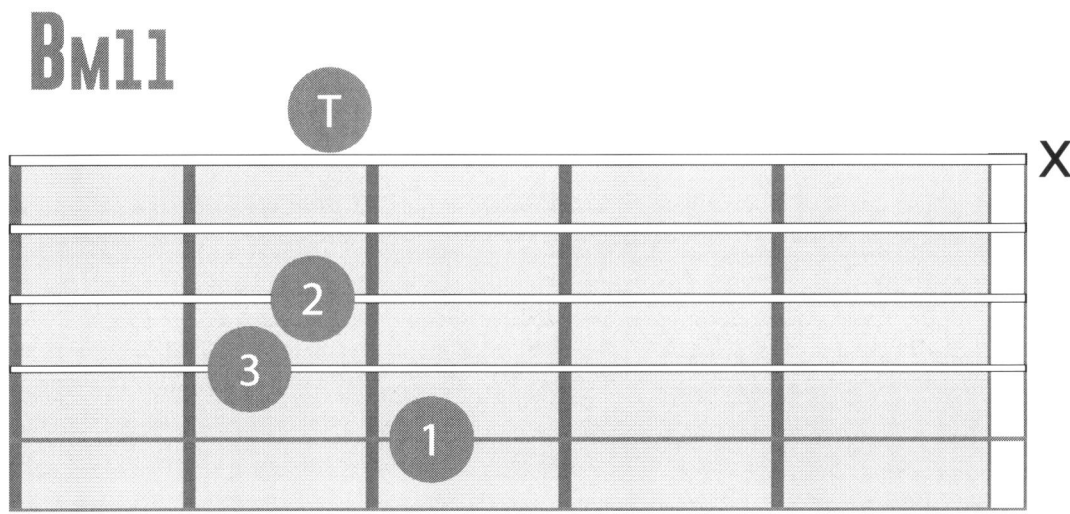

- Sometimes played instead of Bm
- Thumb touching 6th string
- Strum 6 strings - Only 5 sound

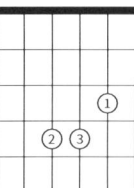

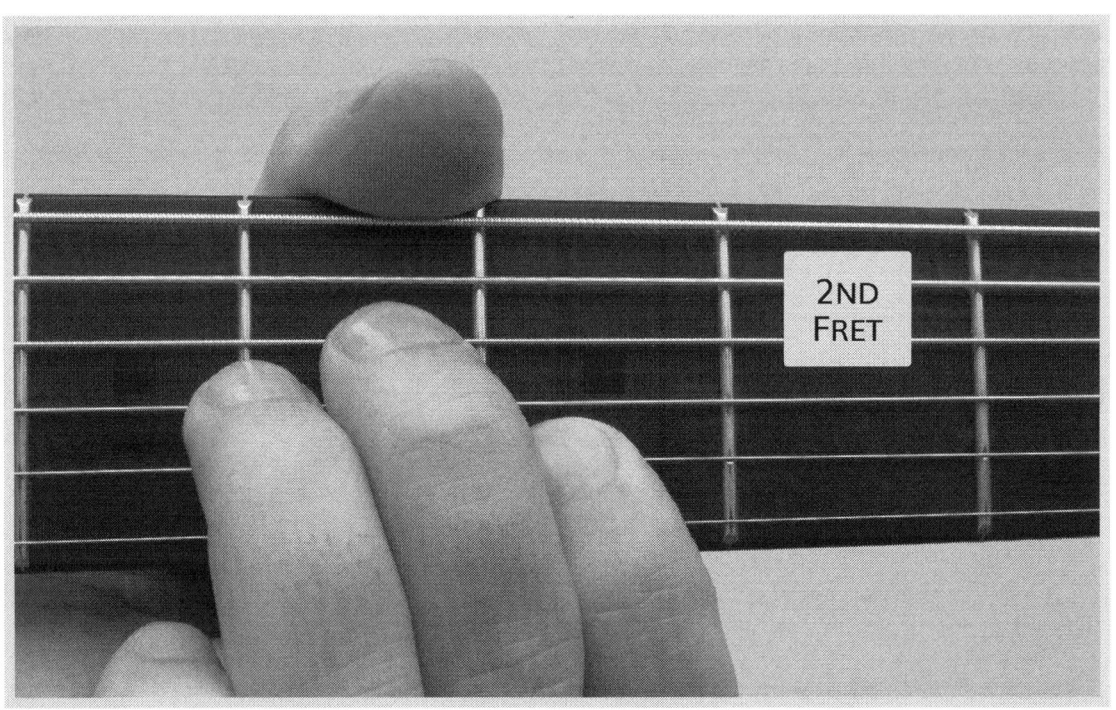

B/E

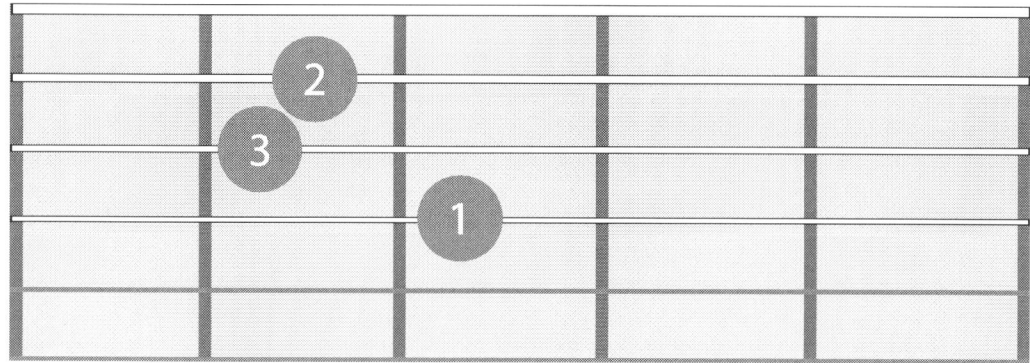

7TH FRET

- Sometimes played instead of B
- Thumb not touching 6th string
- All 6 strings sound

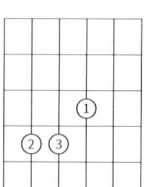

7TH FRET

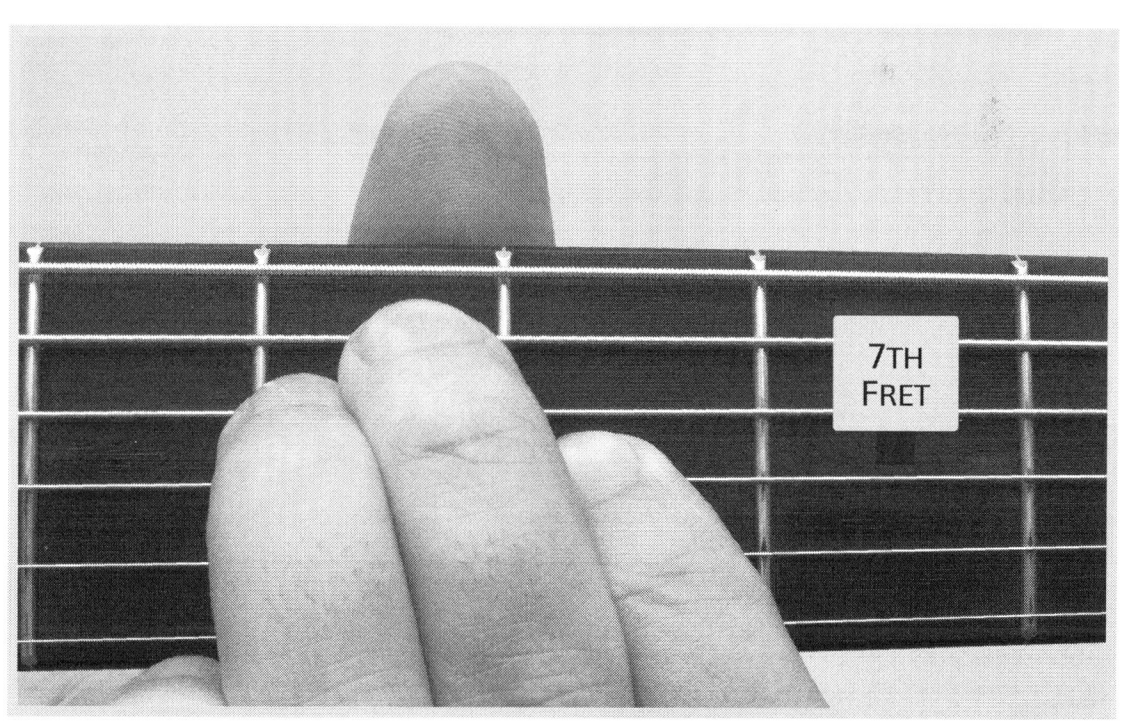

7TH FRET

C

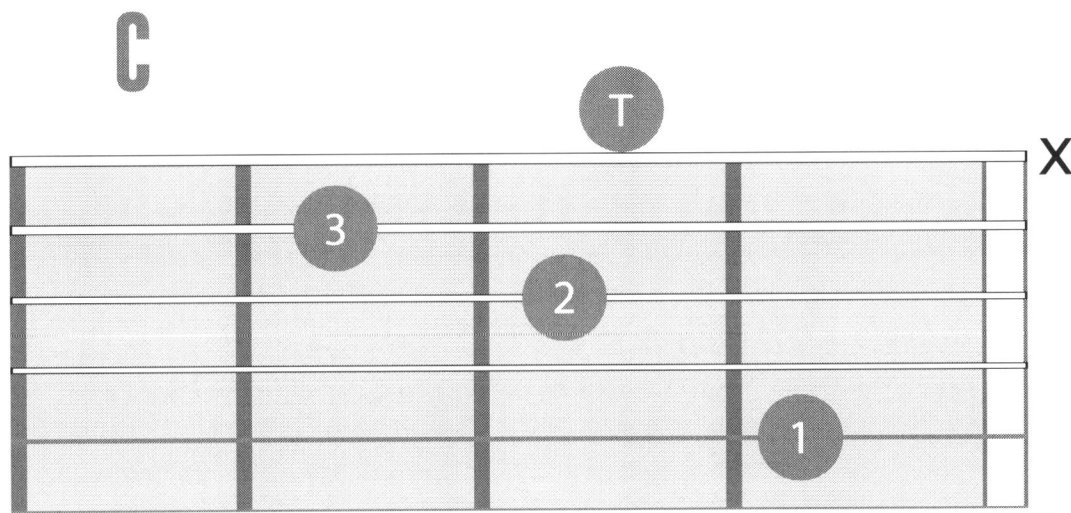

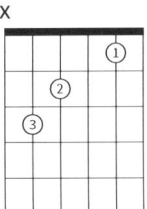

- Thumb touching 6th string
- 1st finger in corner of fret
- Strum 6 strings - Only 5 sound

C ANOTHER WAY

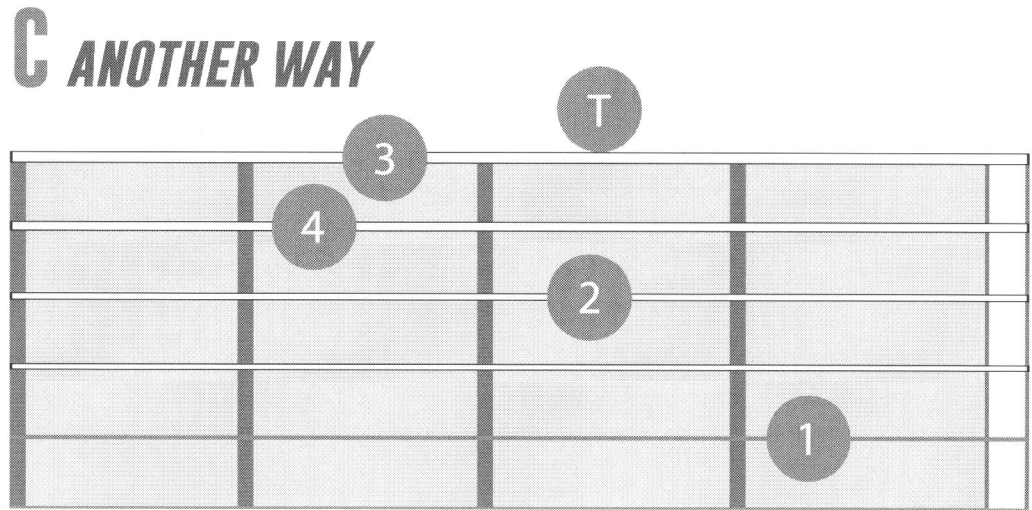

- Thumb touching 6th string
- 1st finger in corner of fret
- All 6 strings sound

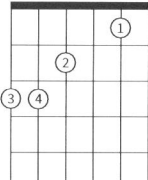

Csus4

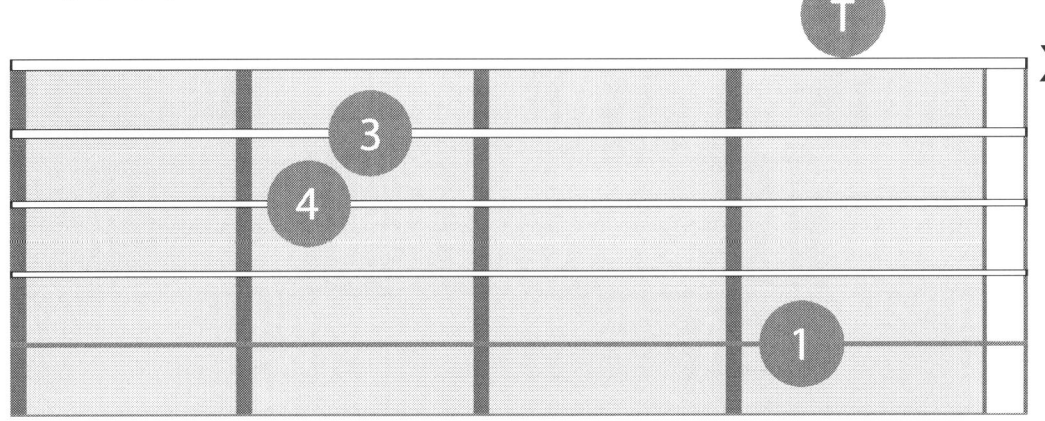

- Thumb touching 6th string
- 1st finger in corner of fret
- Strum 6 strings - Only 5 sound

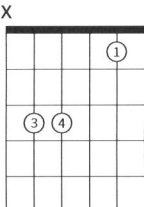

C5

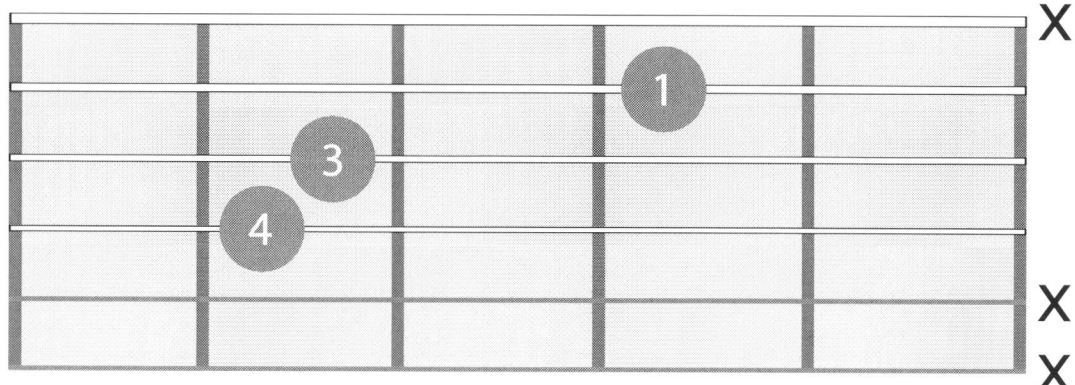

2ND FRET

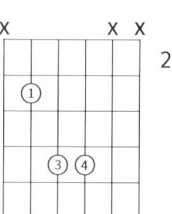

2ND FRET

- Thumb low and centred
- 1st finger touching 6th string
- Strum 5th 4th and 3rd strings

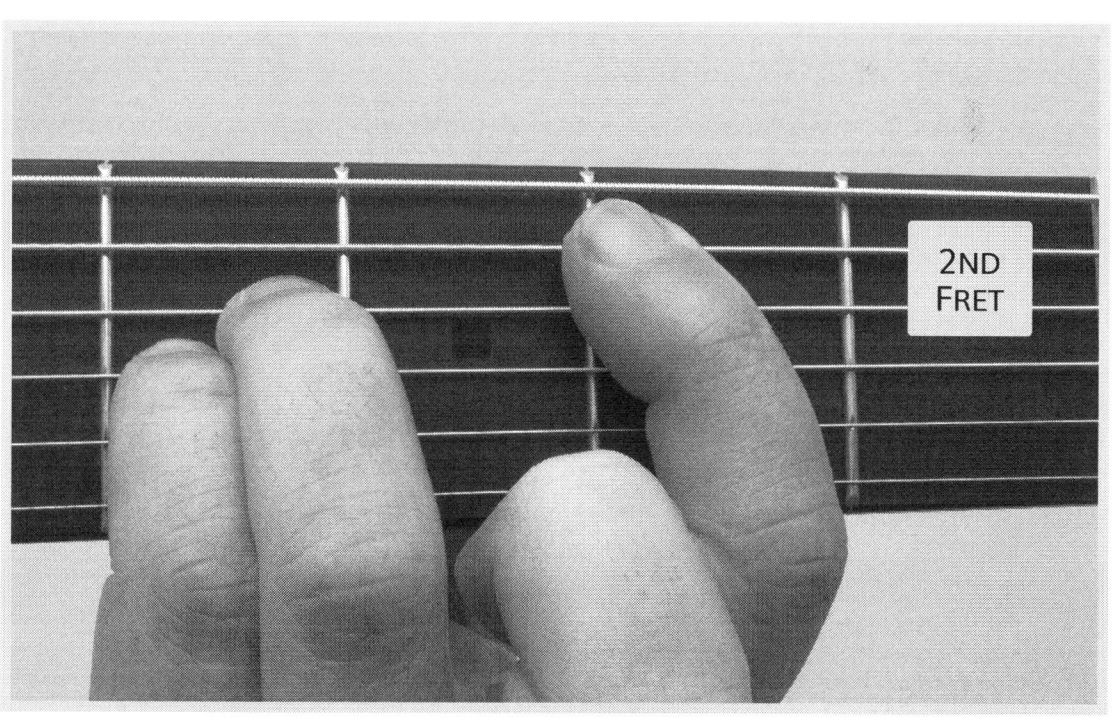

2ND FRET

C7

- Thumb touching 6th string
- 1st finger in corner of fret
- Strum 6 strings - Only 5 sound

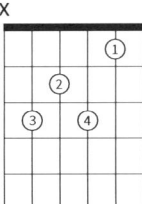

Cm7

2ND FRET

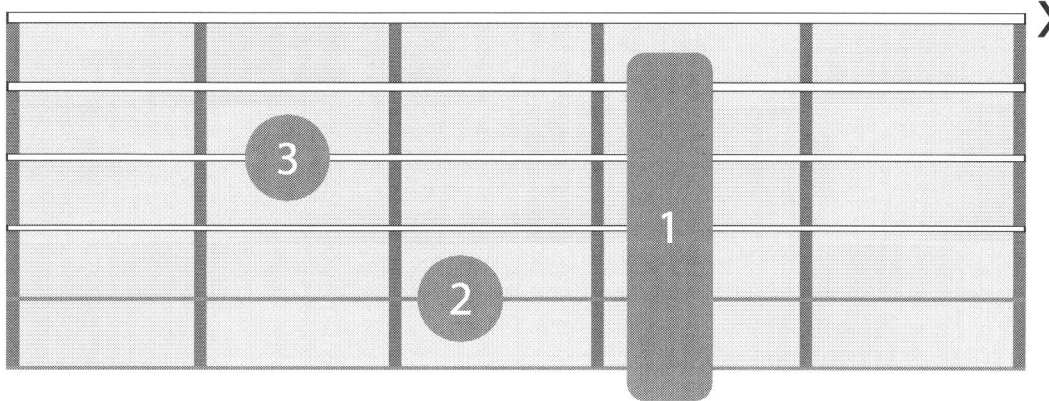

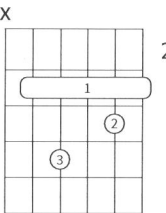

- 1st finger touching 6th string
- Thumb low and centred
- Strum 6 strings - Only 5 sound

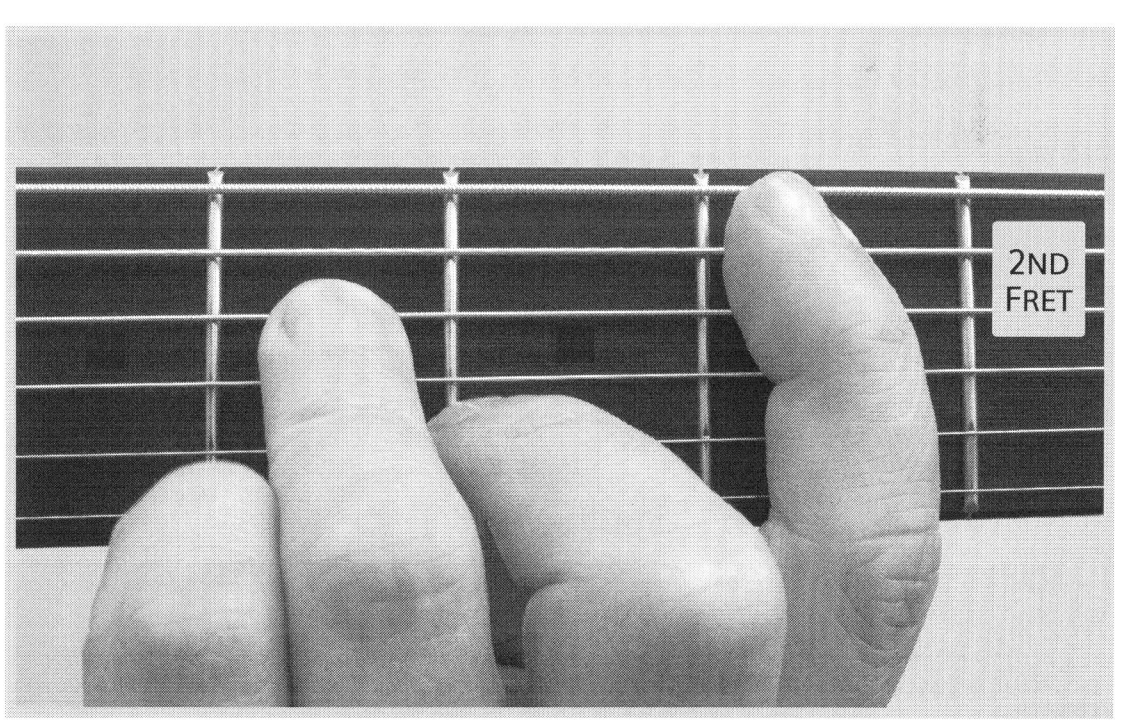

CMAJ7

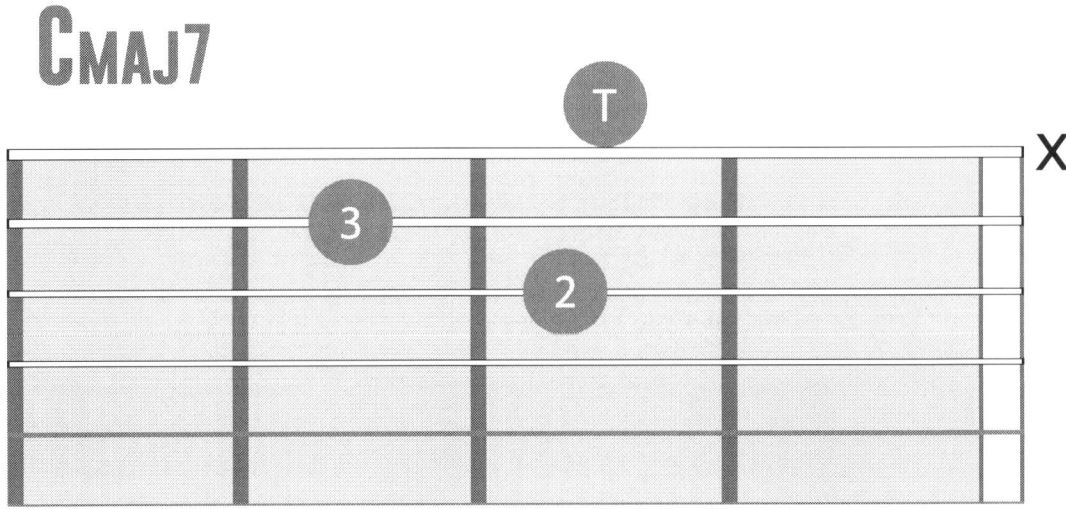

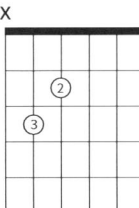

- Thumb touching 6th string
- Can also be played with 1st & 2nd fingers
- Strum 6 strings - Only 5 sound

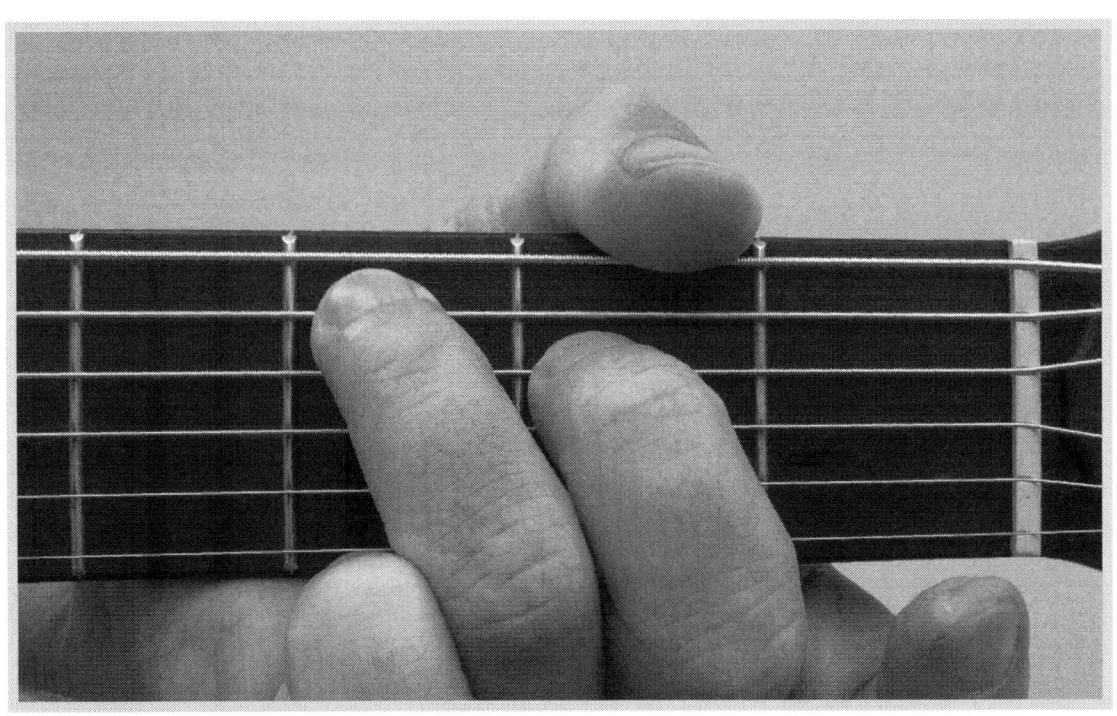

Cmaj7 ANOTHER WAY

6TH FRET

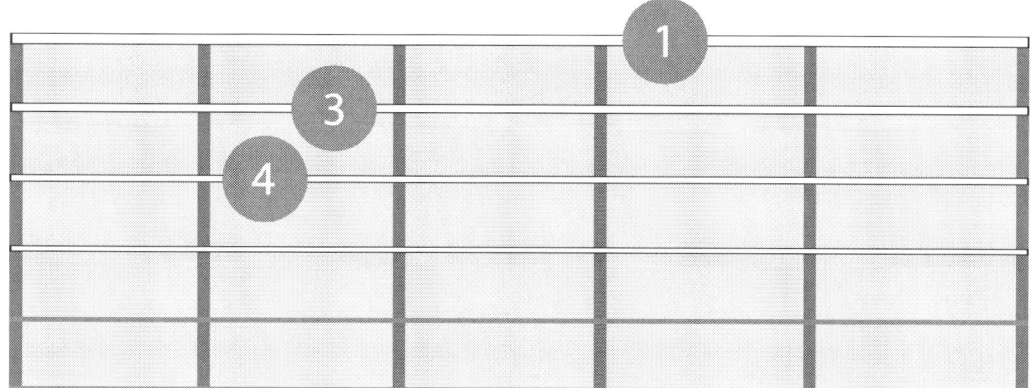

- Stretch your hand
- Thumb low and centred
- All 6 strings sound

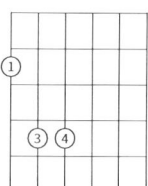

6TH FRET

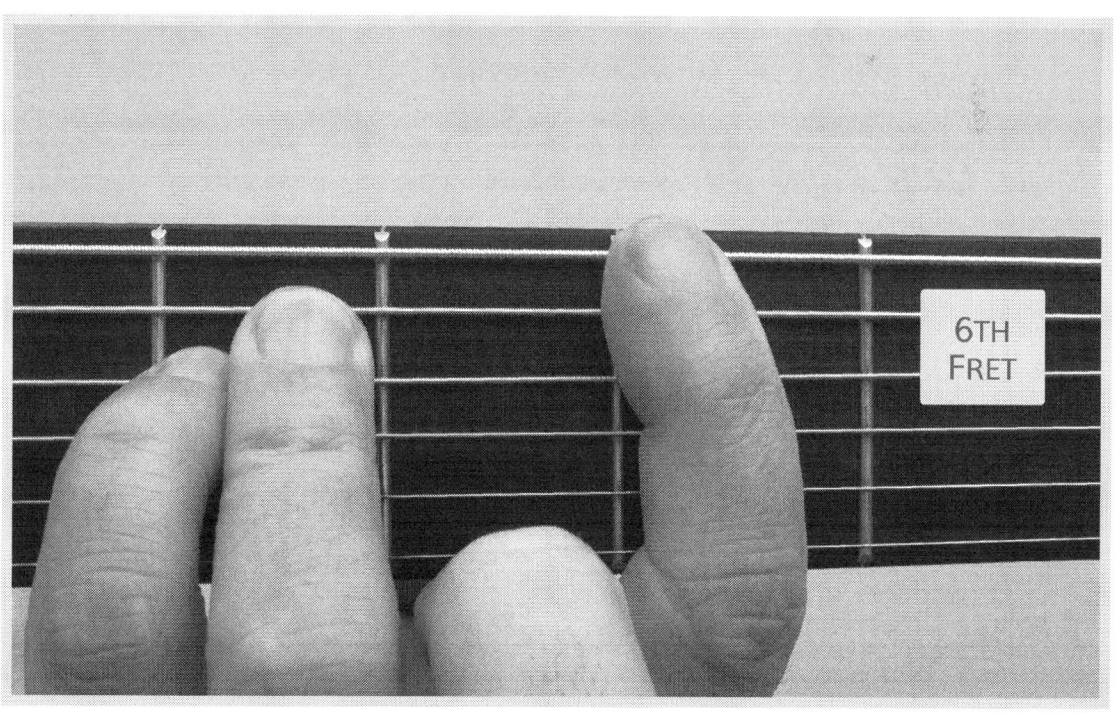

CADD9

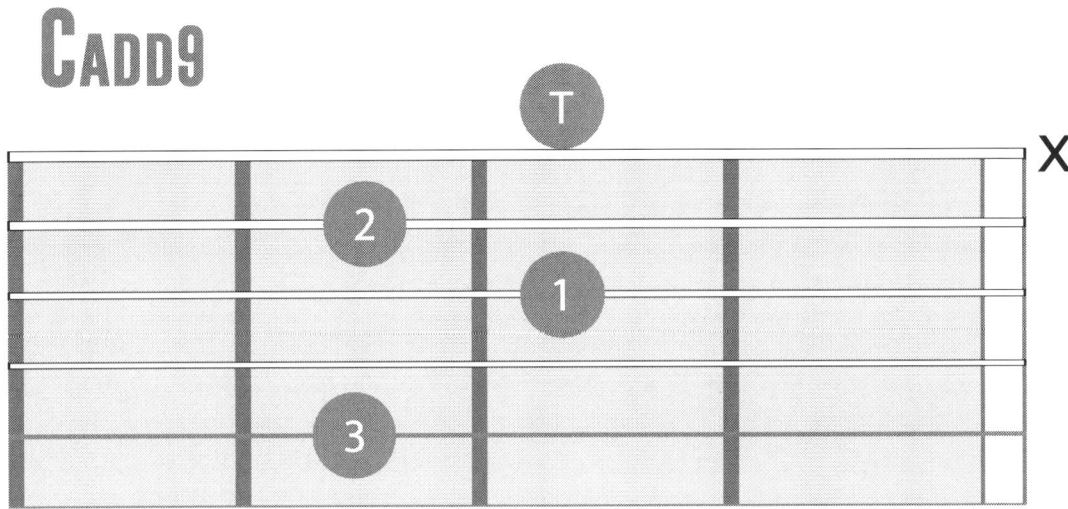

- Sometimes played instead of C
- Thumb touching 6th string
- Strum 6 strings - Only 5 sound

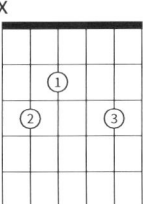

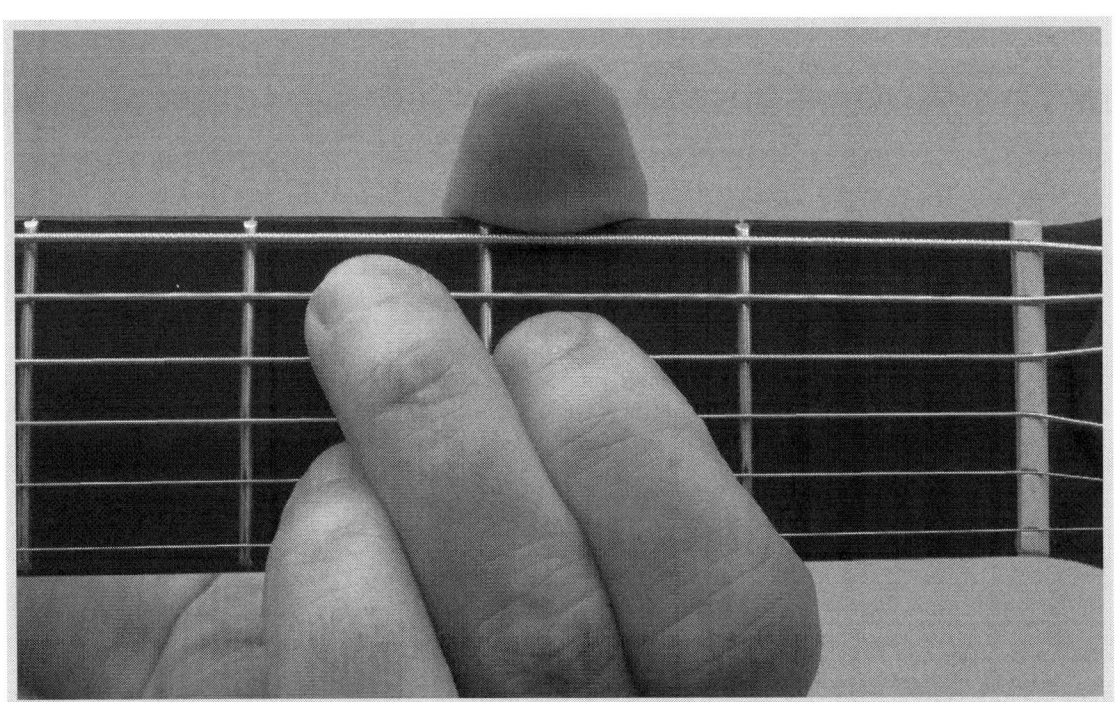

Cadd9 ANOTHER WAY

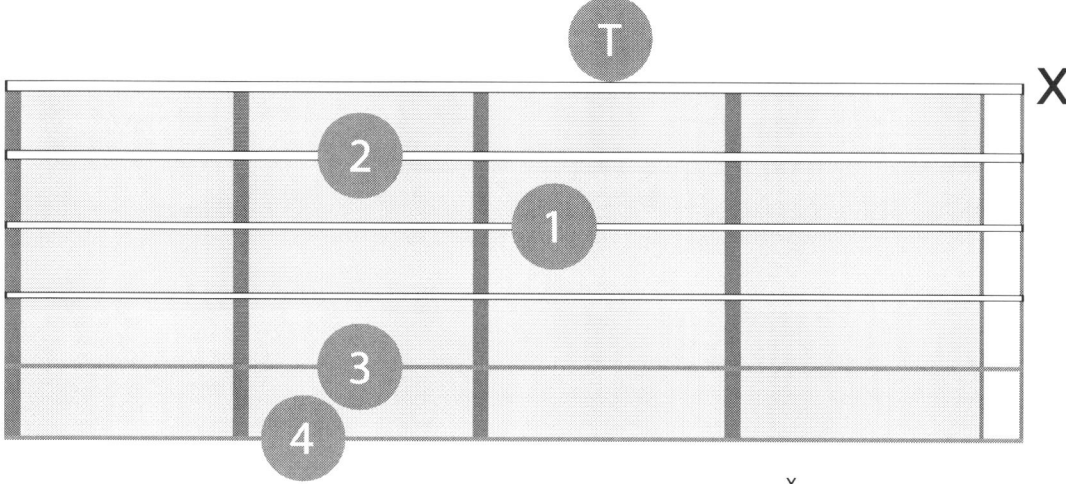

- Thumb touching 6th string
- 3rd finger in middle of fret
- Strum 6 strings - Only 5 sound

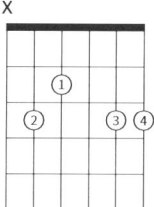

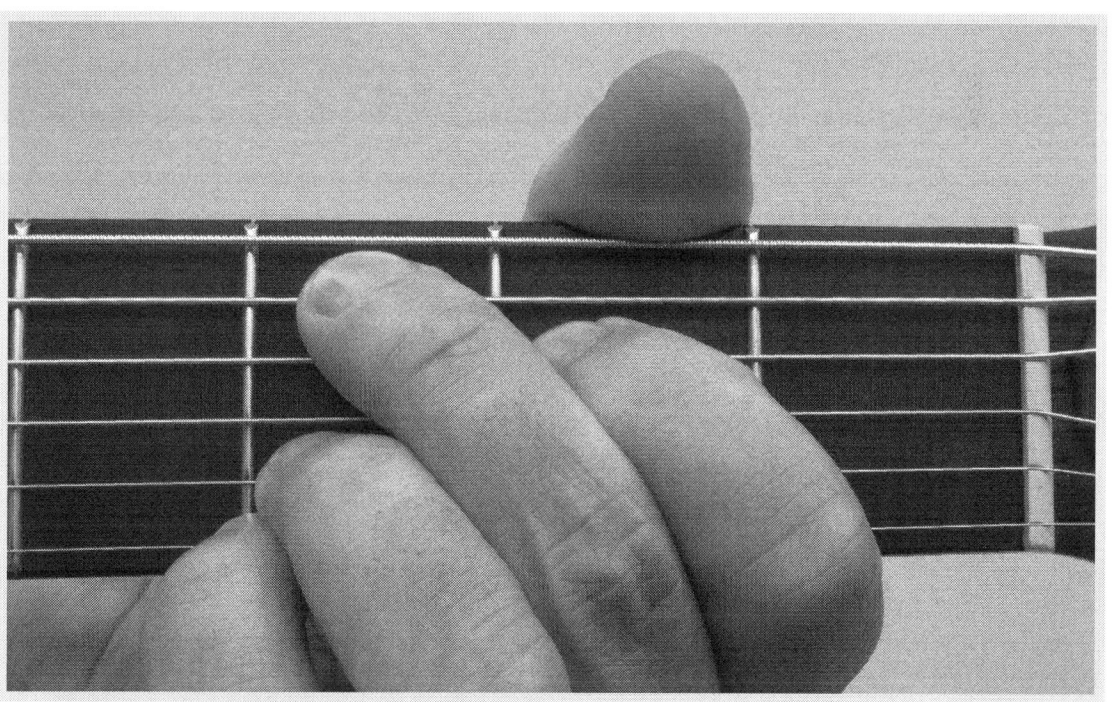

C/B

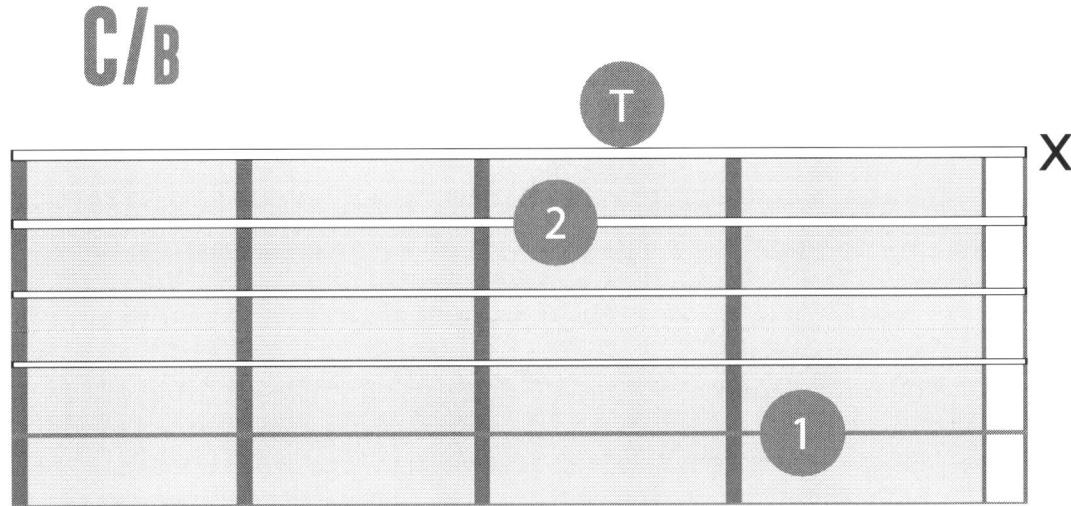

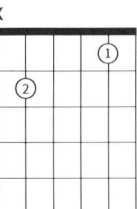

- Thumb touching 6th string
- 1st finger in corner of fret
- Strum 6 strings - Only 5 sound

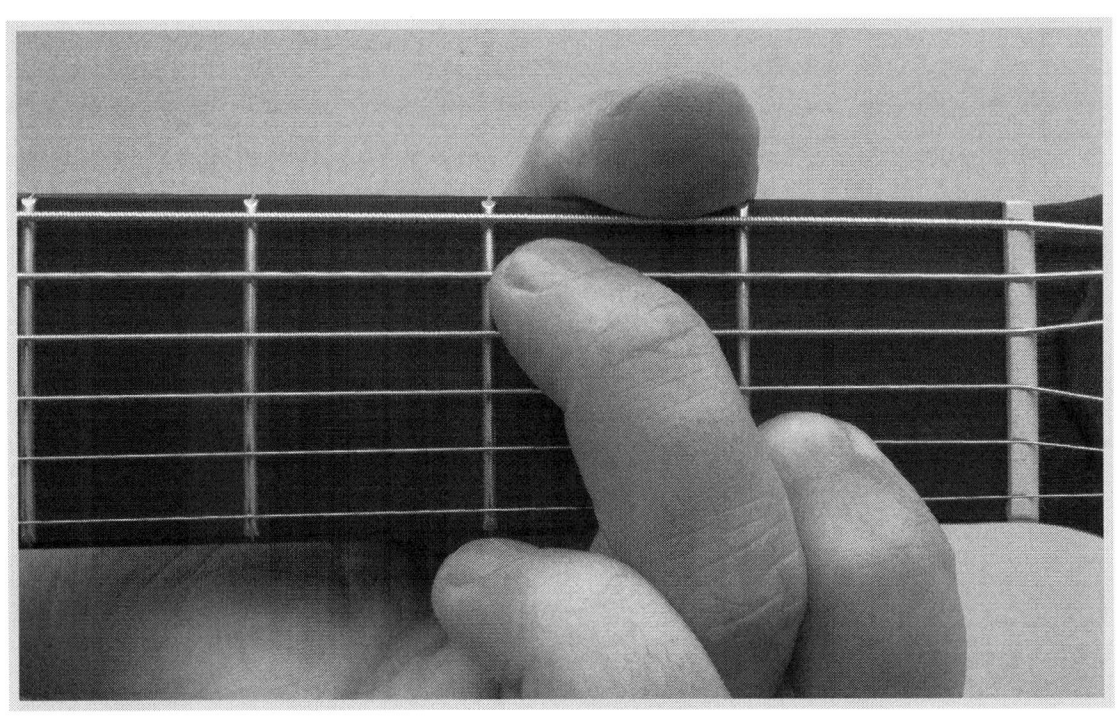

C/G

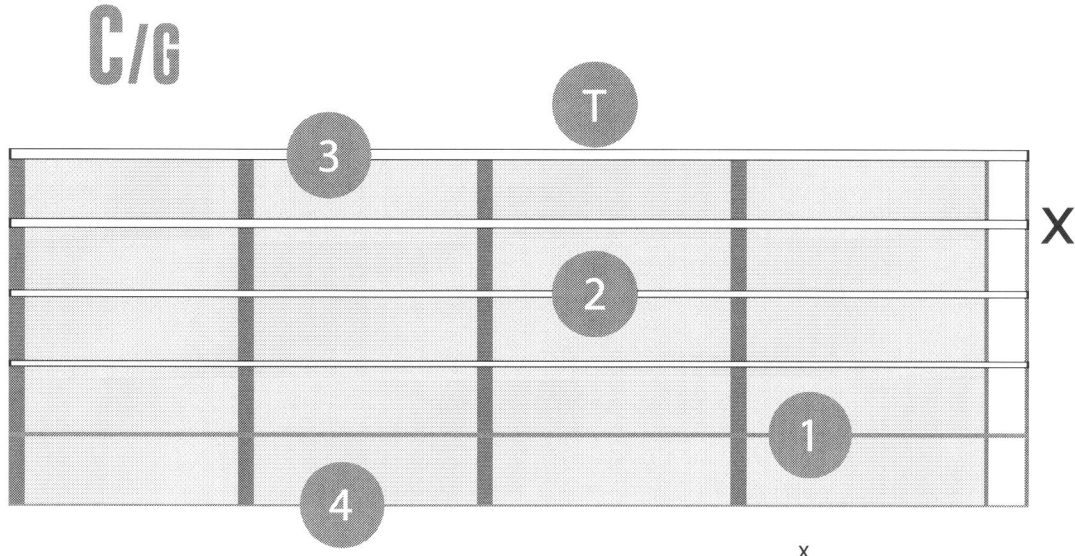

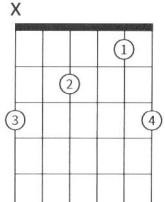

- Thumb may or may not touch 6th string
- 5th string muted by inside of 3rd finger
- Strum 6 strings - Only 5 sound

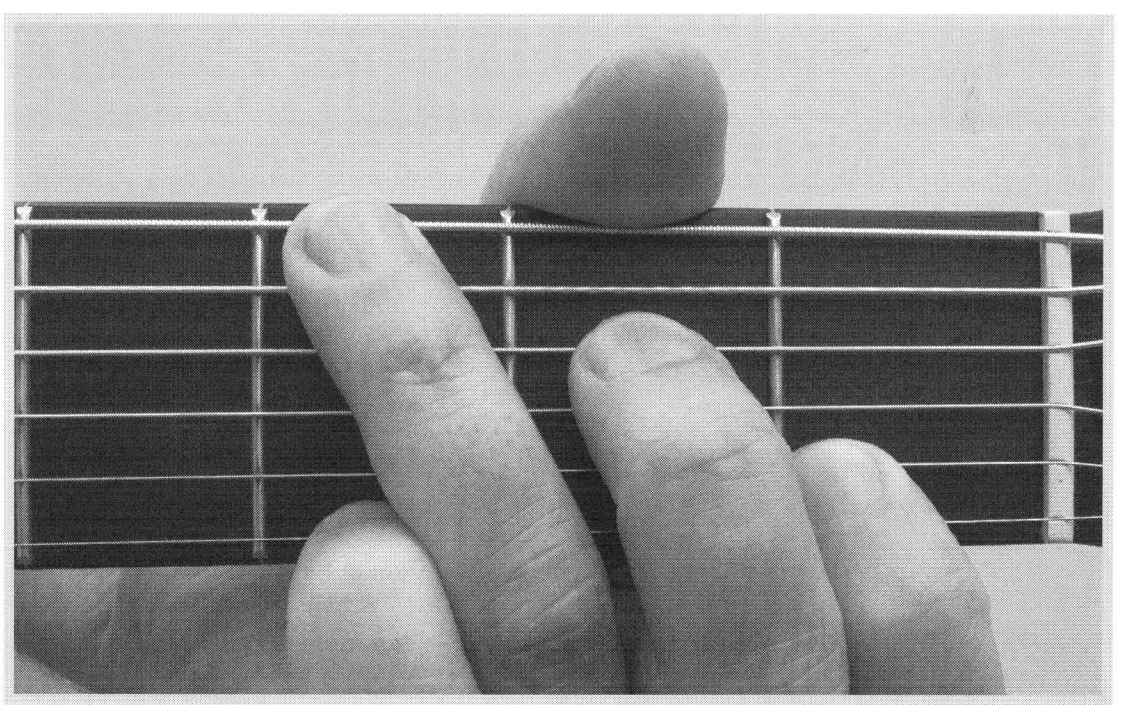

C/E

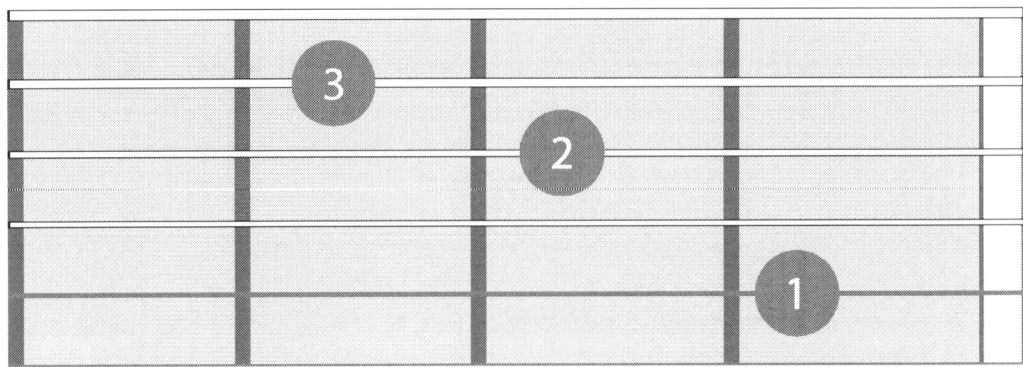

- Thumb not touching 6th string
- 1st finger in corner of fret
- All 6 strings sound

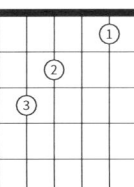

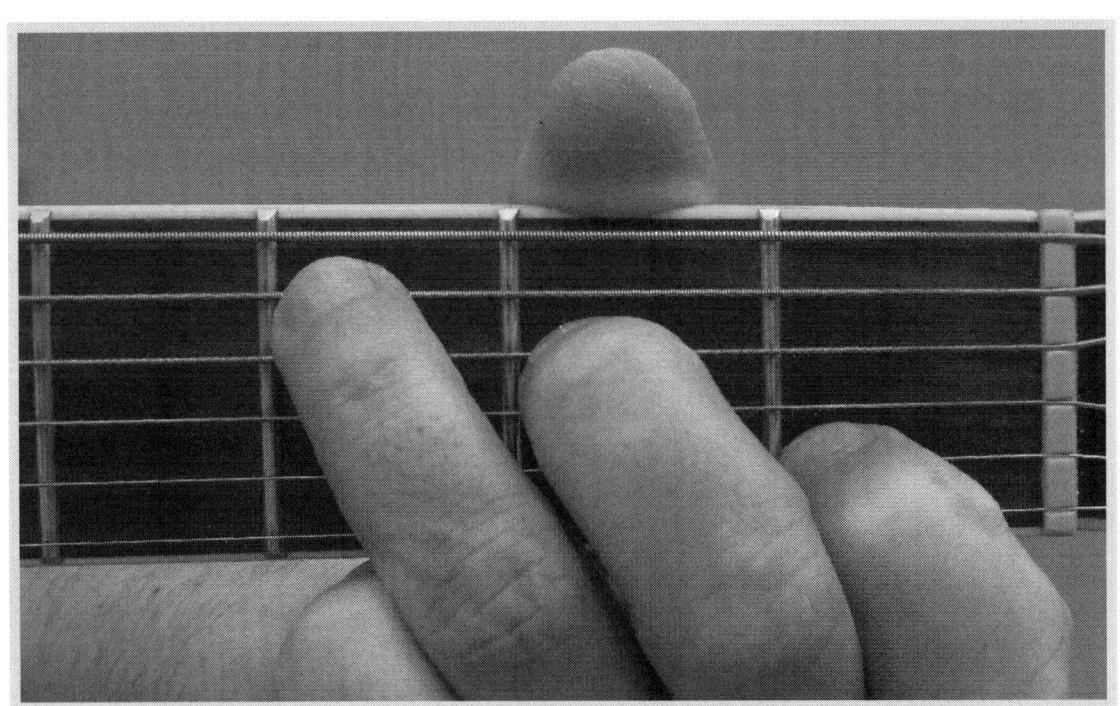

C/E *EASIER*

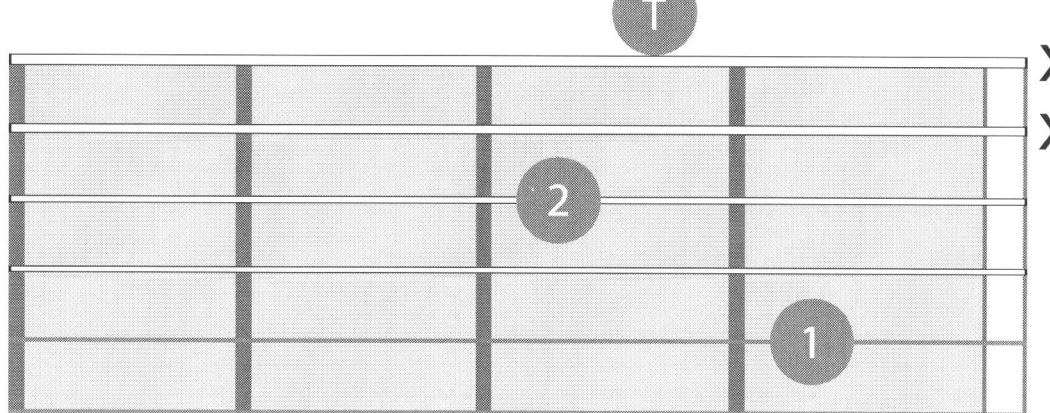

- Thumb touching 6th string
- 1st finger in corner of fret
- Strum bottom 4 strings

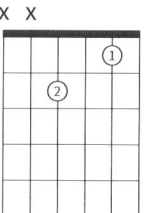

C#m

3RD FRET

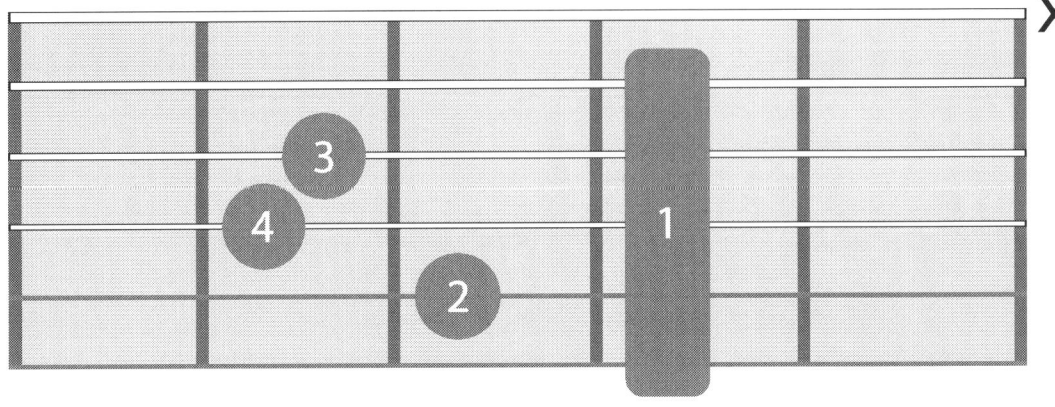

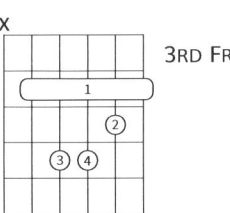

- Thumb low and centred
- 1st finger touching 6th string
- Strum 6 strings - Only 5 sound

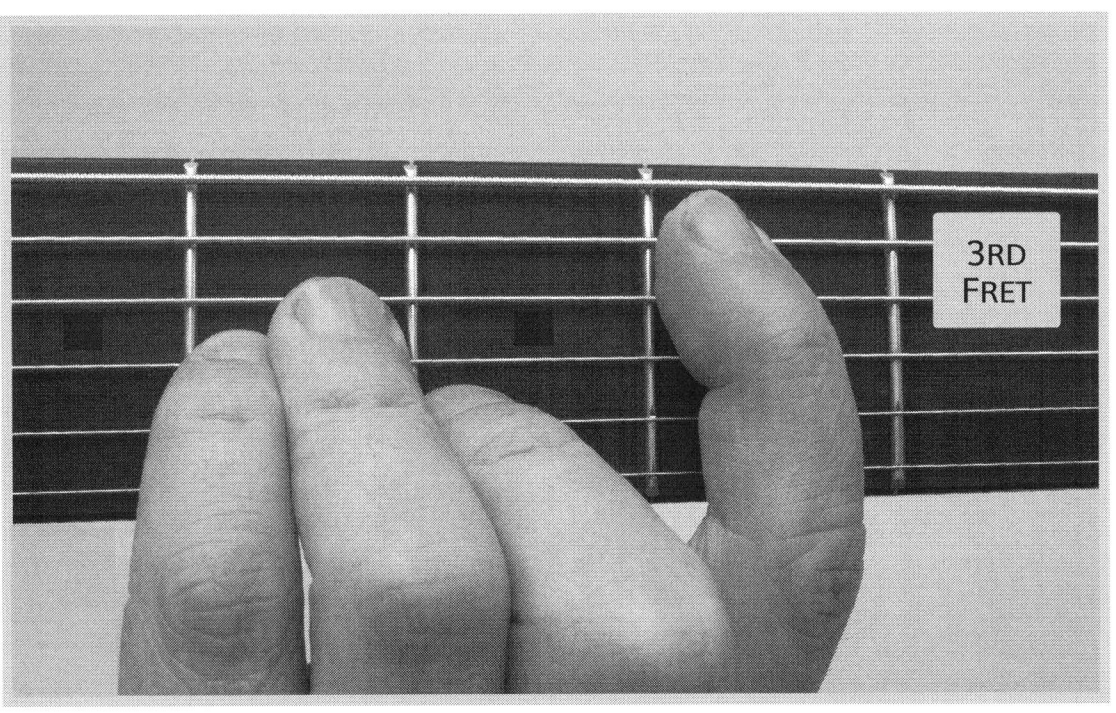

C#m *EASIER*

3RD FRET

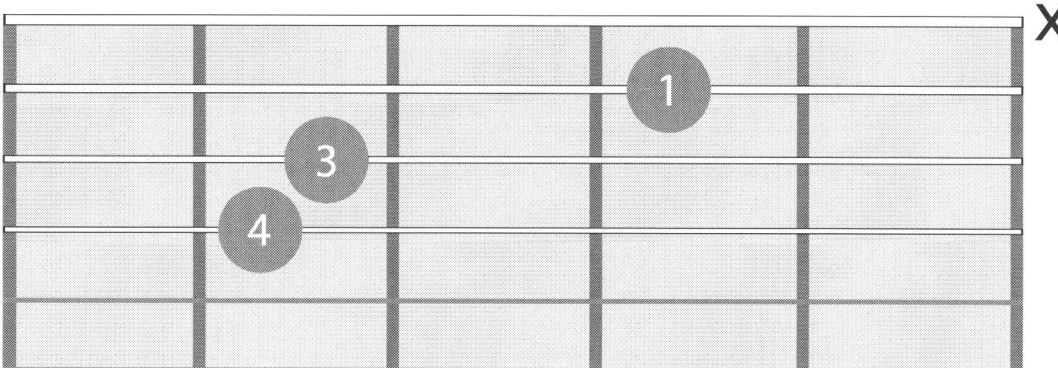

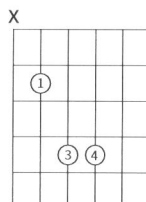

3RD FRET

- Thumb low and centred
- 1st finger touching 6th string
- Strum 6 strings - Only 5 sound

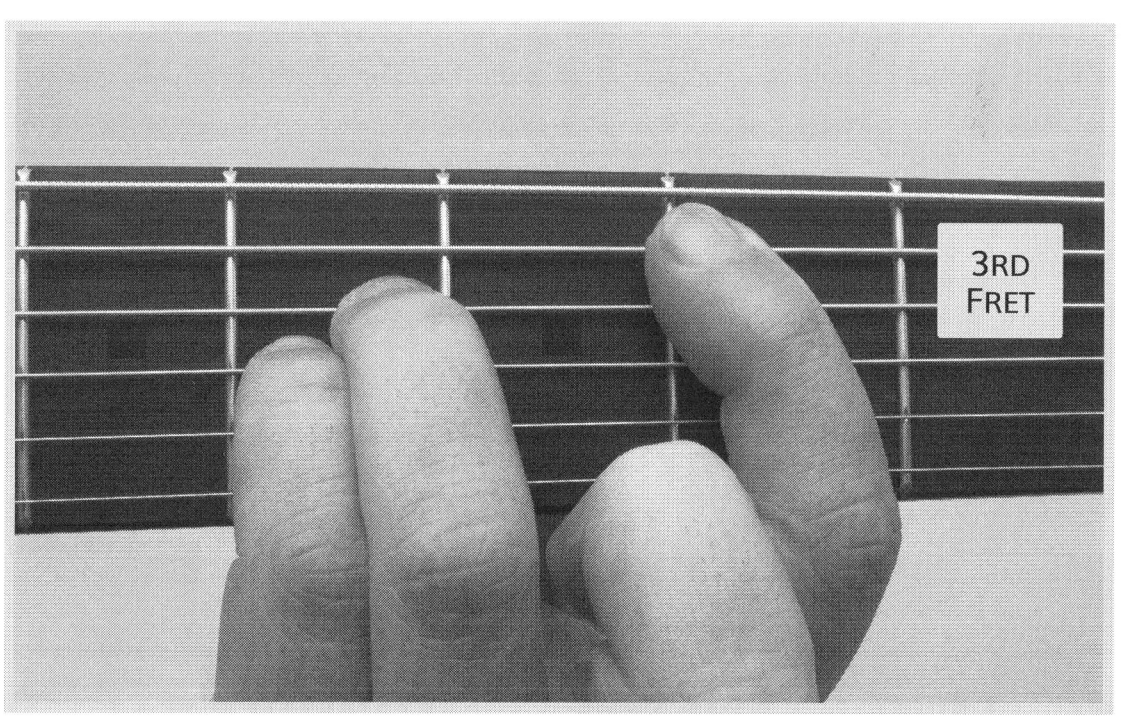

C#5

3RD FRET

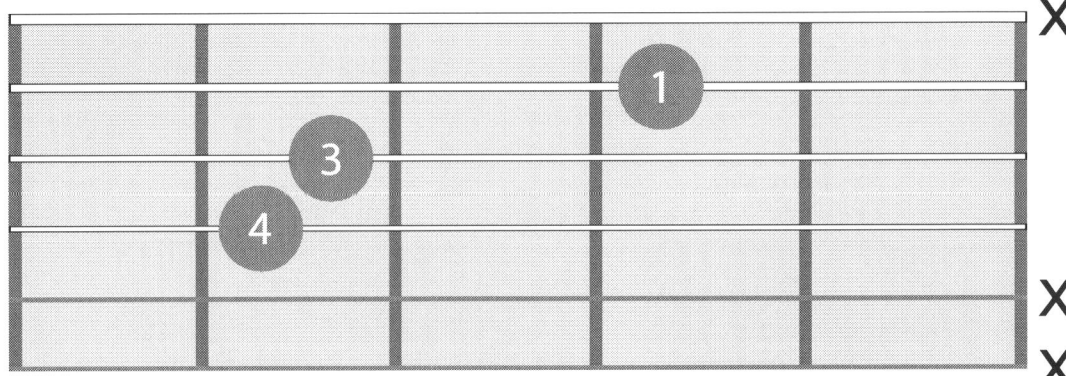

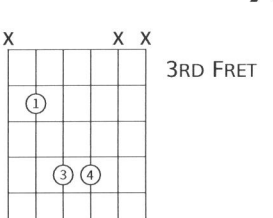

3RD FRET

- Thumb low and centred
- 1st finger touching 6th string
- Strum 5th 4th and 3rd strings

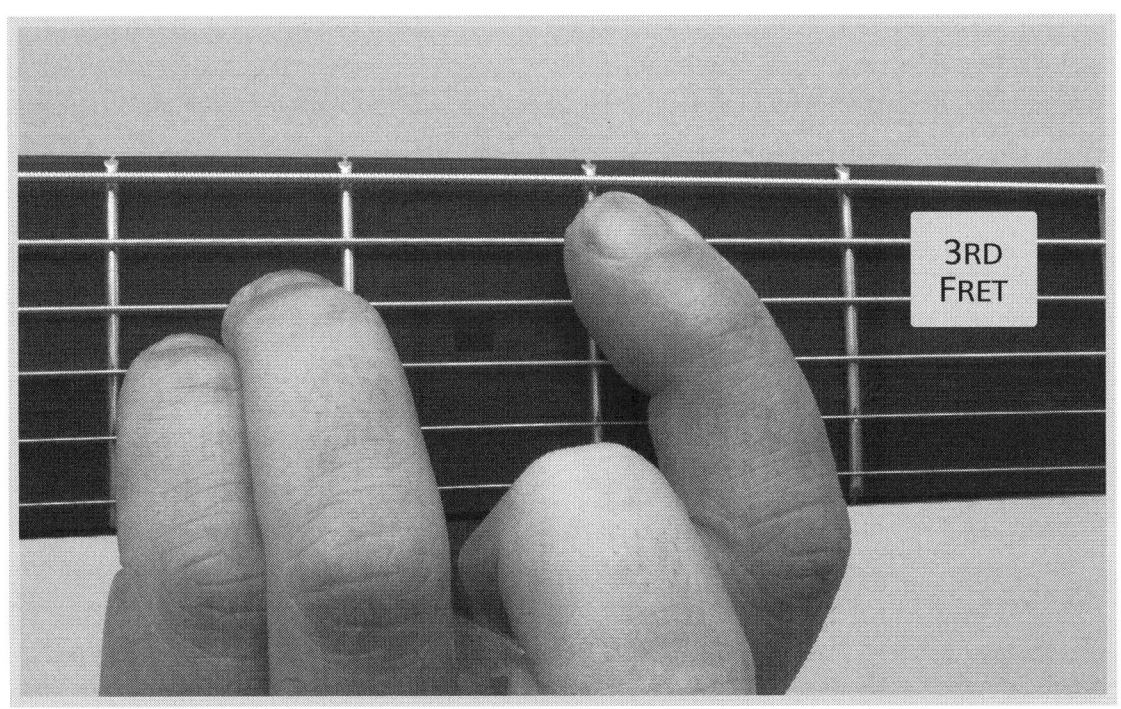

C#m7

3RD FRET

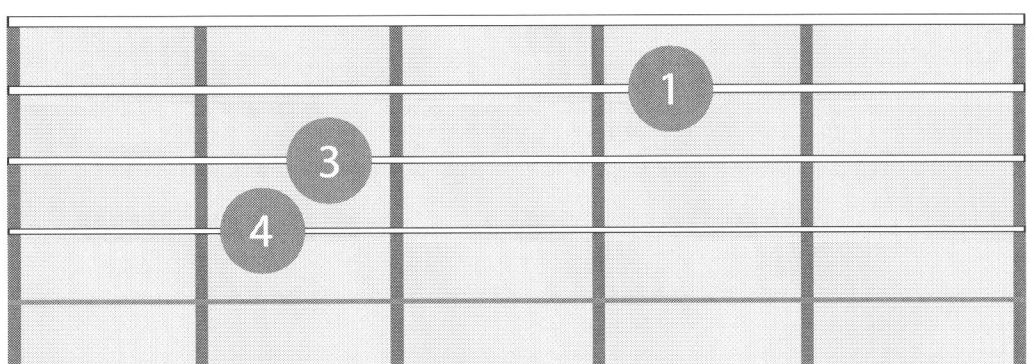

- Sometimes played instead of C#m
- Thumb low and centred
- Strum 6 strings - Only 5 sound

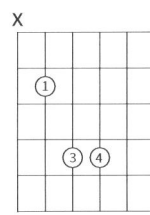

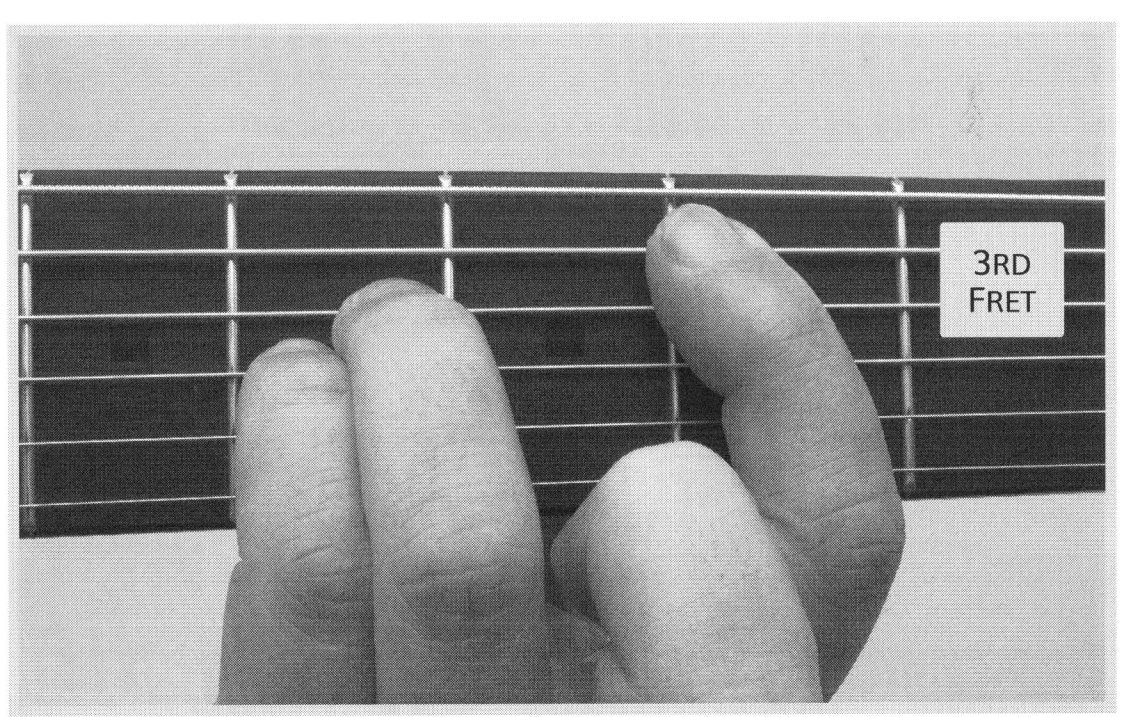

D

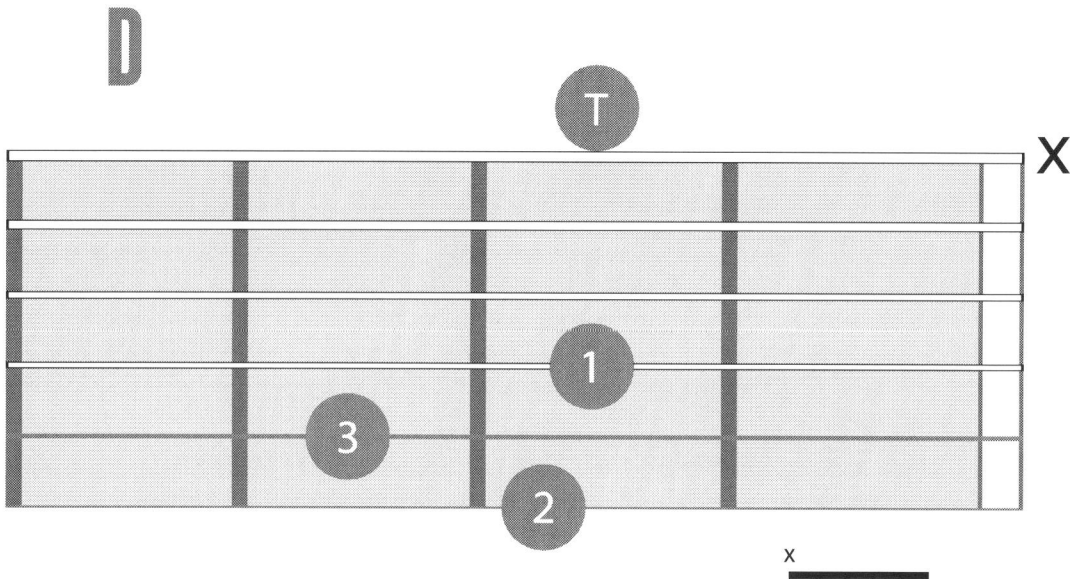

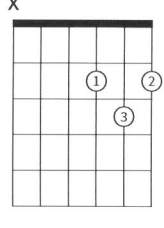

- Thumb touching 6th string
- 3rd finger in middle of fret
- Strum 6 strings - Only 5 sound

Dm

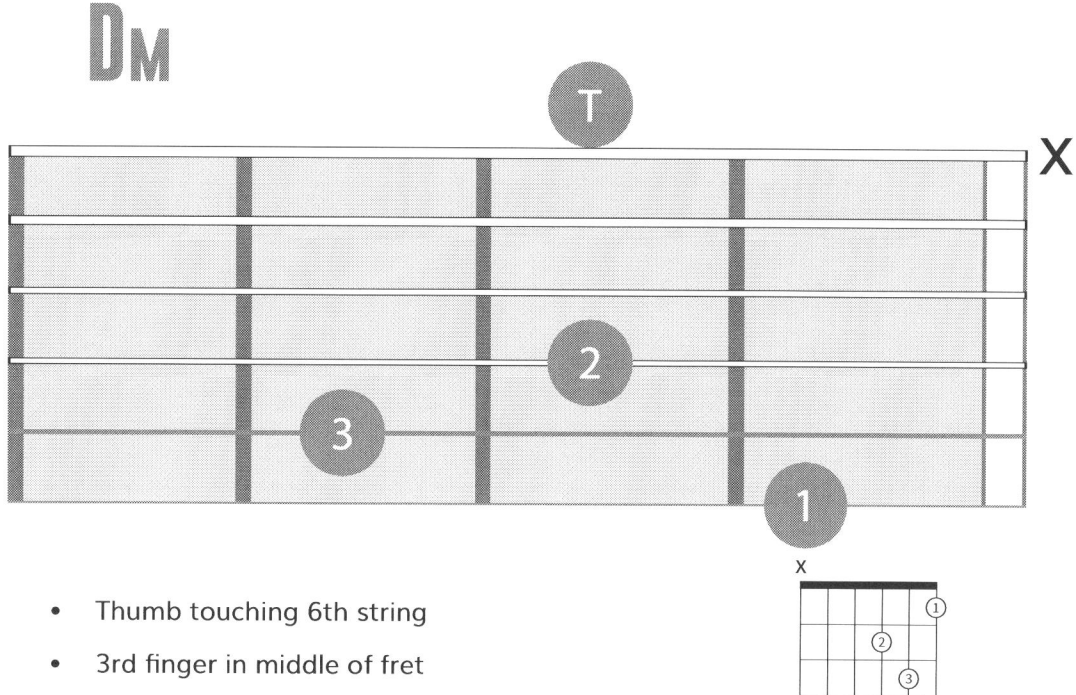

- Thumb touching 6th string
- 3rd finger in middle of fret
- Strum 6 strings - Only 5 sound

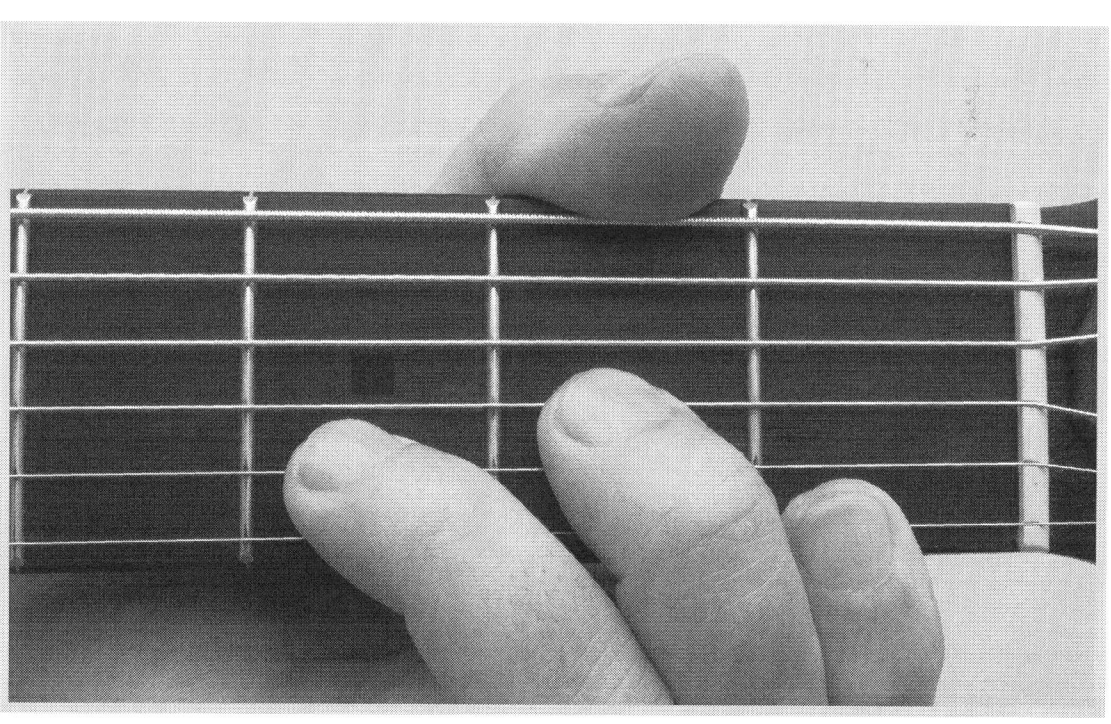

D/B

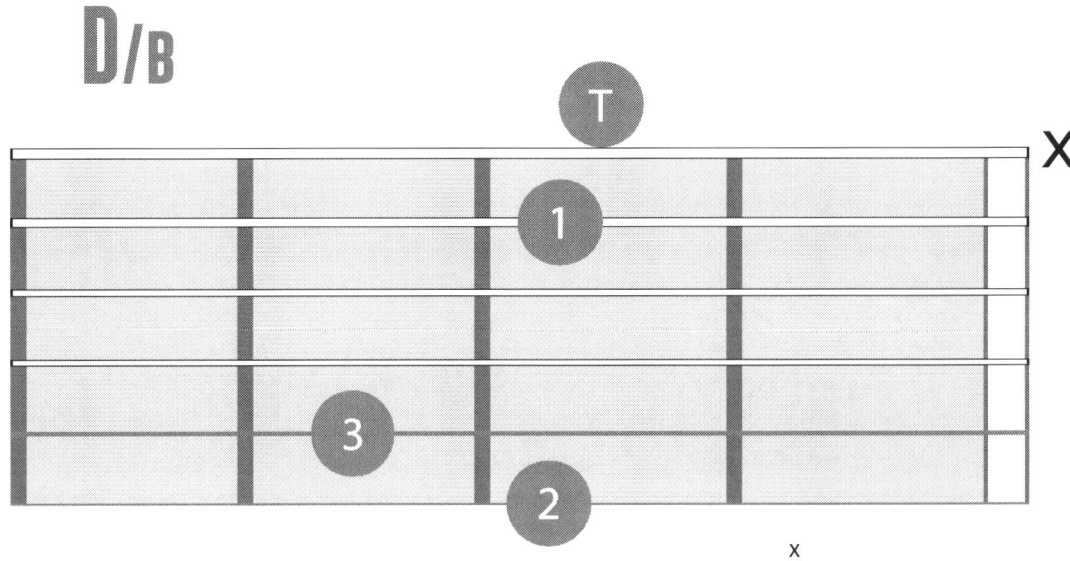

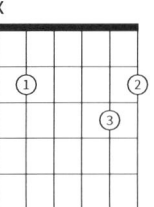

- Thumb may or may not touch 6th string
- 3rd finger in middle of fret
- Strum 6 strings - Only 5 sound

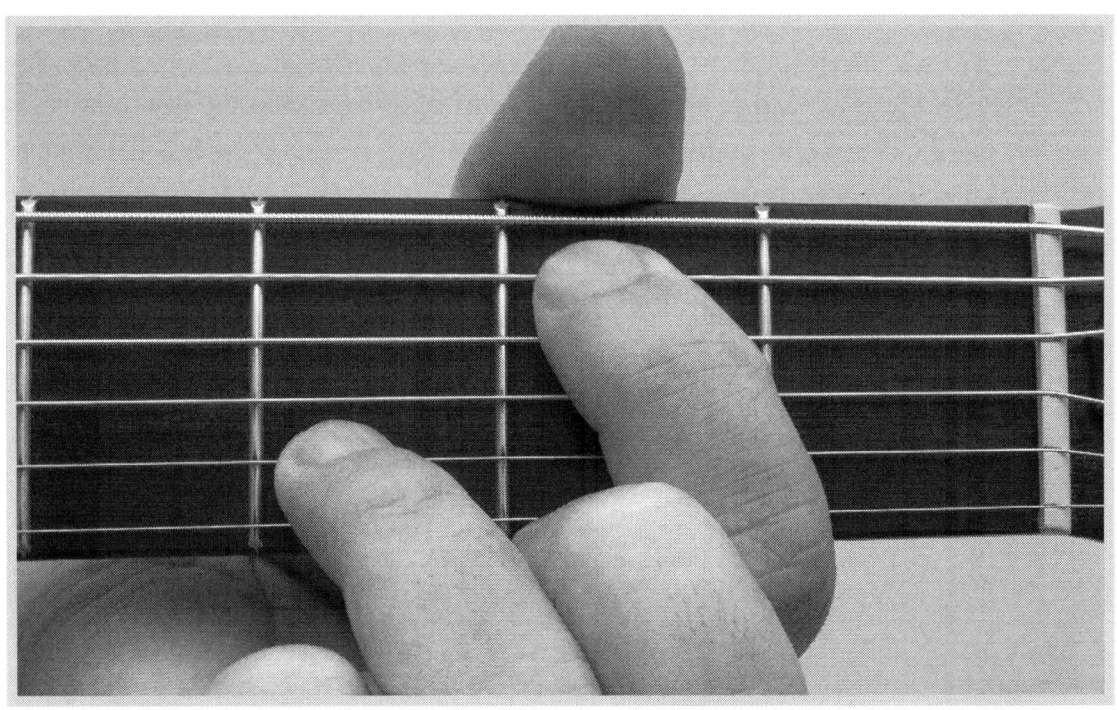

D/C

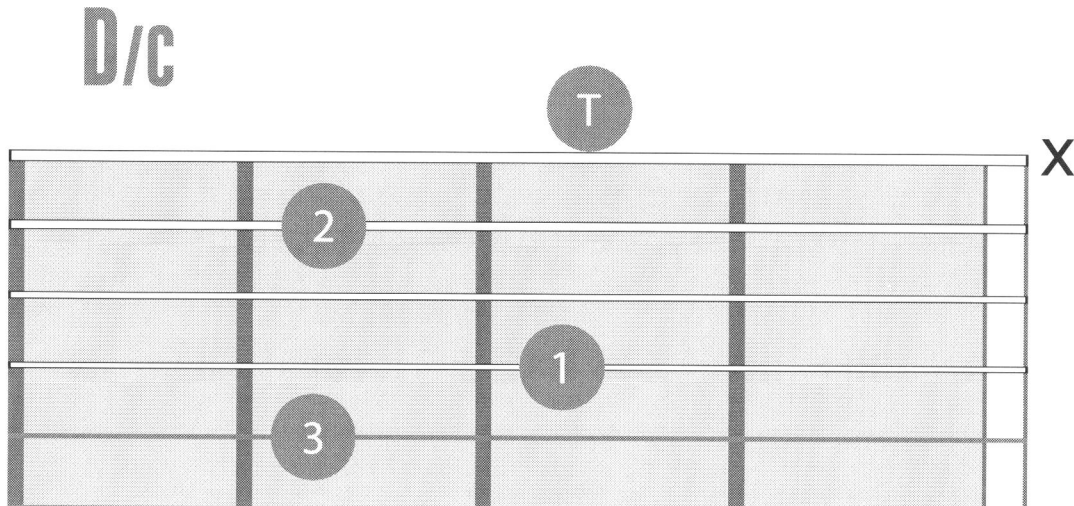

- Thumb touching 6th string
- 3rd finger in middle of fret
- Strum 6 strings - Only 5 sound

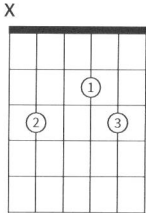

Dsus2

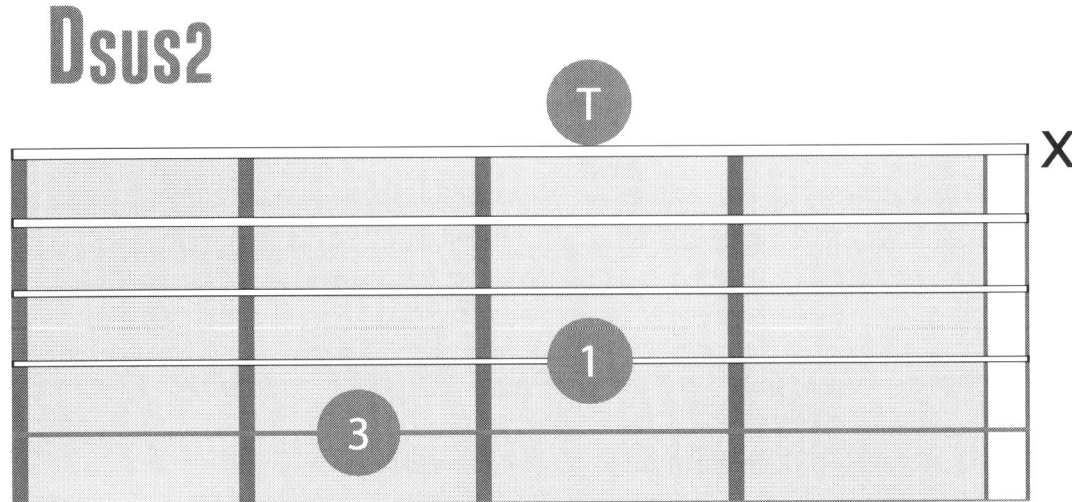

- Thumb touching 6th string
- 3rd finger in middle of fret
- Strum 6 strings - Only 5 sound

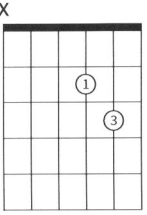

Dsus2 ANOTHER WAY

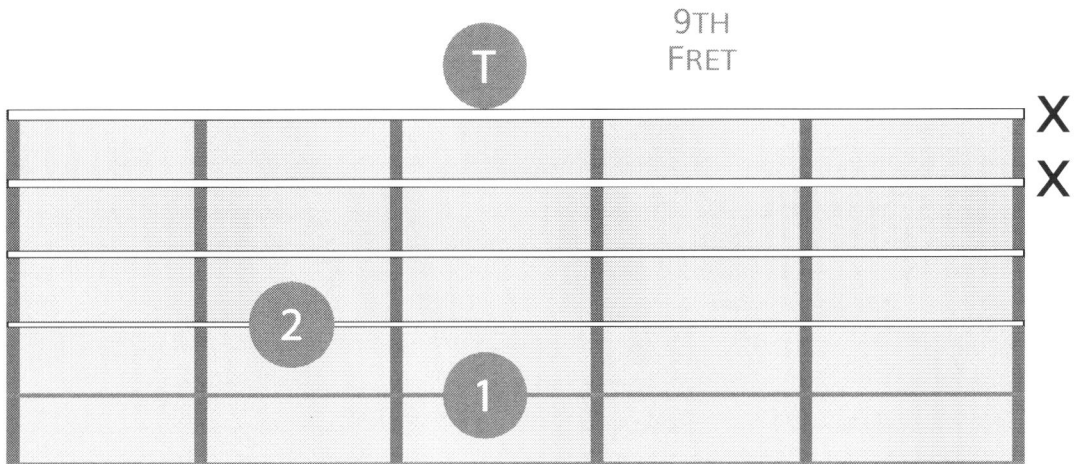

- Thumb touching 6th string
- 1st finger in corner of fret
- Strum bottom 4 strings

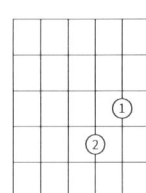

9TH FRET

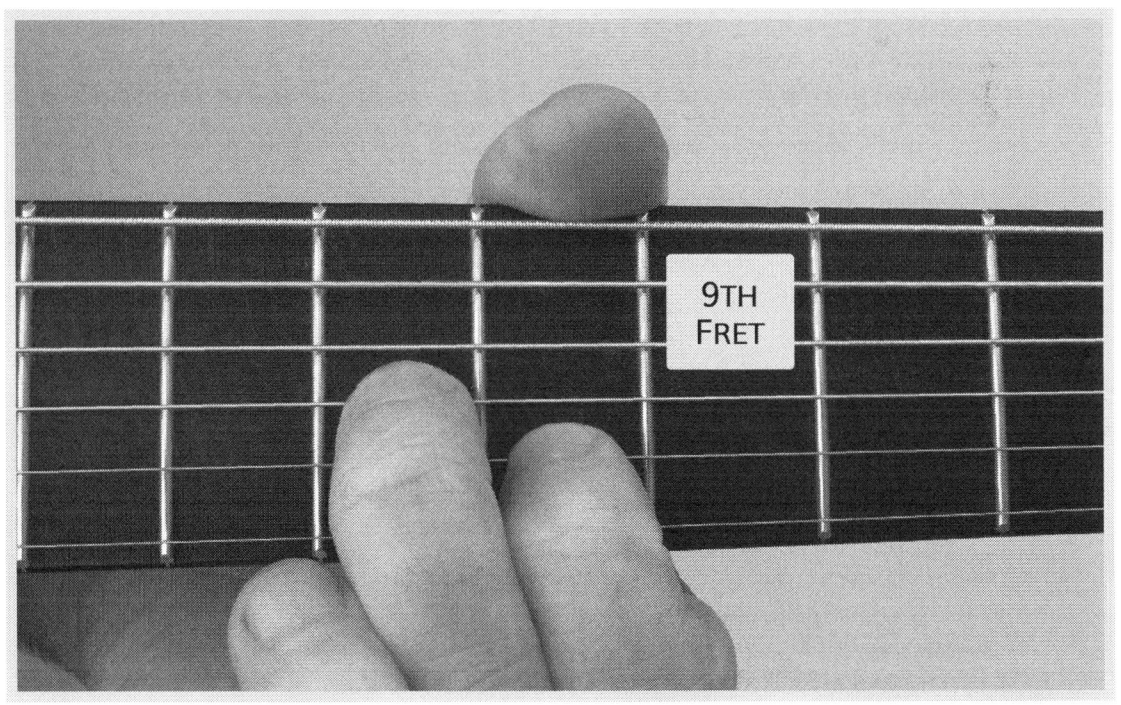

Dsus4

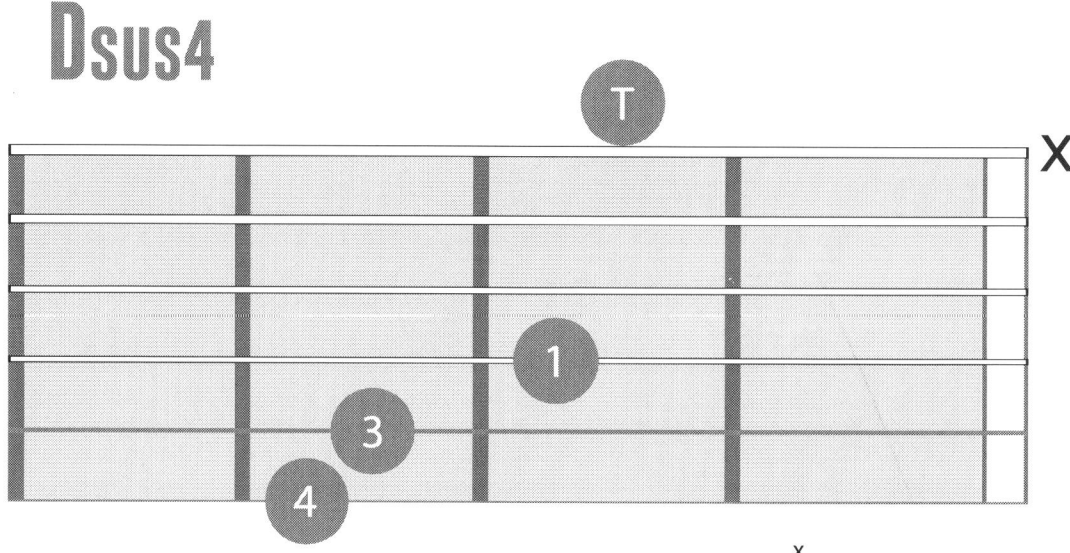

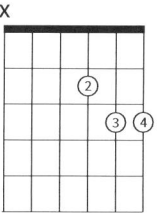

- Thumb touching 6th string
- 3rd finger in middle of fret
- Strum 6 strings - Only 5 sound

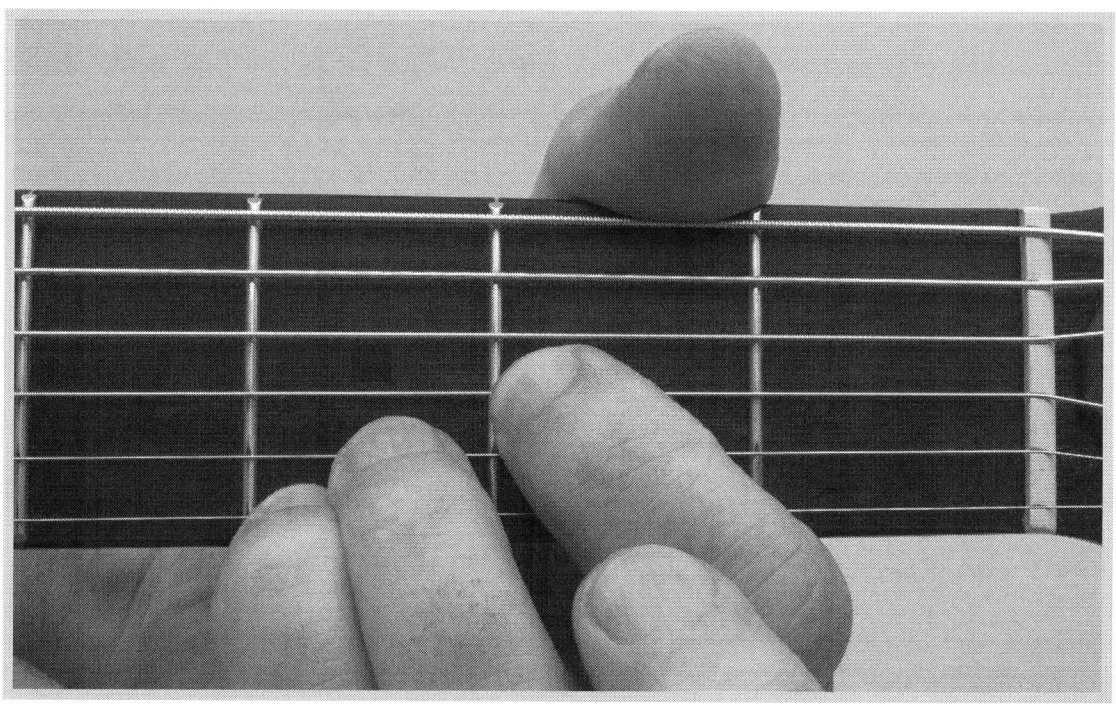

D5

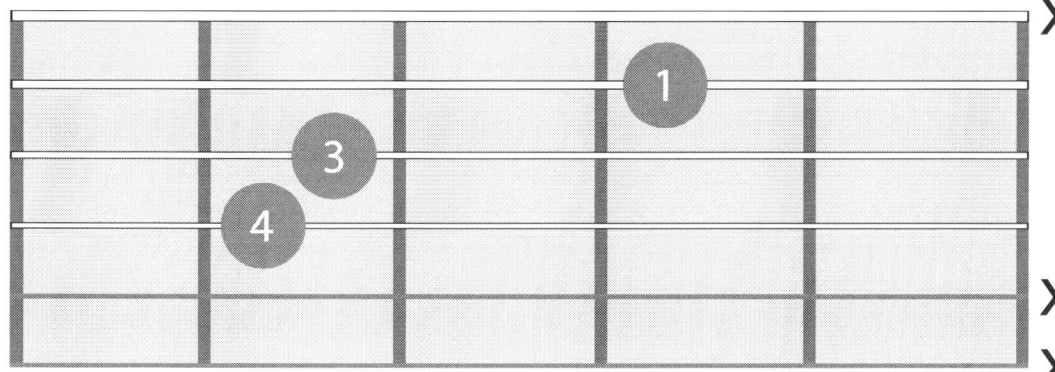

- Thumb low and centred
- 1st finger touching 6th string
- Strum 5th 4th and 3rd strings

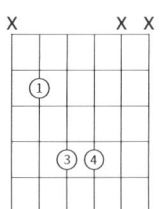

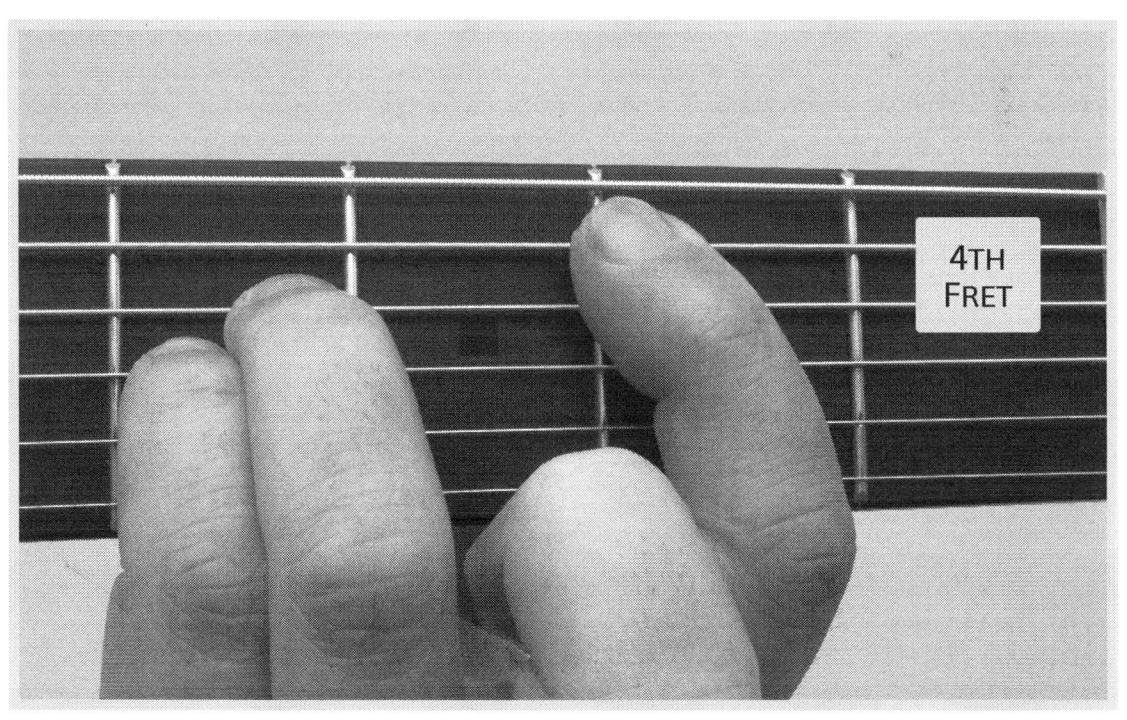

D6

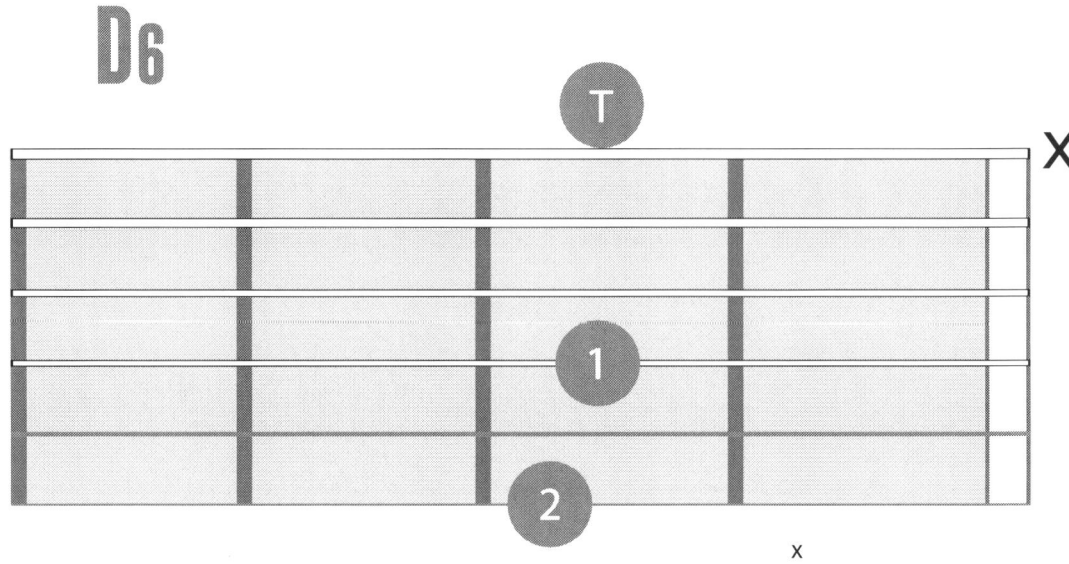

- Thumb touching 6th string
- Can also be played with 2nd and 3rd finger
- Strum 6 strings - Only 5 sound

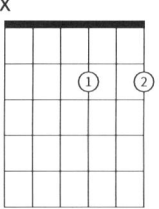

D6/9

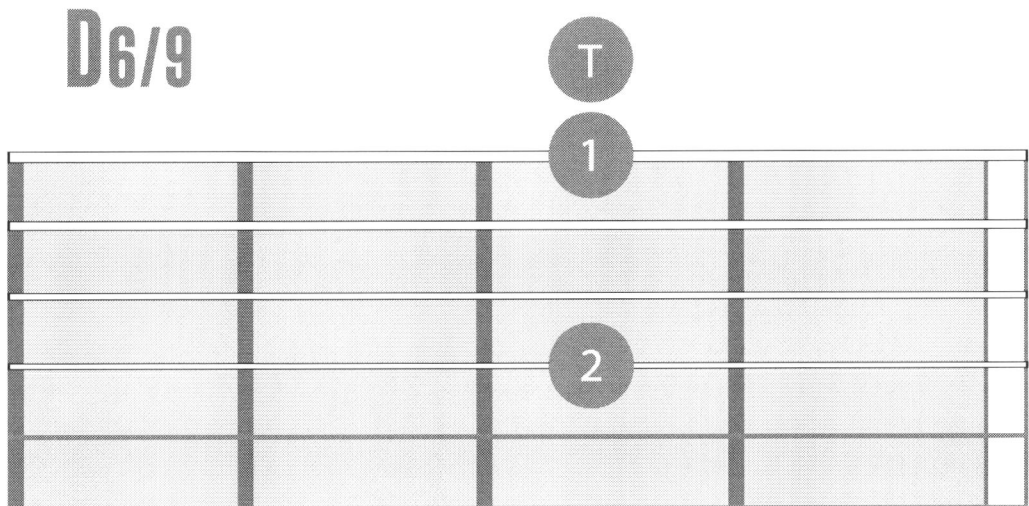

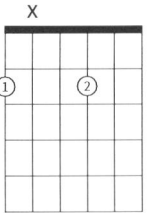

- 5th string muted by inside of 1st finger
- Can also be played with 2nd and 3rd finger
- Strum 6 strings - Only 5 sound

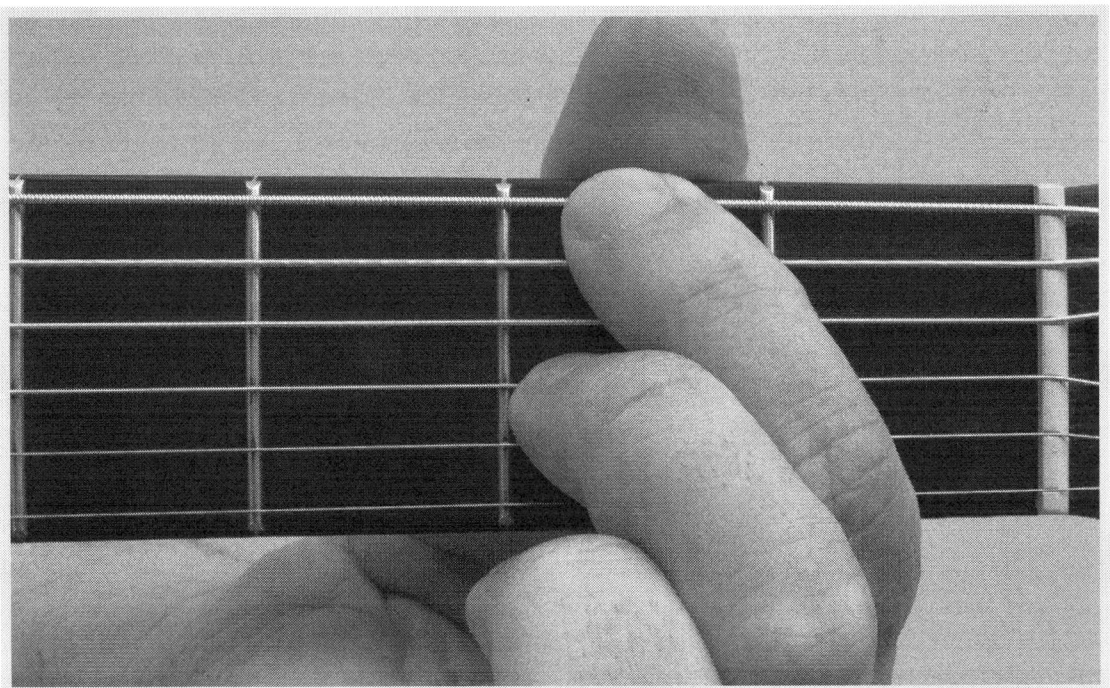

D7

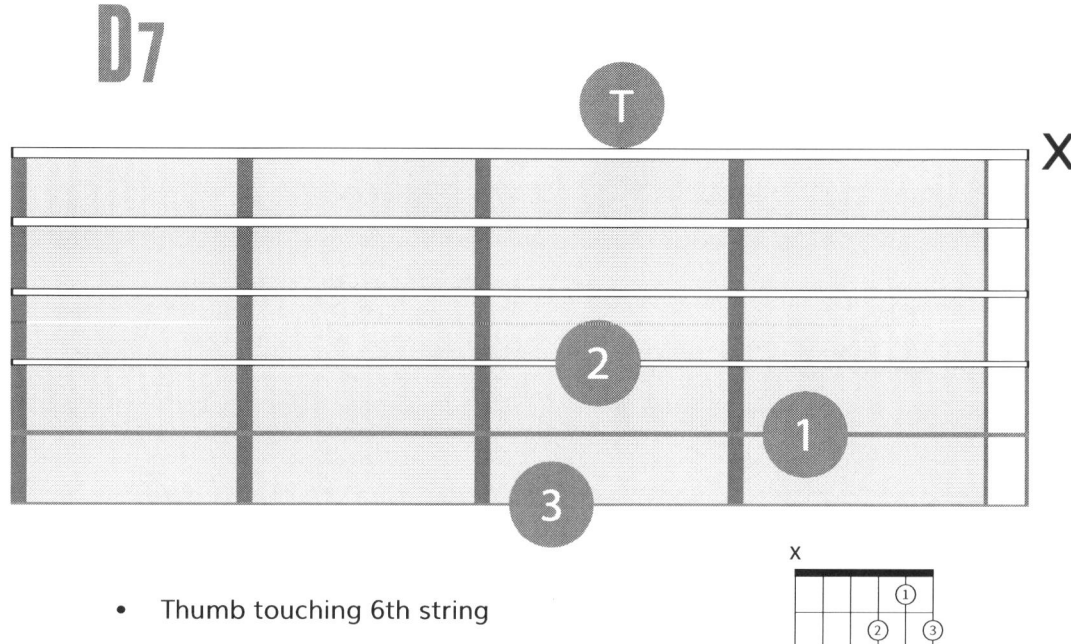

- Thumb touching 6th string
- 1st finger in corner of fret
- Strum 6 strings - Only 5 sound

D7 ANOTHER WAY

2ND FRET

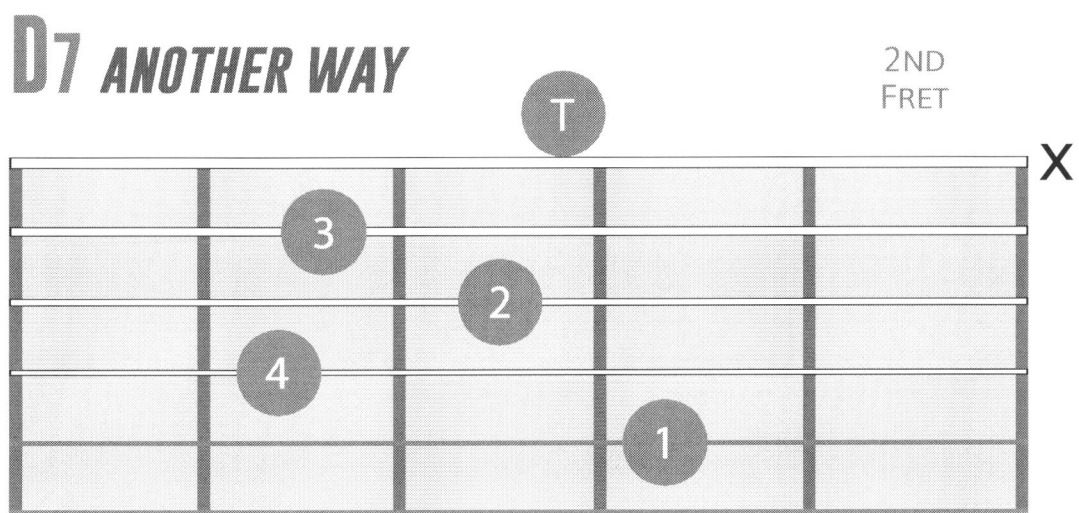

- Thumb touching 6th string
- 1st finger in corner of fret
- Strum 6 strings - Only 5 sound

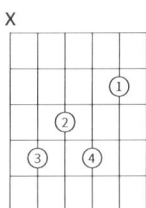

2ND FRET

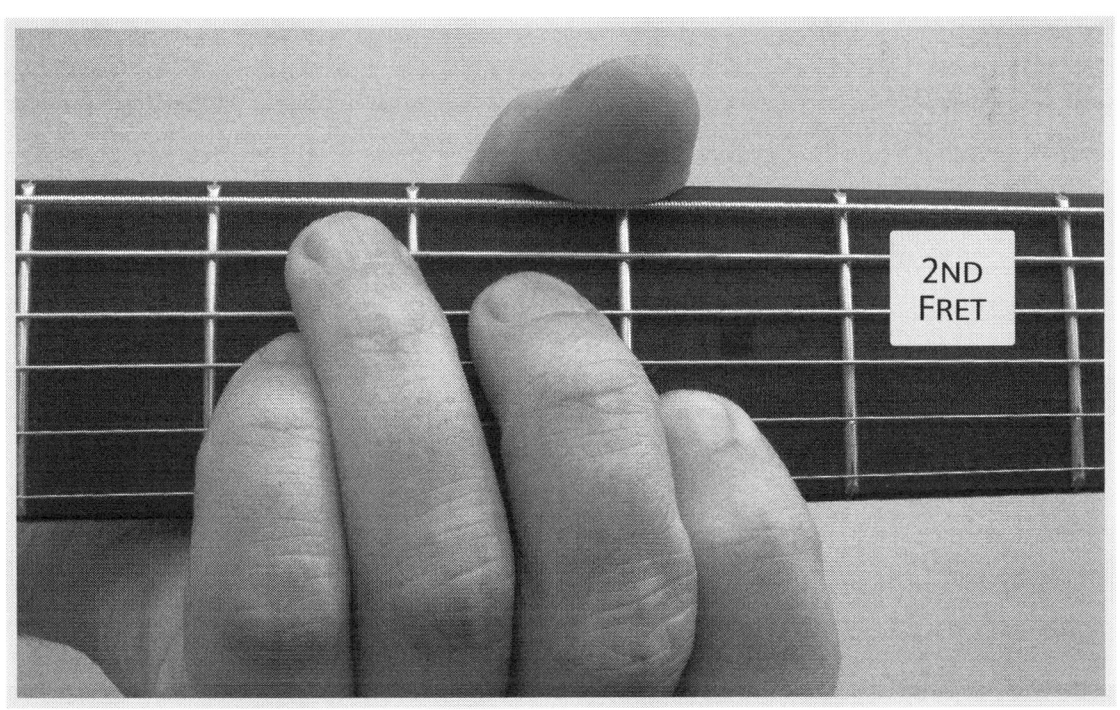

DM7

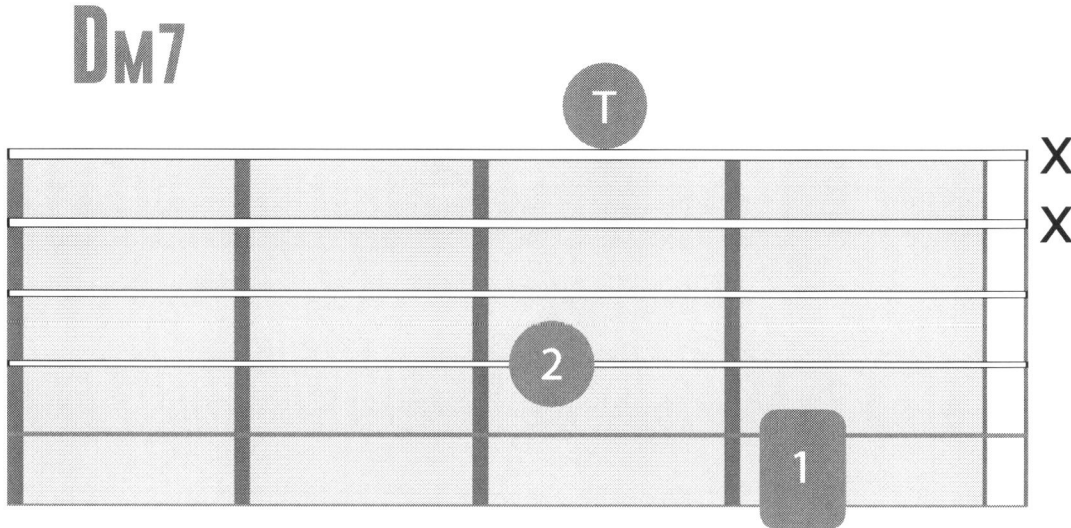

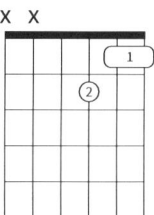

- Grab the guitar neck
- 1st finger pressing 2 strings
- Strum bottom 4 strings

Dm7 ANOTHER WAY

4TH FRET

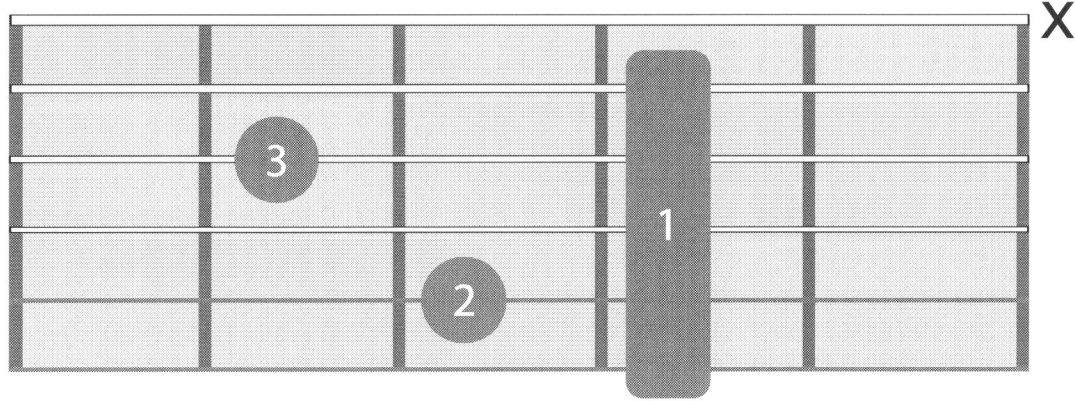

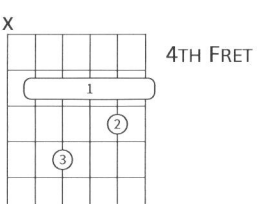

4TH FRET

- Thumb low and centred
- 1st finger touching 6th string
- Strum 6 strings - Only 5 sound

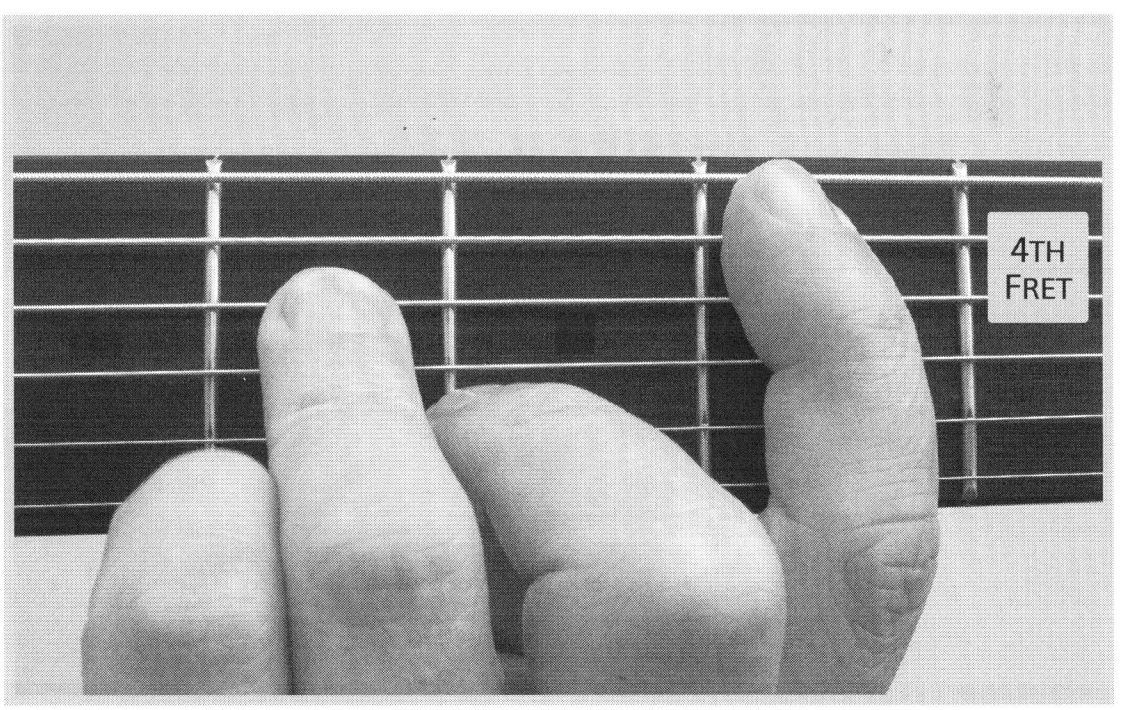

D_{MAJ7}

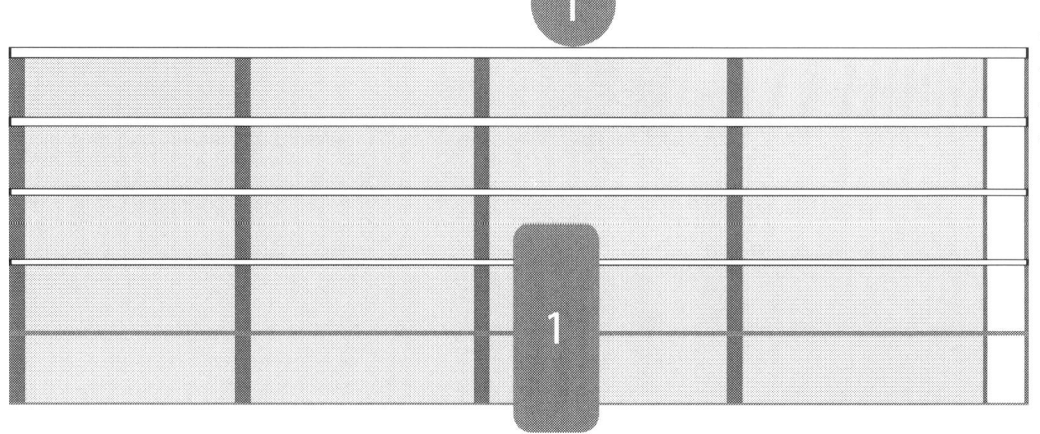

- Sometimes played instead of D
- 1st finger pressing 3 strings
- Strum bottom 4 strings

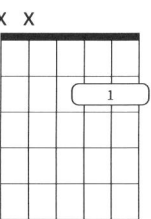

DMAJ9

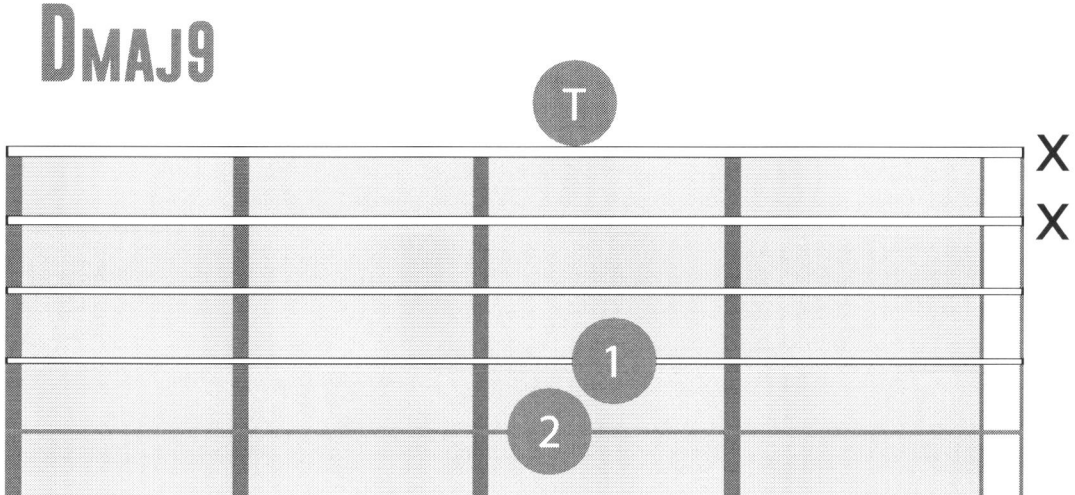

- Thumb touching 6th string
- Can also be played with 2nd & 3rd fingers
- Strum bottom 4 strings

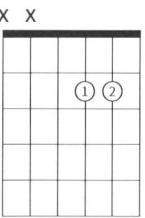

D/E

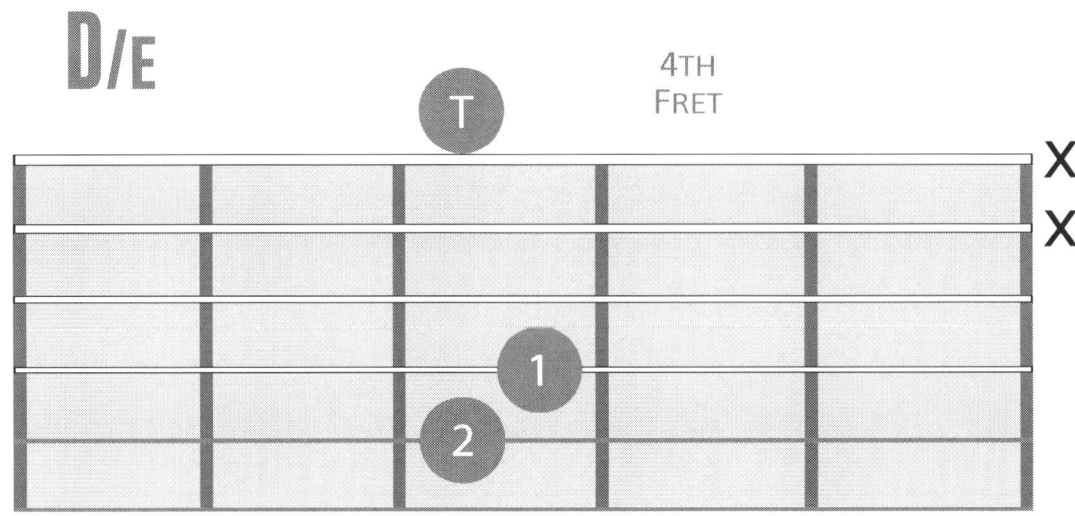

4TH FRET

- Thumb touching 6th string
- Can also be played with 2nd & 3rd fingers
- Strum bottom 4 strings

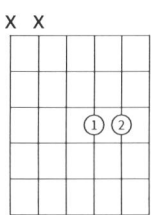

4TH FRET

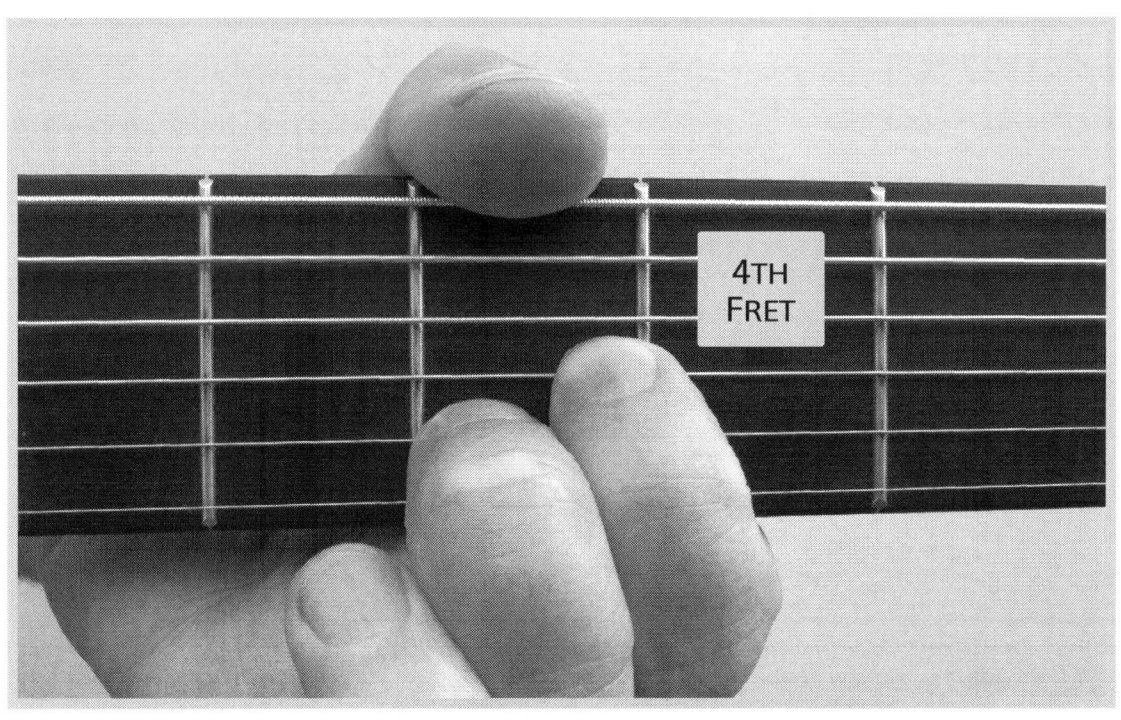

4TH FRET

E

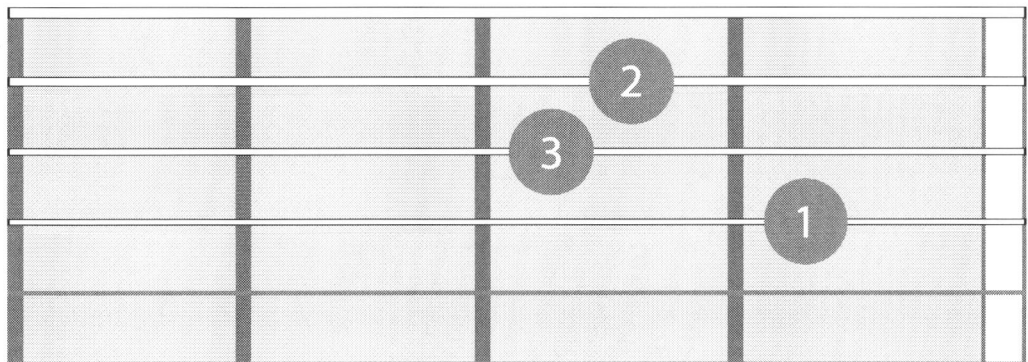

- Thumb not touching 6th string
- 1st finger in corner of fret
- All 6 strings sound

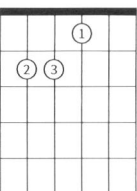

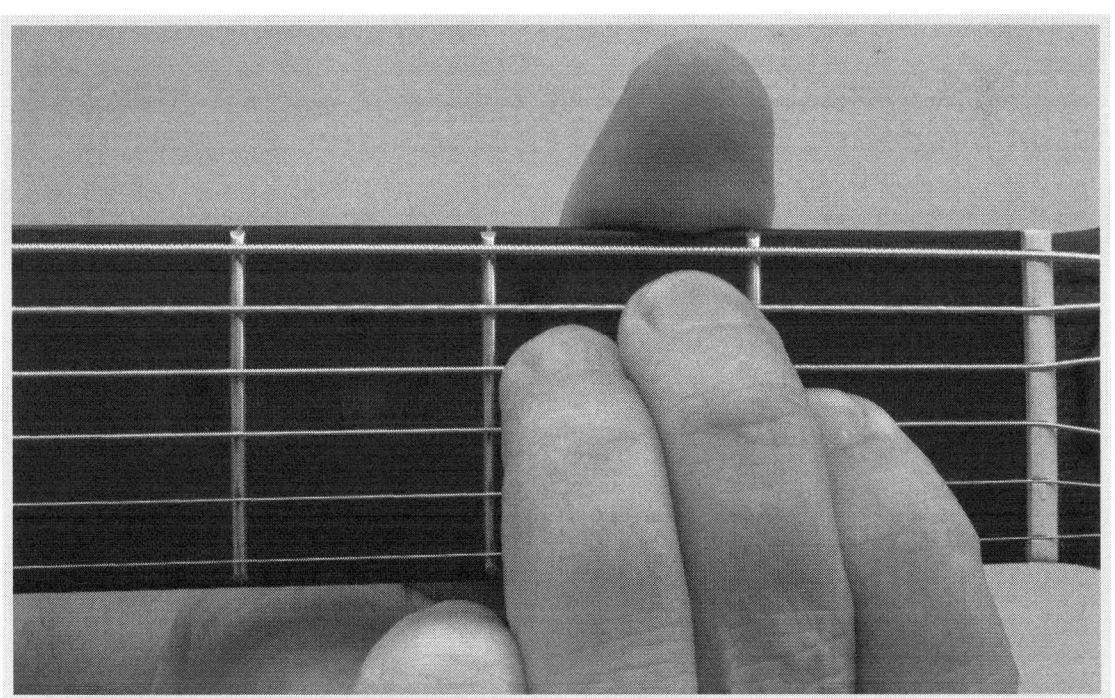

Em

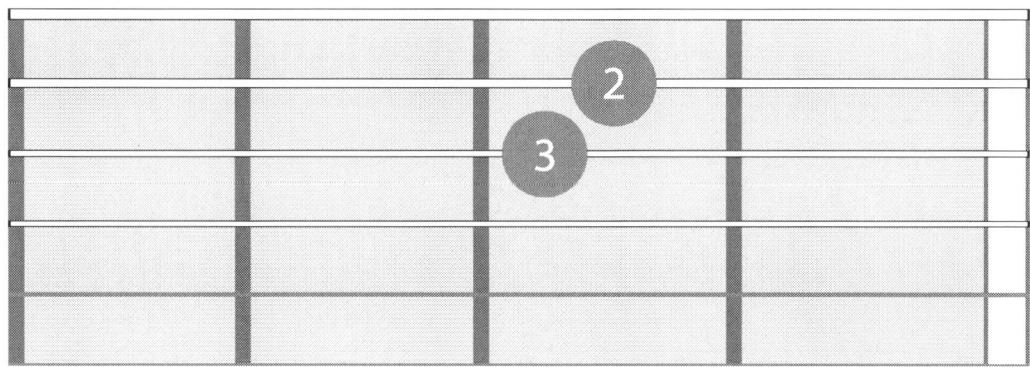

- Thumb not touching 6th string
- Can also be played with 1st and 2nd finger
- All 6 strings sound

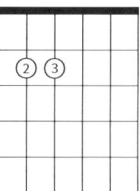

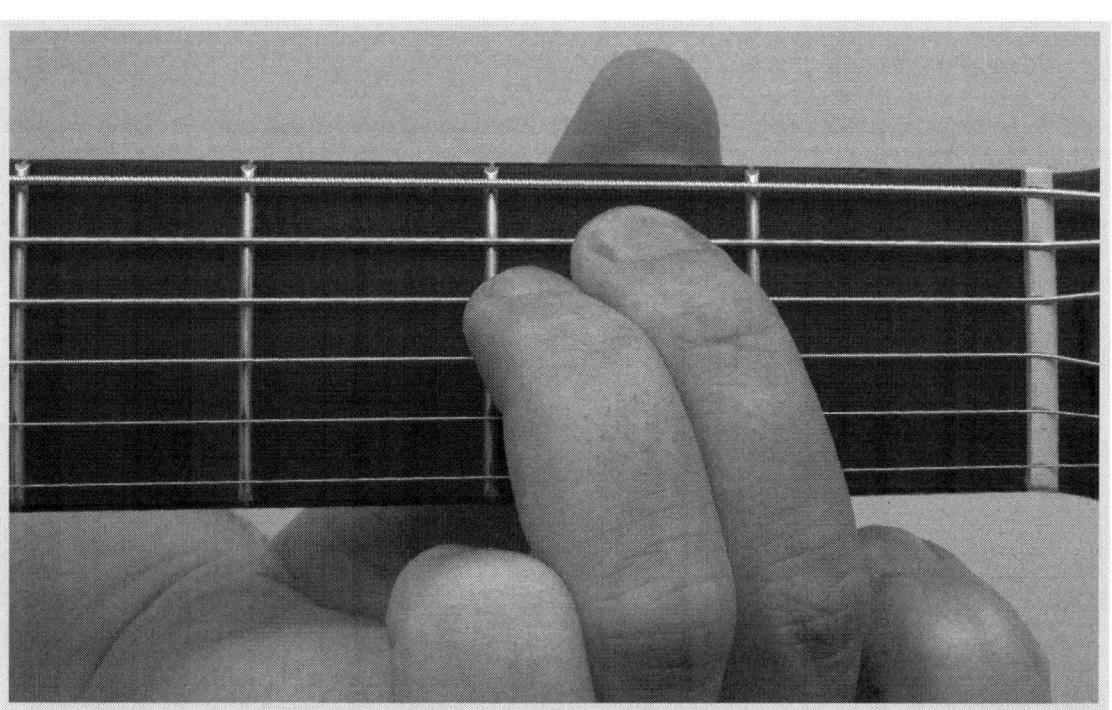

Em *ANOTHER WAY*

6TH FRET

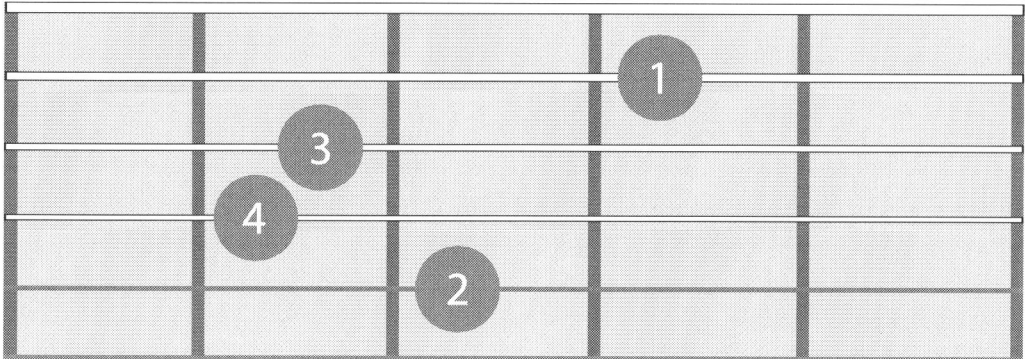

- Thumb low and centred
- 1st finger not touching 6th string
- All 6 strings sound

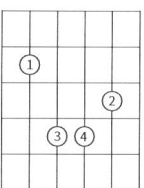

6TH FRET

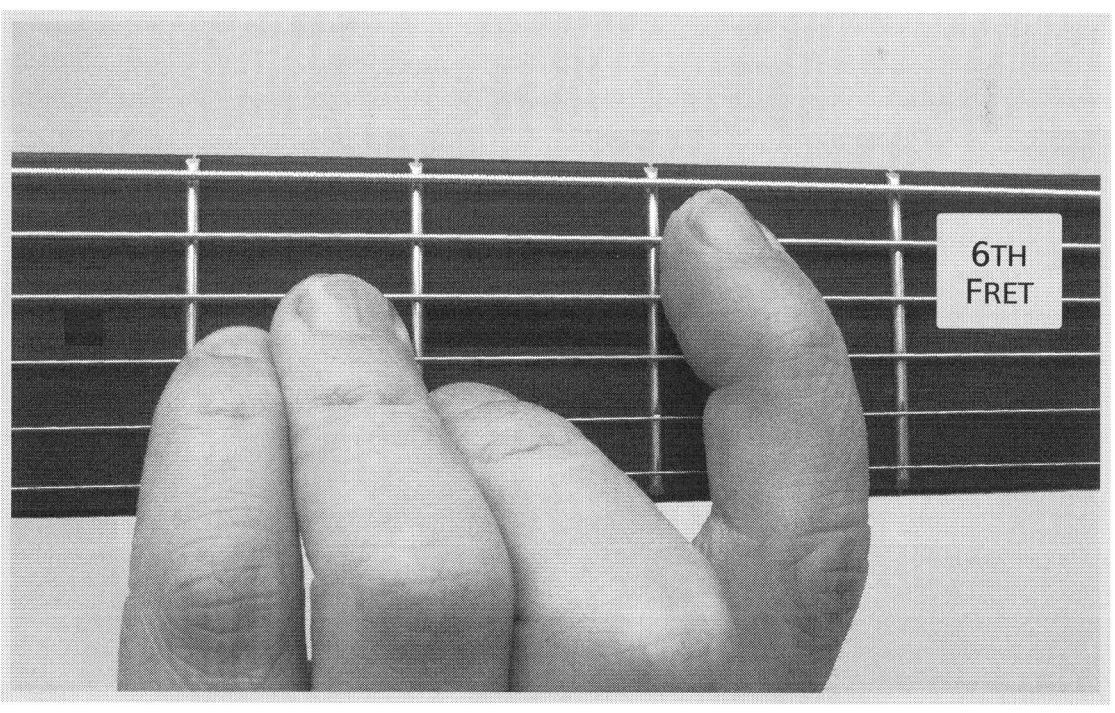

Esus4

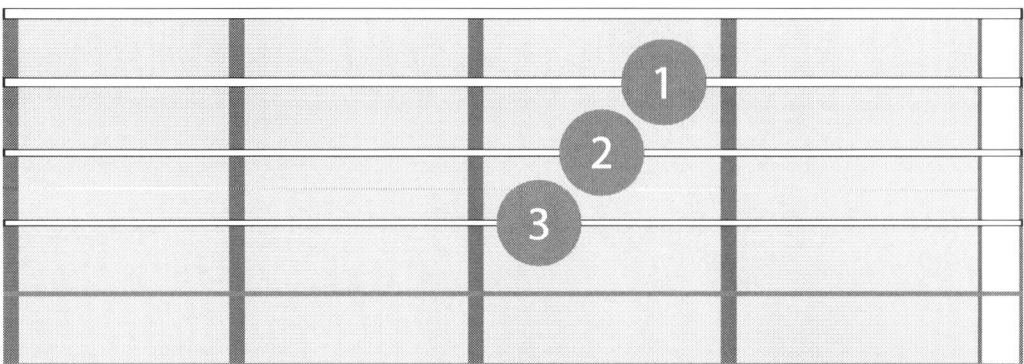

- Thumb not touching 6th string
- Can also be played with 2nd 3rd and 4th finger
- All 6 strings sound

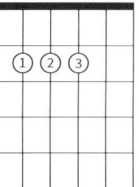

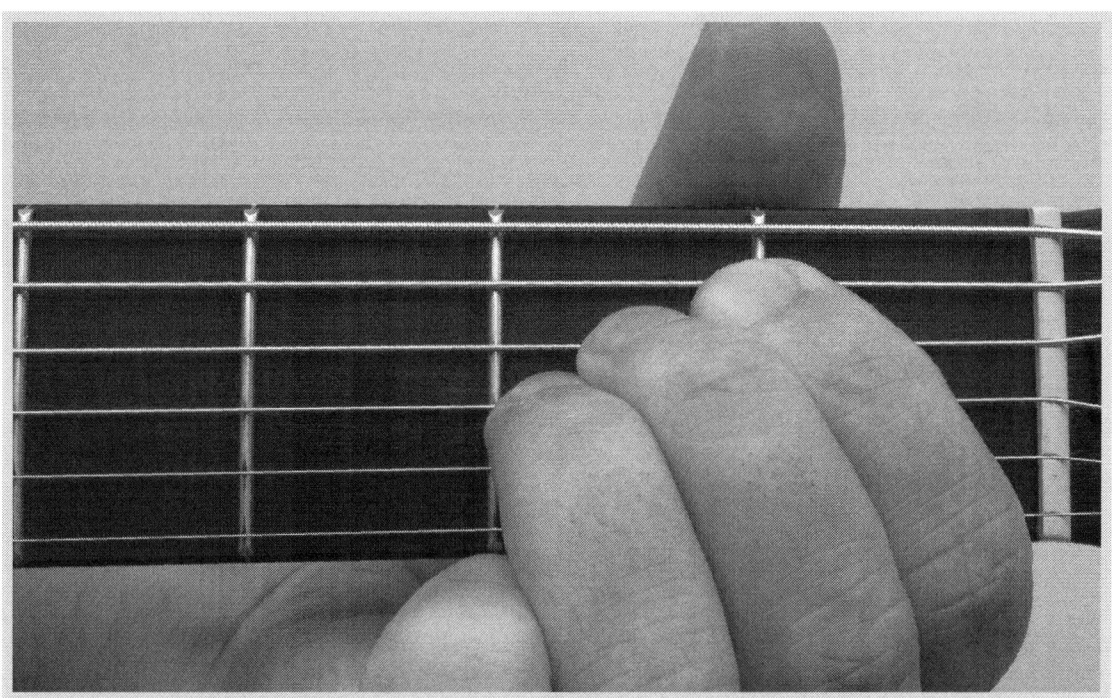

E7sus4

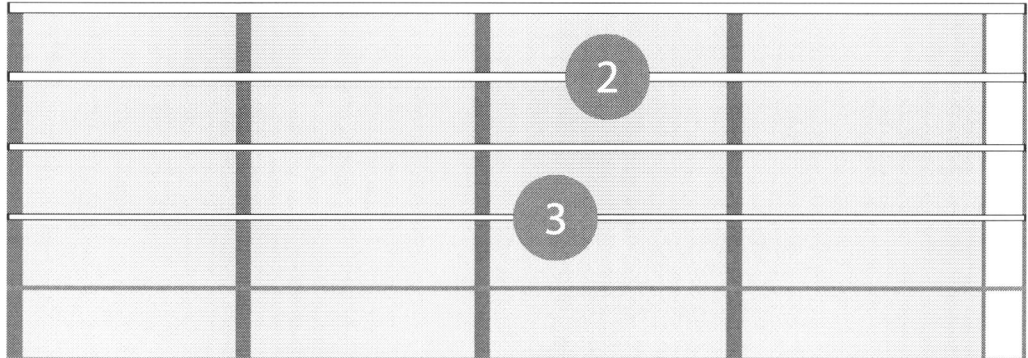

- Thumb not touching 6th string
- Can also be played with 1st and 2nd finger
- All 6 strings sound

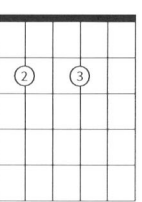

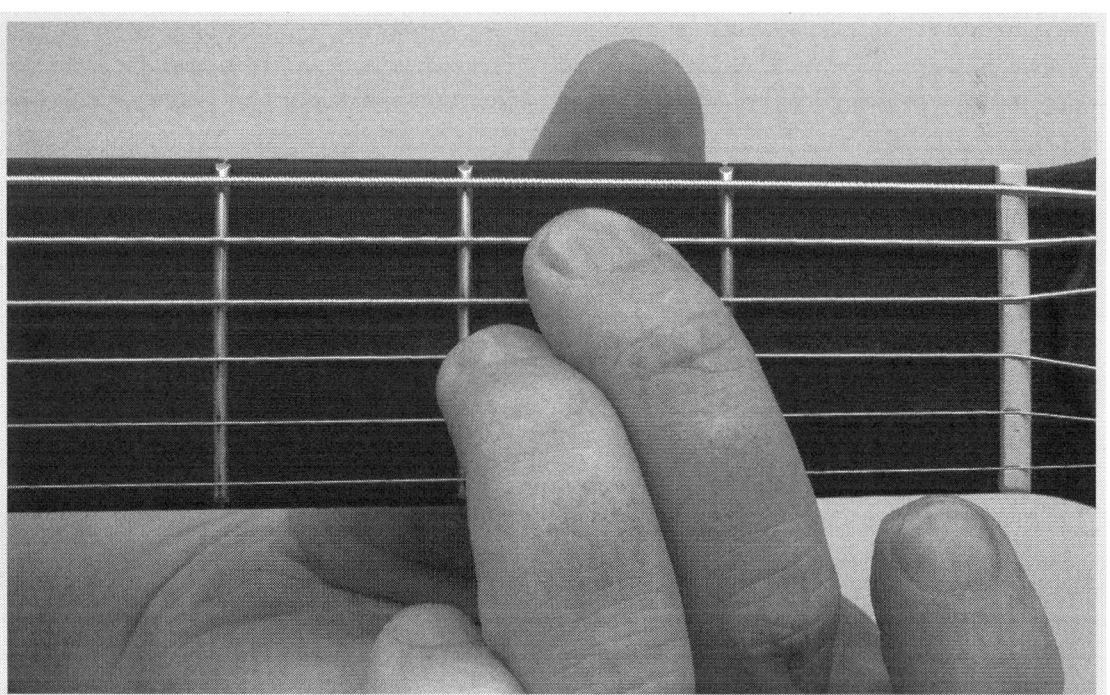

E5

6TH FRET

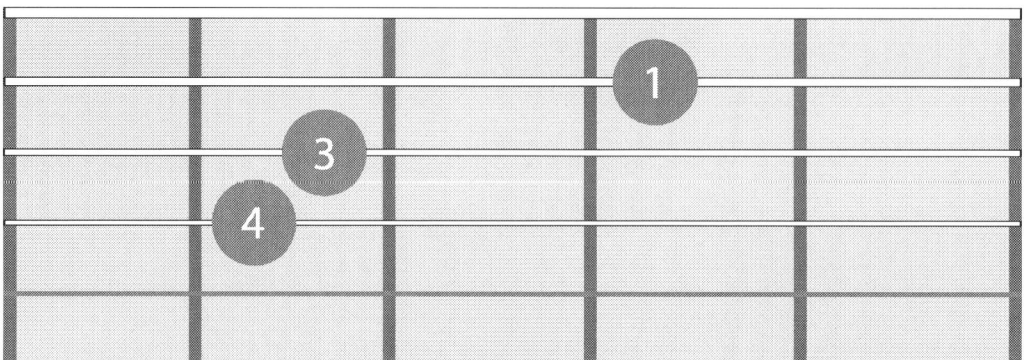

- Thumb low and centred
- 1st finger not touching 6th string
- All 6 strings sound

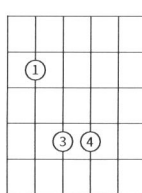

6TH FRET

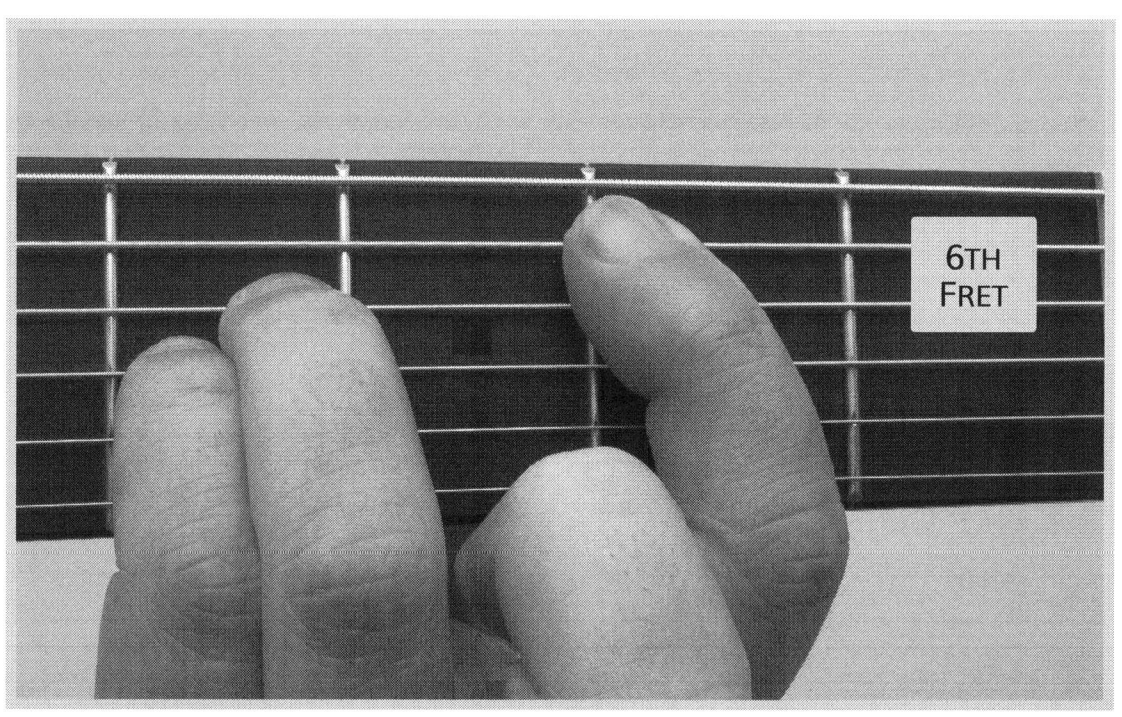

Emaj7

3rd Fret

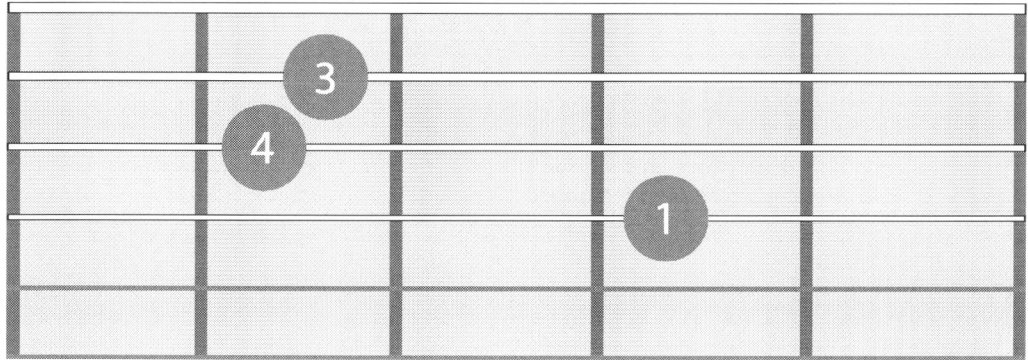

- Sometimes played instead of E
- Thumb not touching 6th string
- All 6 strings sound

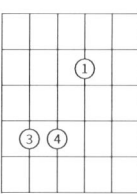

3rd Fret

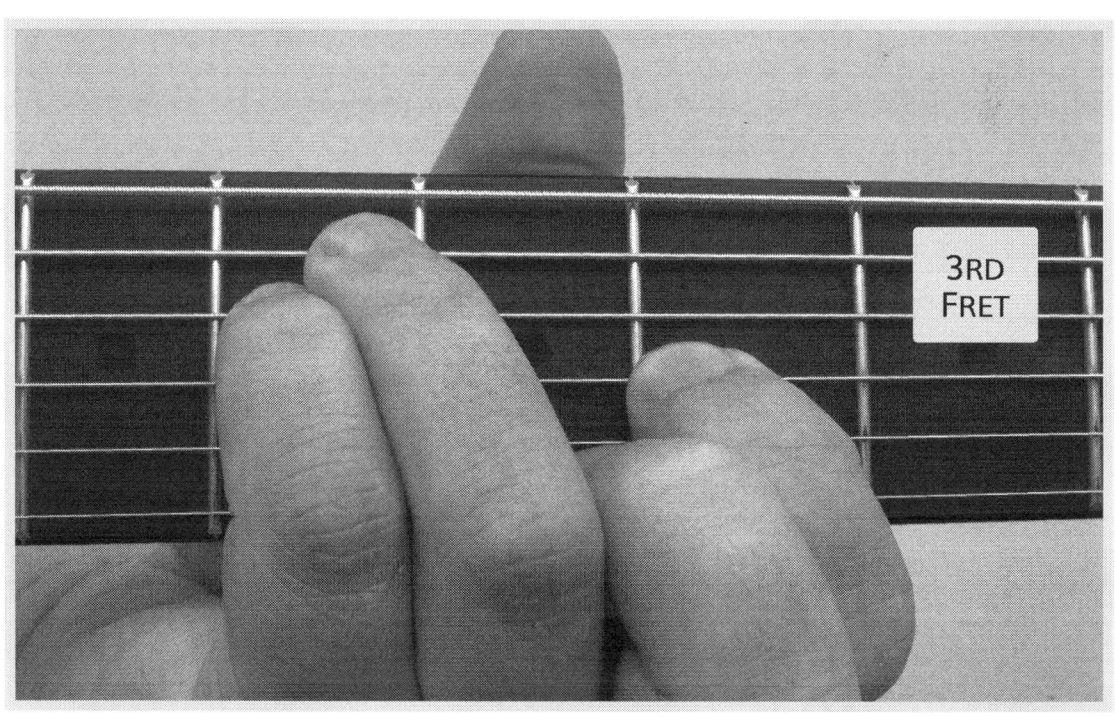

E7

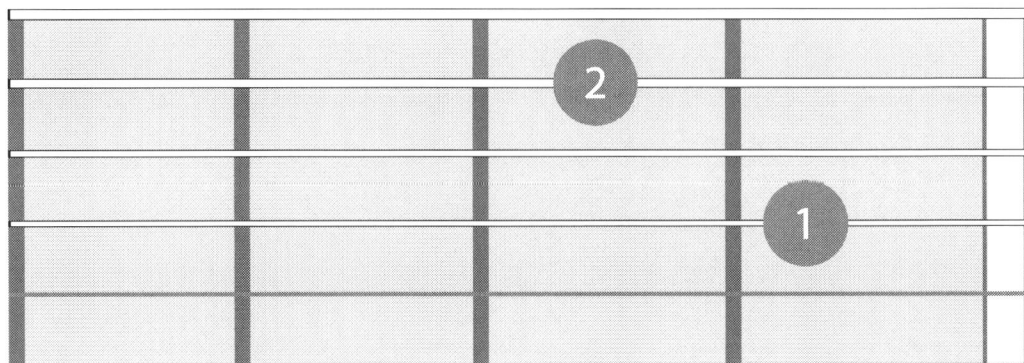

- Thumb not touching 6th string
- 1st finger in corner of fret
- All 6 strings sound

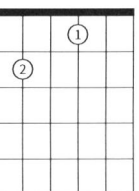

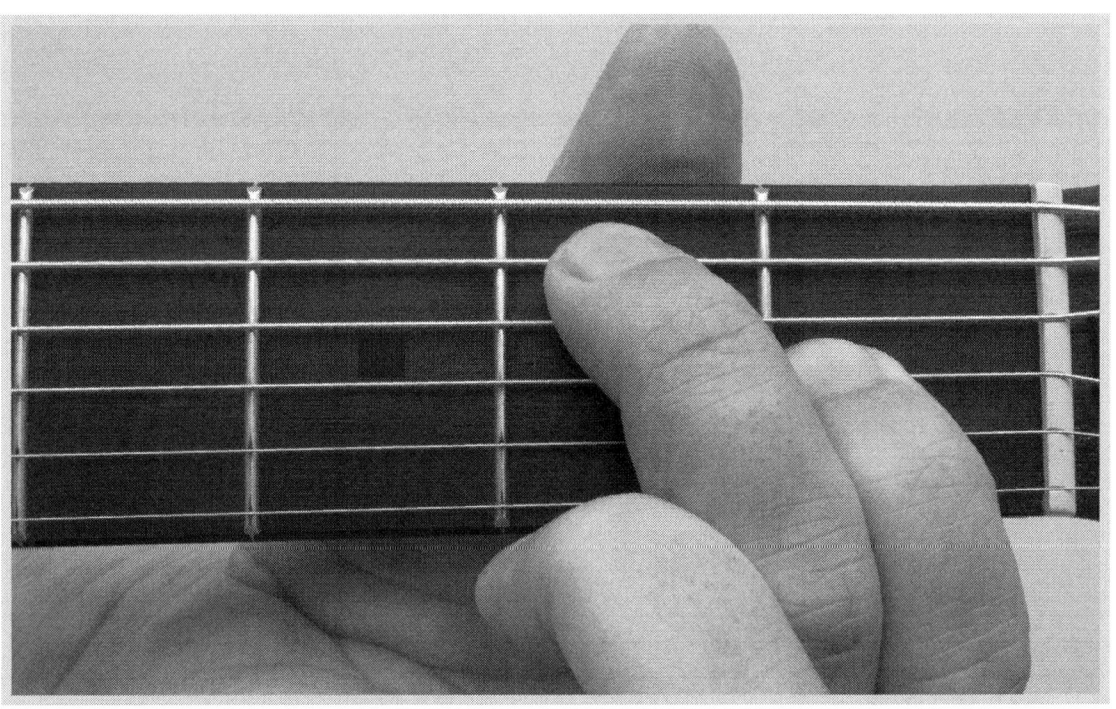

E7 ANOTHER WAY

4TH FRET

- Thumb touching 6th string
- 1st finger in corner of fret
- All 6 strings sound

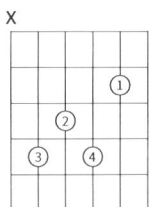

4TH FRET

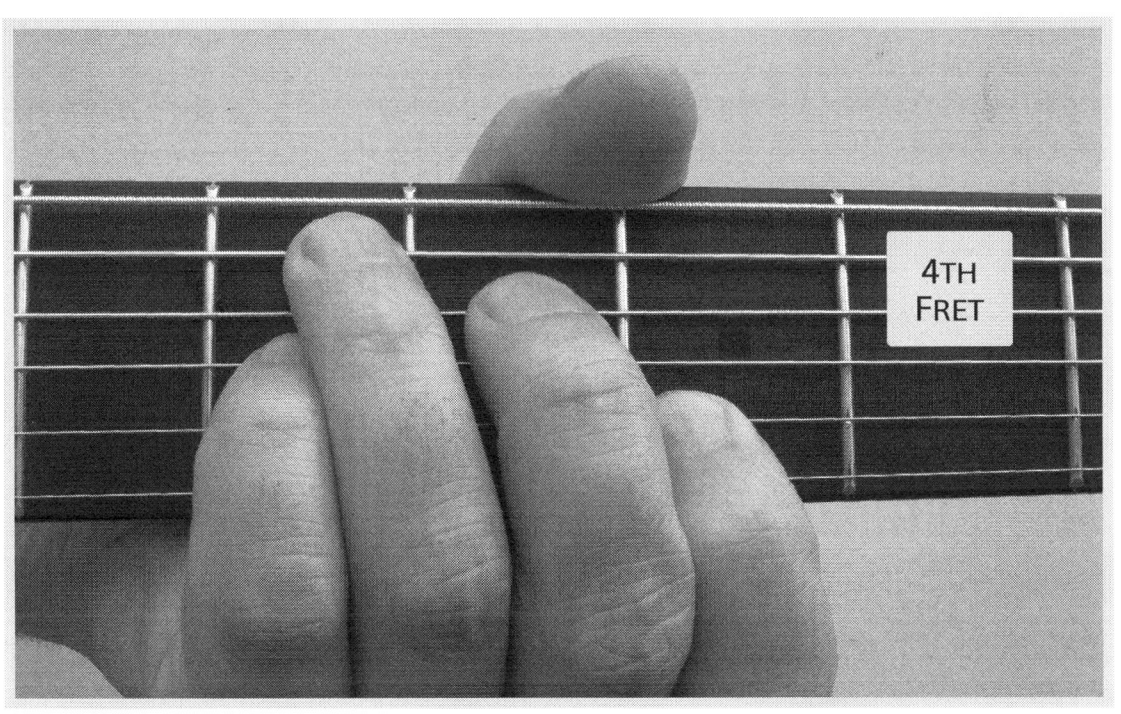

Em7

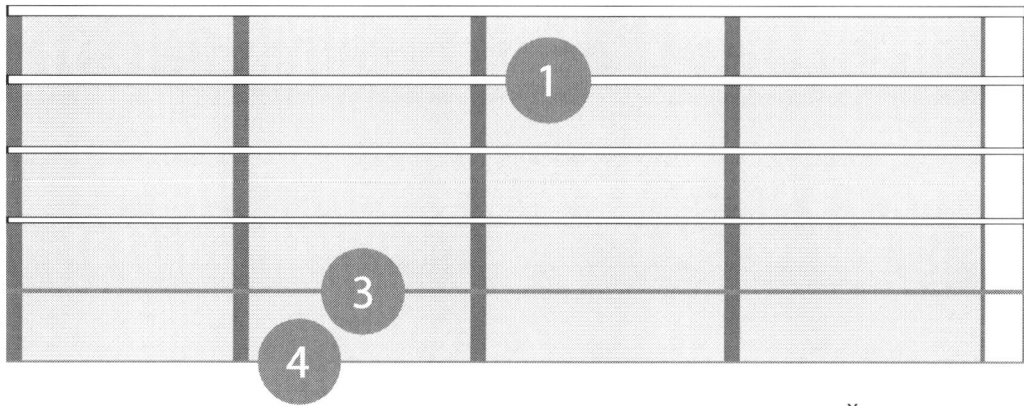

- Thumb not touching 6th string
- 4th string muted by inside of 2nd finger
- Strum 6 strings - Only 5 sound

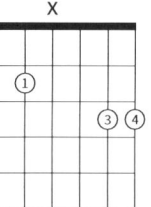

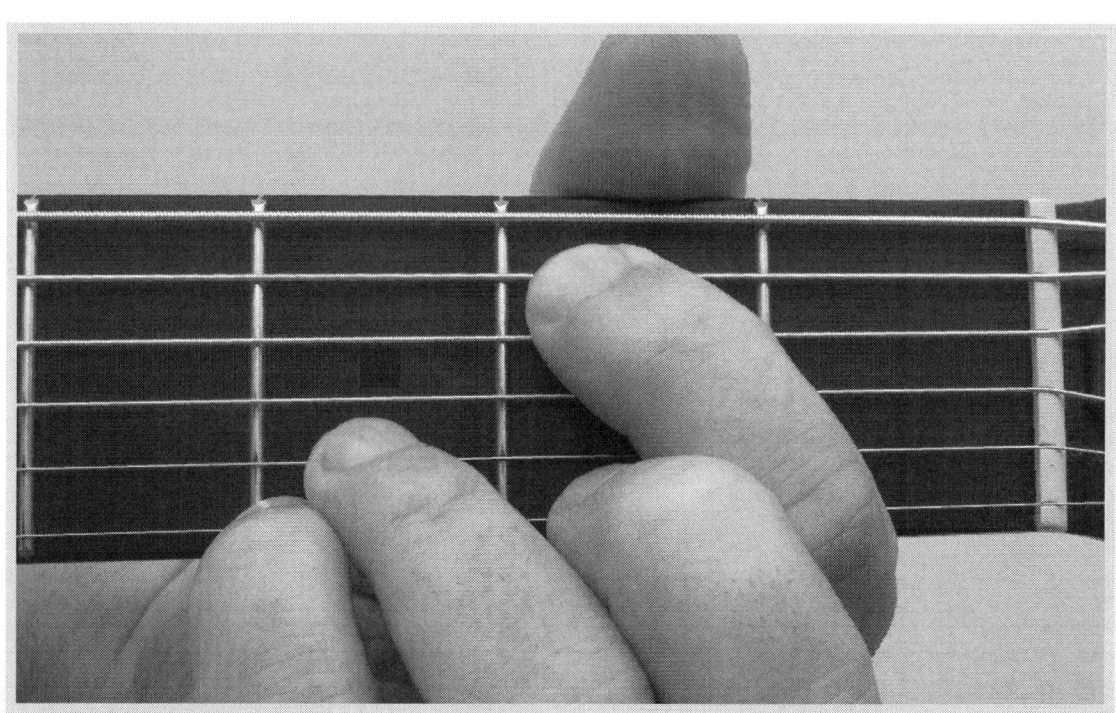

Em7 *EASIER*

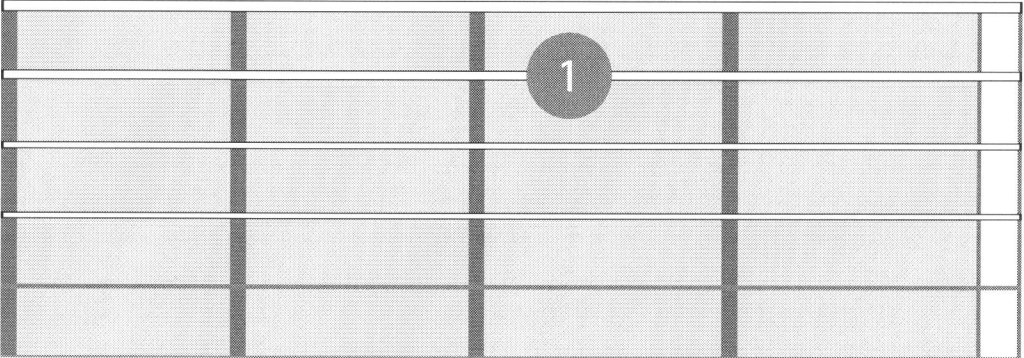

- Thumb not touching 6th string
- Also played with 2nd finger
- All 6 strings sound

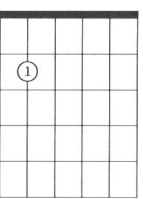

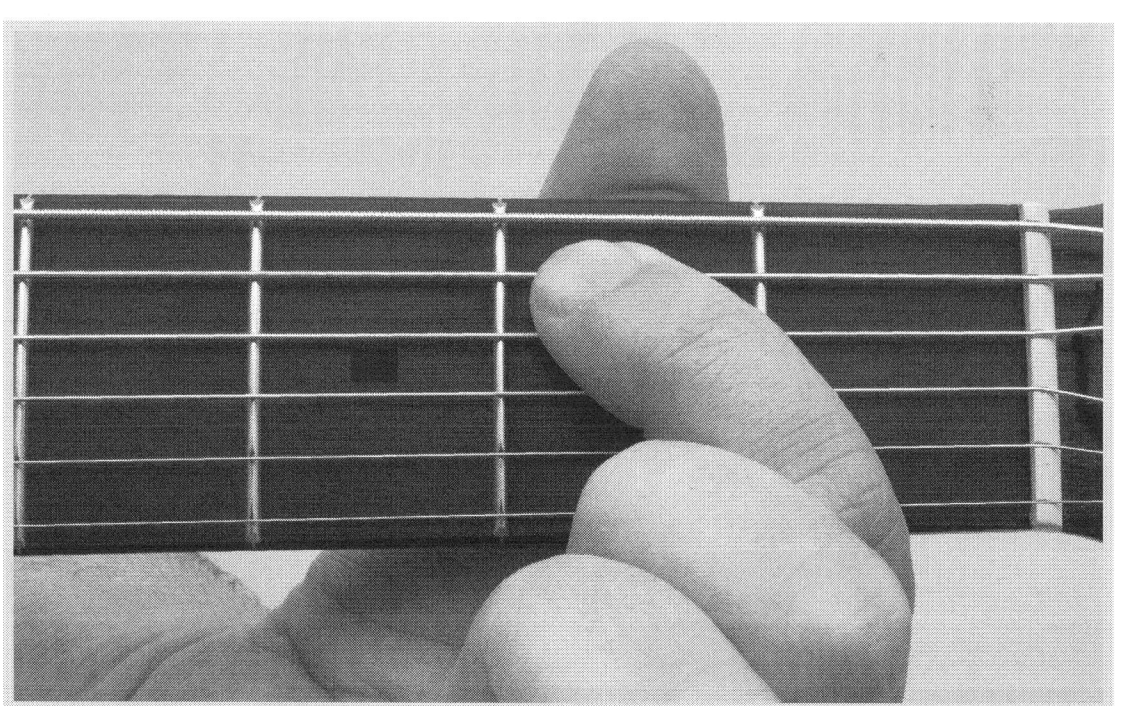

E<small>M</small>/G

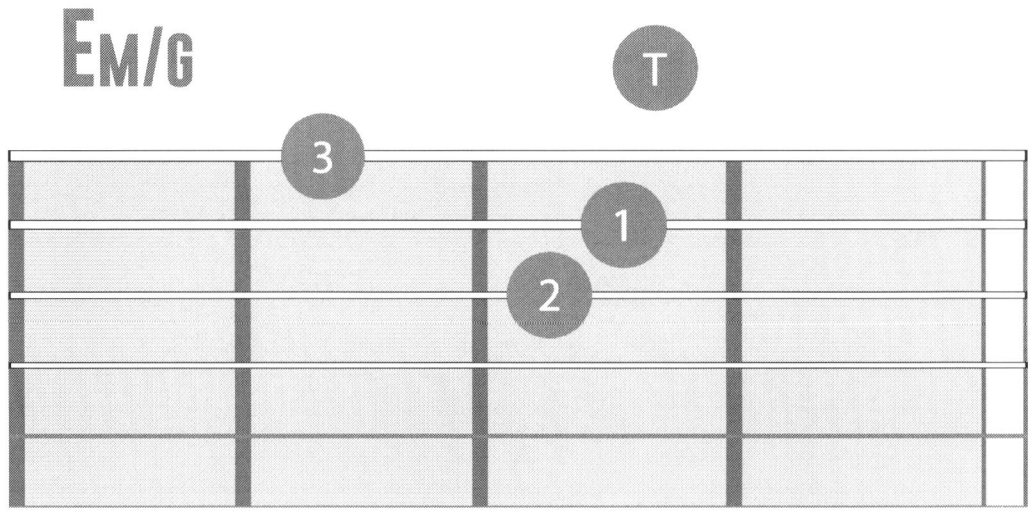

- Thumb may or may not touch 6th string
- Can also be played with 2nd 3rd and 4th finger
- All 6 strings sound

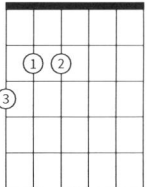

Em11

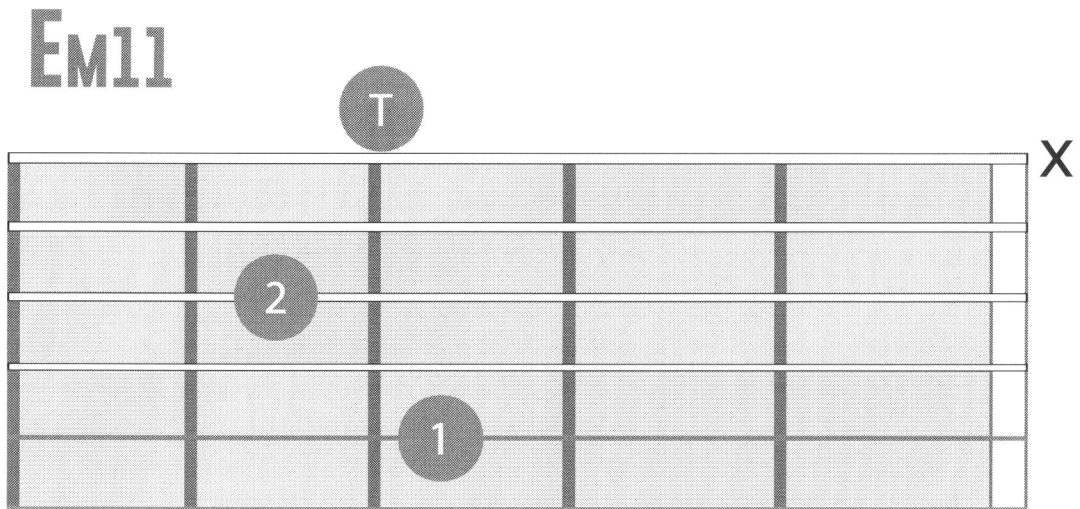

- Sometimes played instead of Em
- Thumb touching 6th string
- Strum 6 strings - Only 5 sound

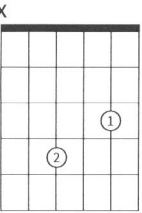

F

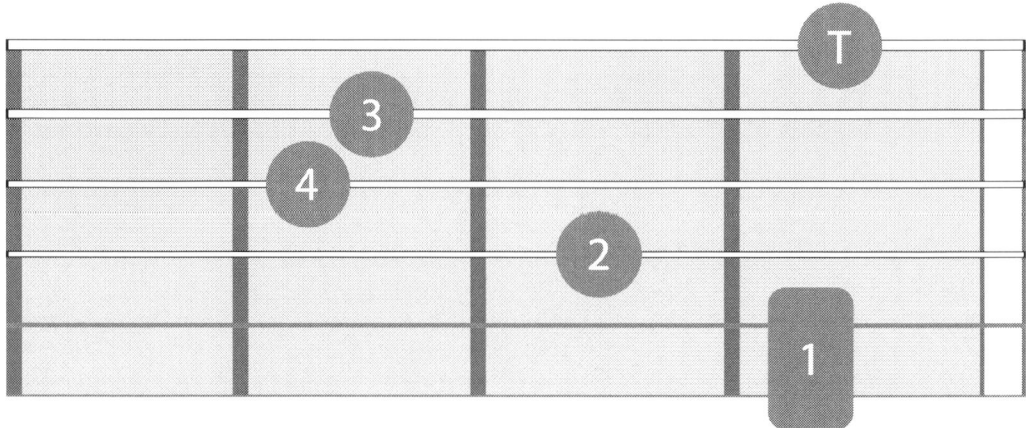

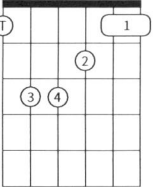

- Grab the guitar neck
- Thumb pressing 6th string
- All 6 strings sound

F *EASIER*

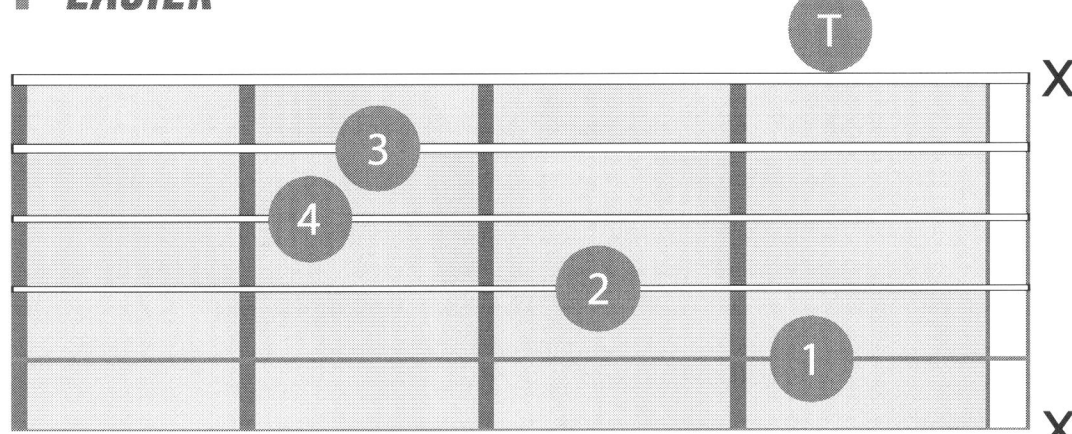

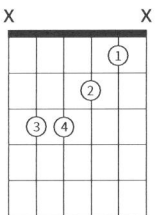

- Grab the guitar neck
- Thumb touching 6th string
- Strum 6 strings - Only 4 sound

F BARRE CHORD

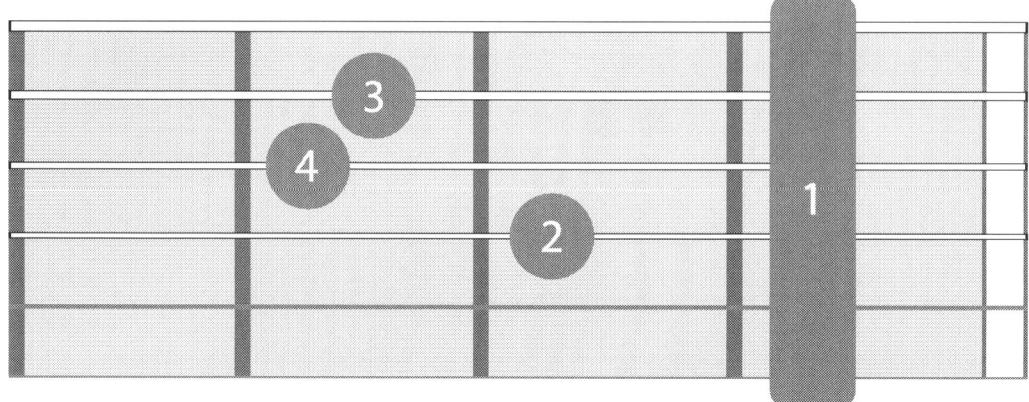

- Thumb low and centred
- Thumb pressing 6th string
- All 6 strings sound

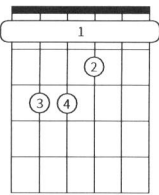

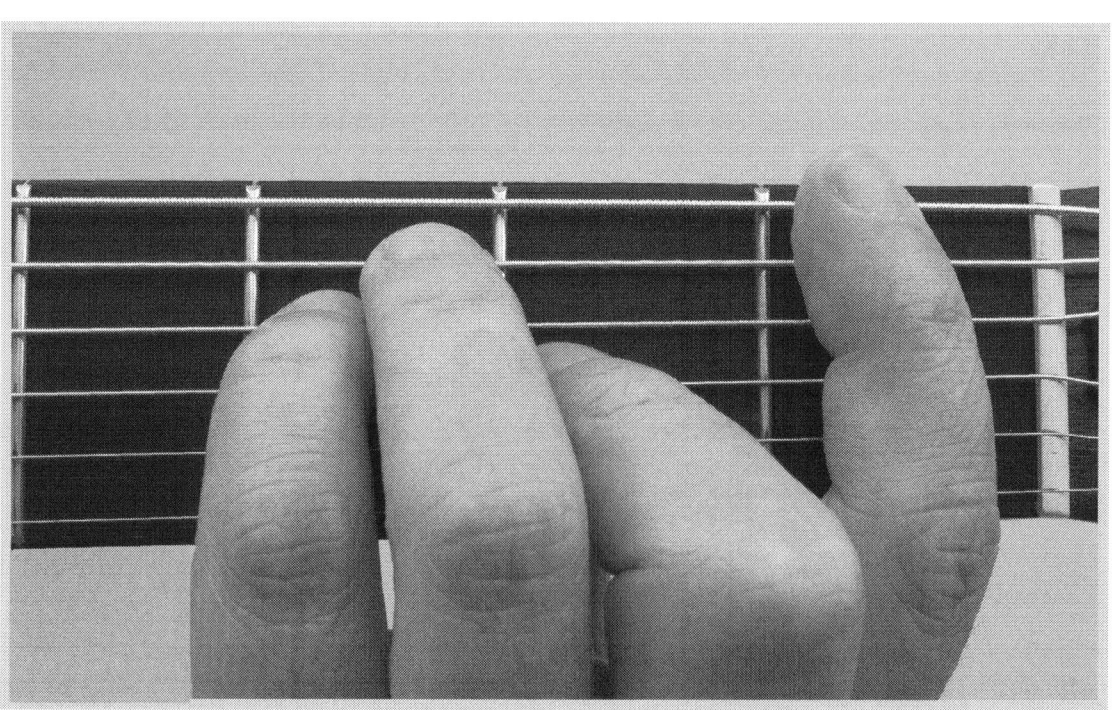

Fm

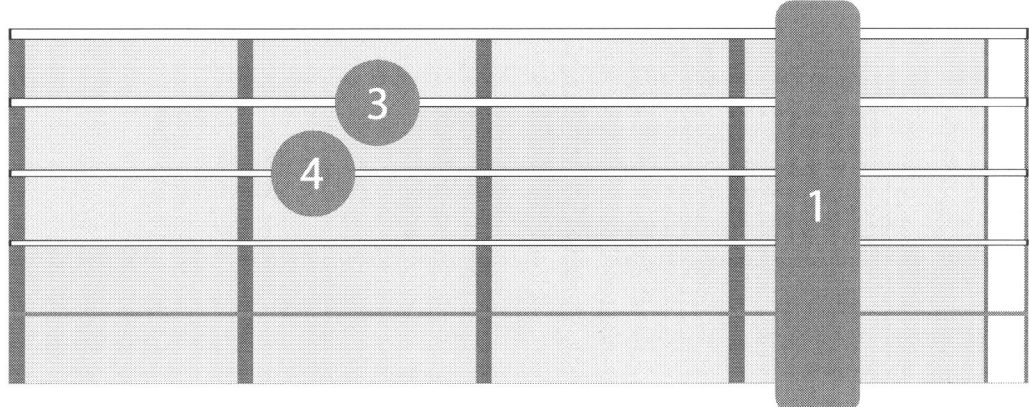

- Stretch your hand
- Thumb low and centred
- All 6 strings sound

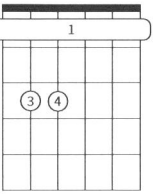

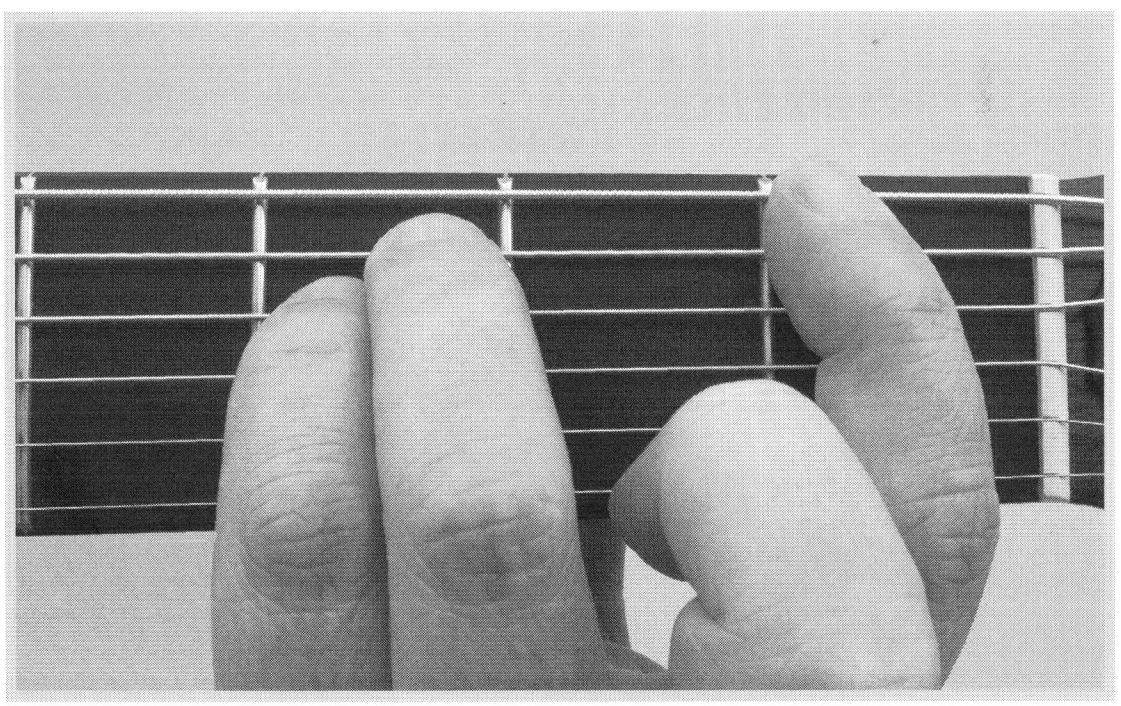

Fsus2

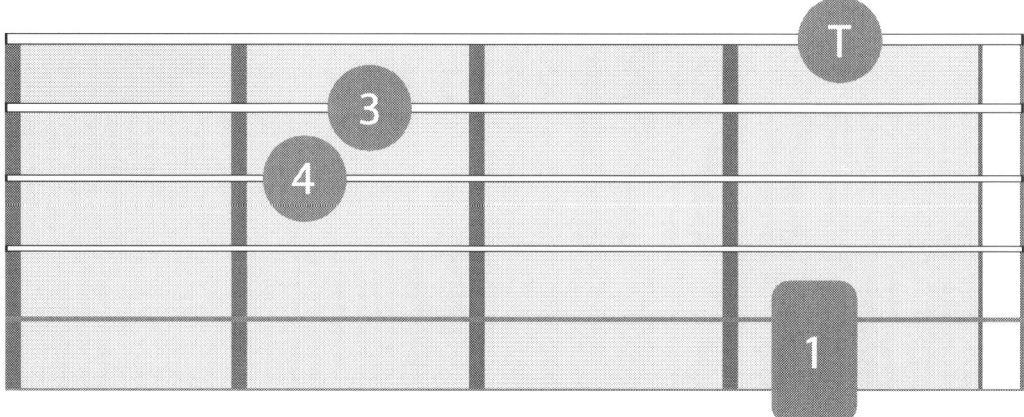

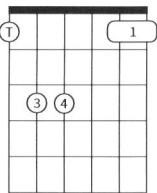

- Grab the guitar neck
- Thumb pressing 6th string
- All 6 strings sound

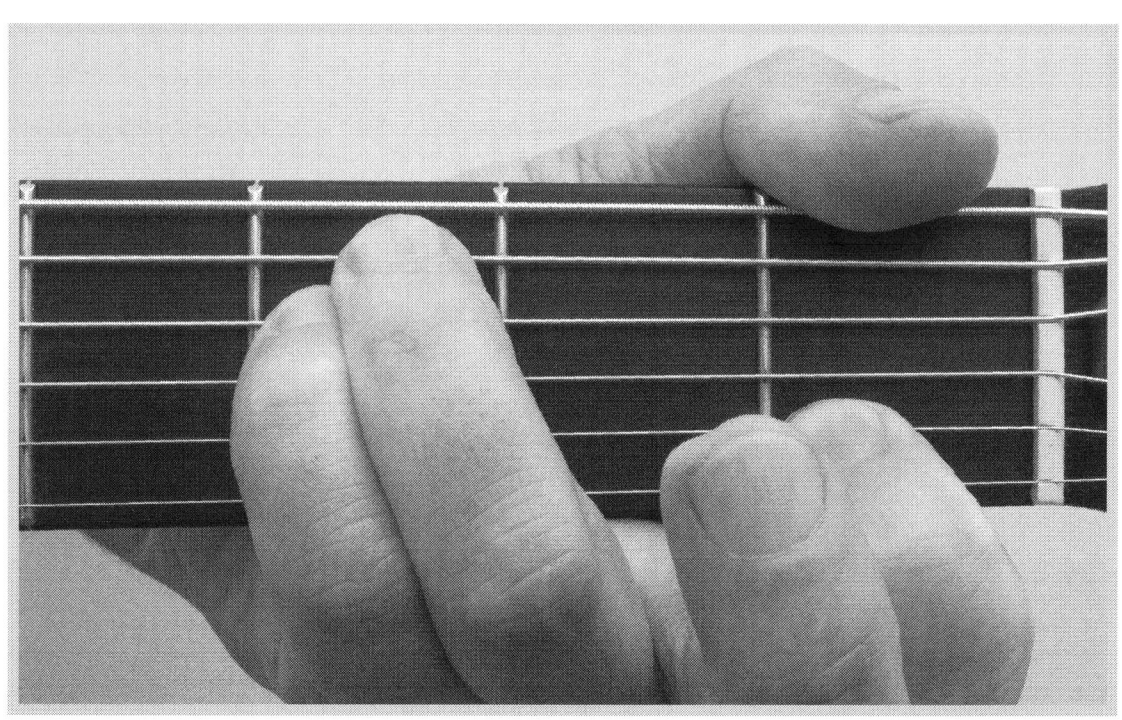

F5

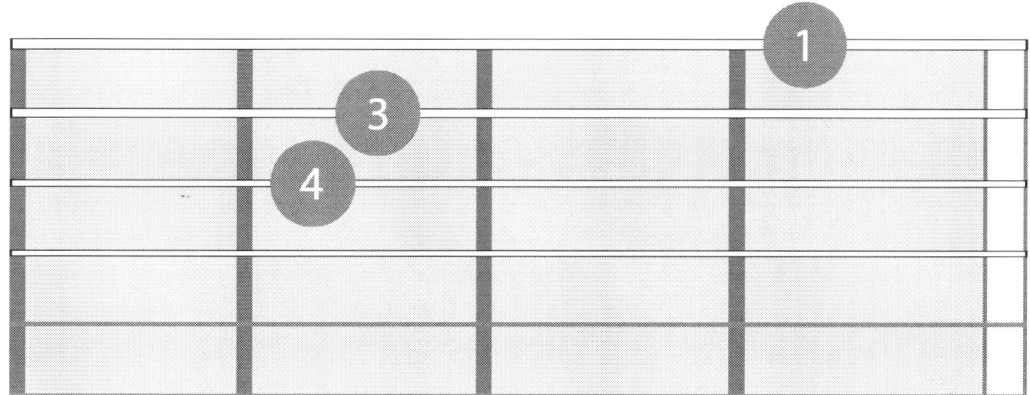

- Stretch your hand
- Thumb low and centred
- Strum 6th 5th and 4th strings

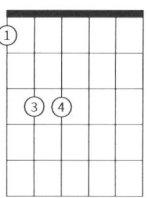

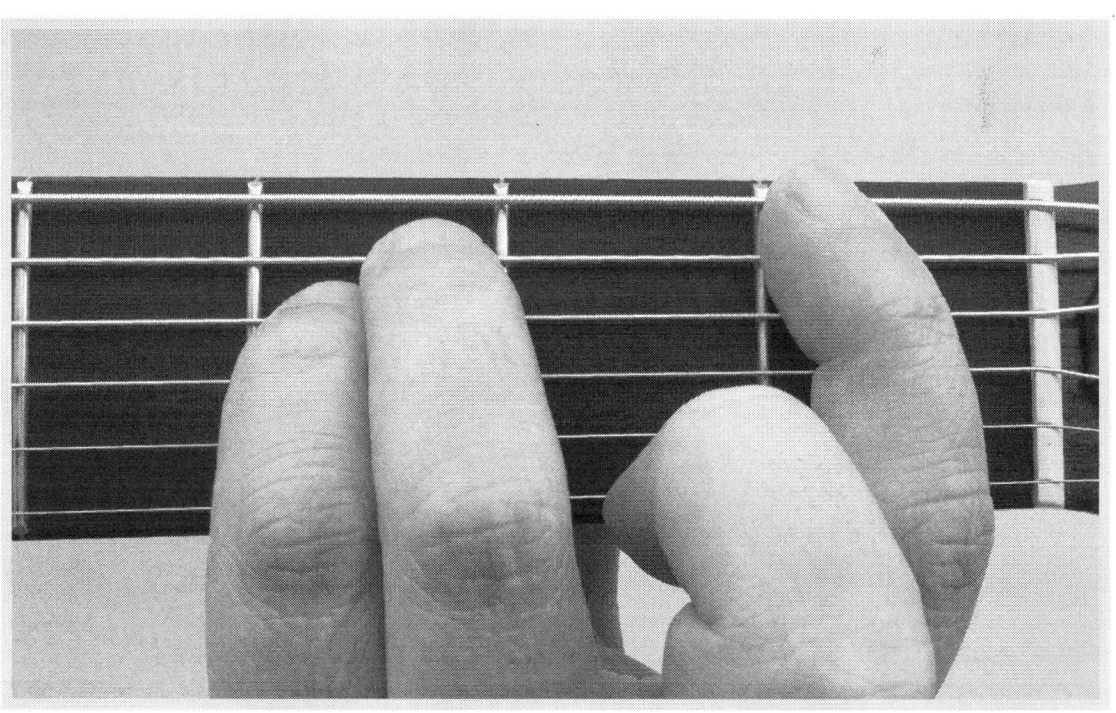

F6

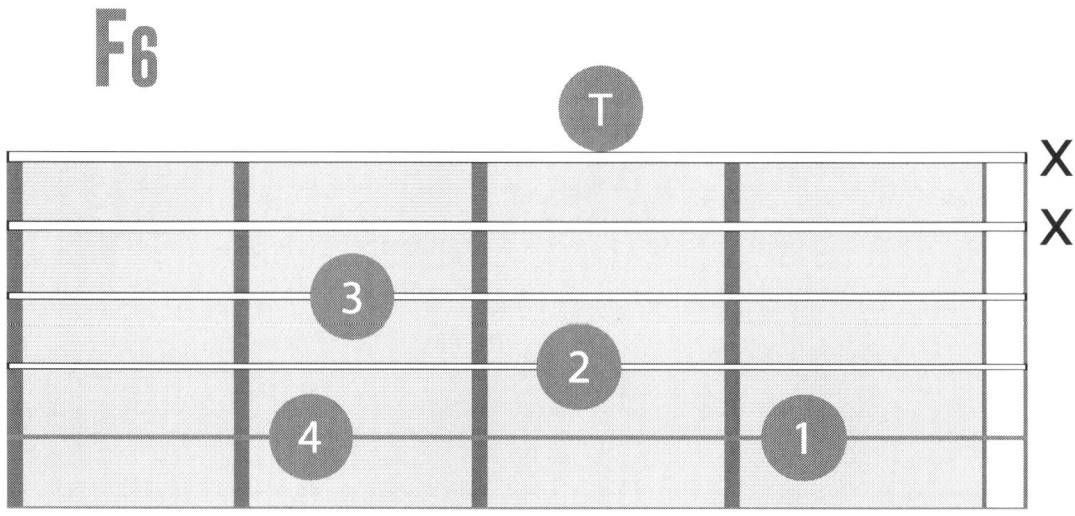

- Thumb touching 6th string
- 1st finger also on 2nd string (makes chord changing easier)
- Strum bottom 4 strings

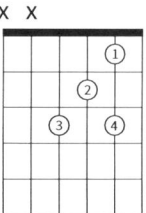

FM7

7TH
FRET

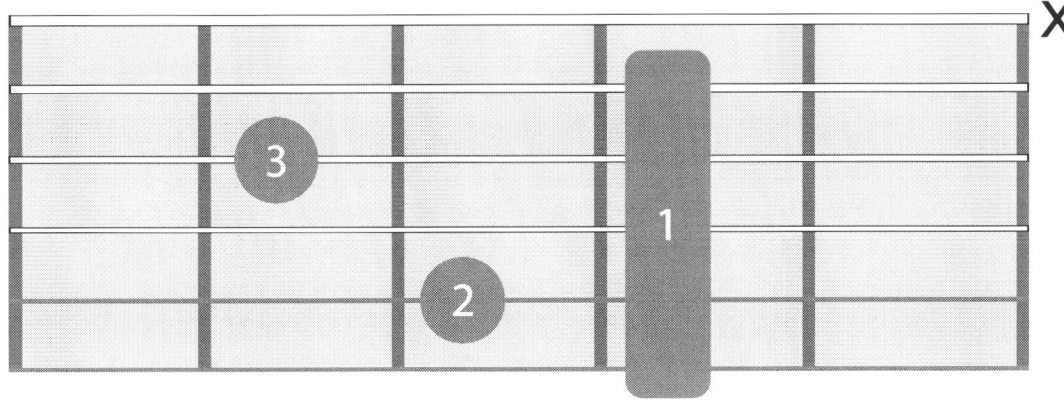

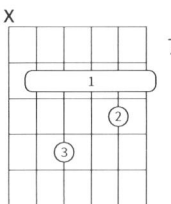

- Thumb low and centred
- 1st finger touching 6th string
- Strum 6 strings - Only 5 sound

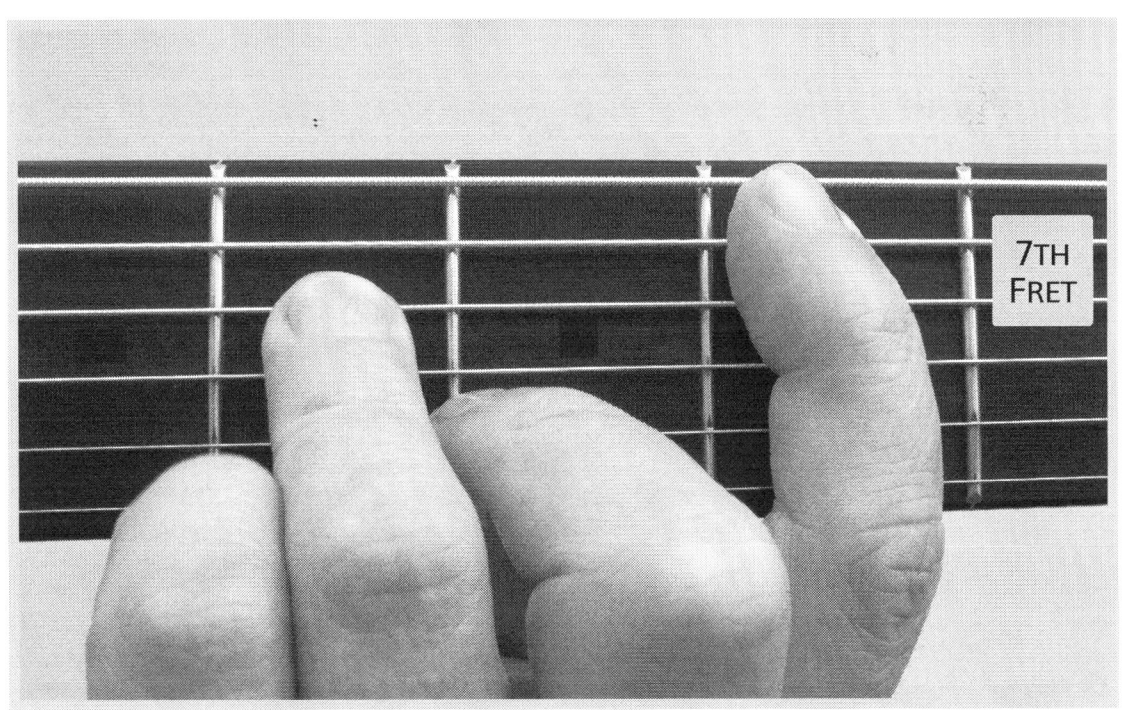

Fmaj7

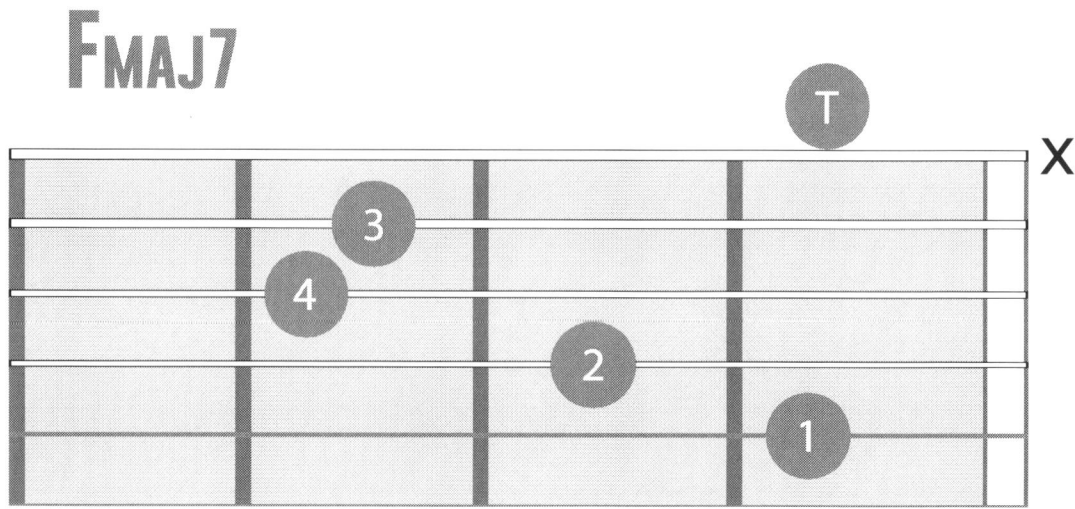

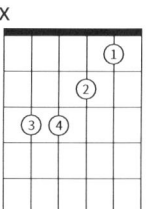

- Grab the guitar neck
- Thumb touching 6th string
- Strum 6 strings - Only 5 sound

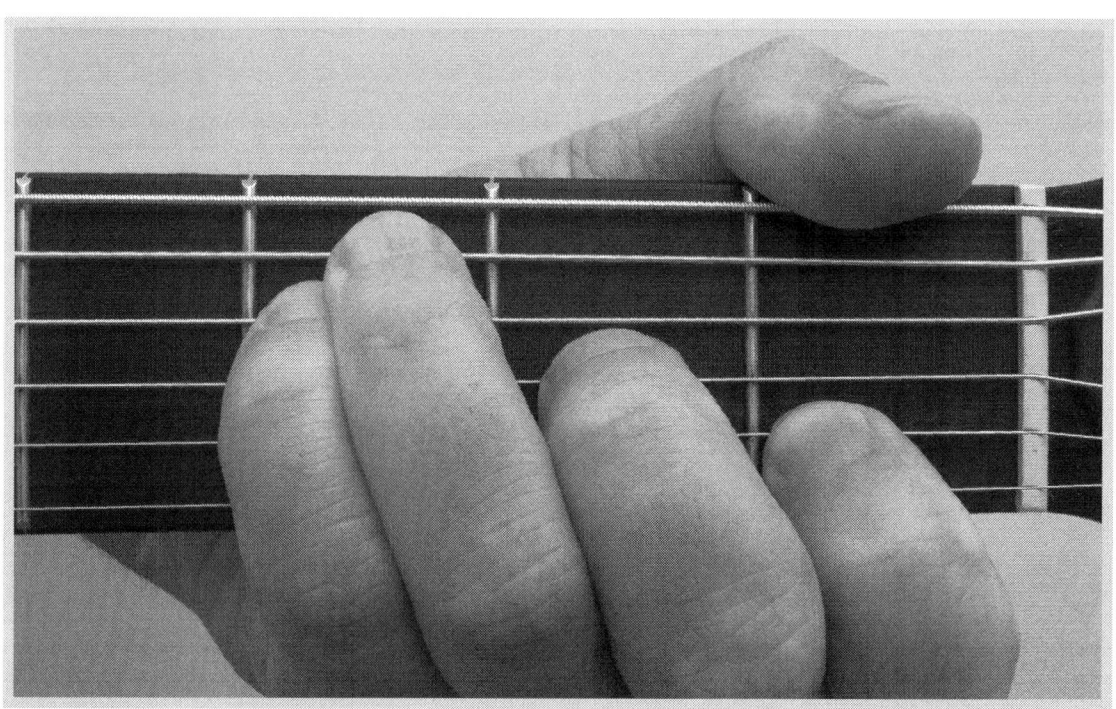

FMAJ7 *EASIER*

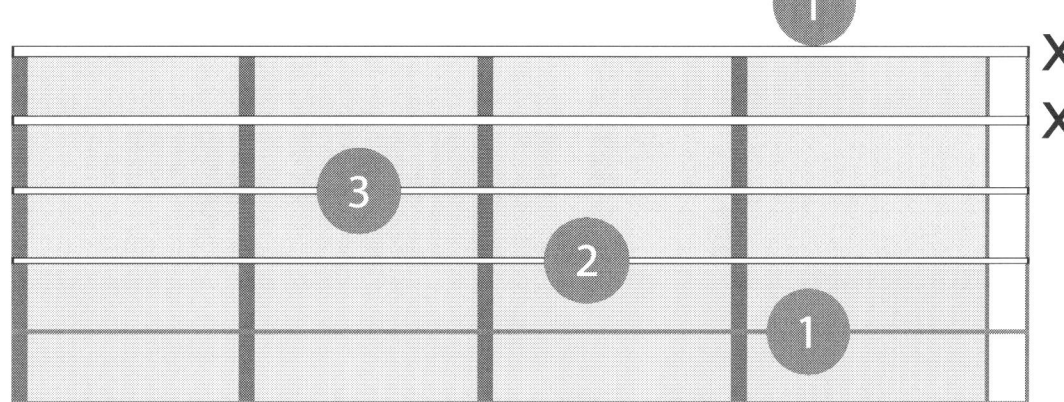

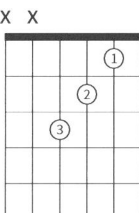

- Sometimes played instead of F
- Thumb touching 6th string
- Strum bottom 4 strings

Fmaj7 ANOTHER WAY

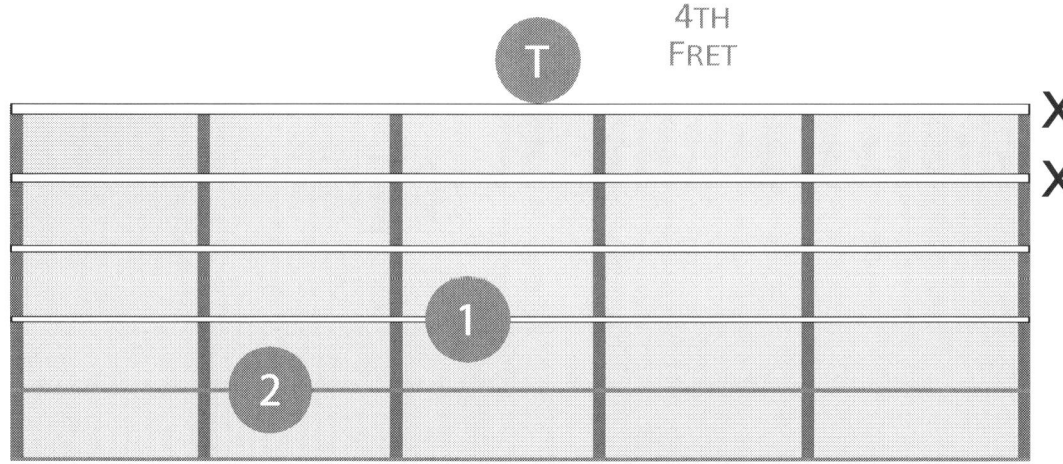

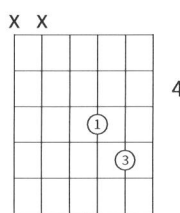

- Thumb touching 6th string
- Can also be played with 1st and 2nd finger
- Strum bottom 4 strings

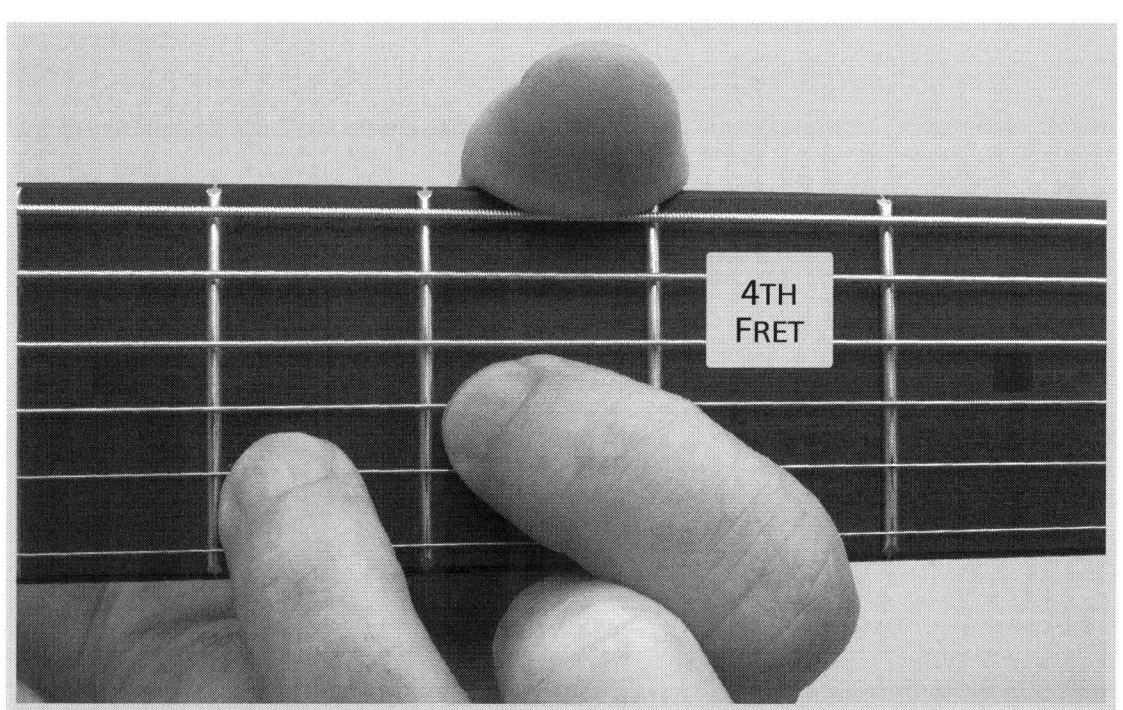

F#

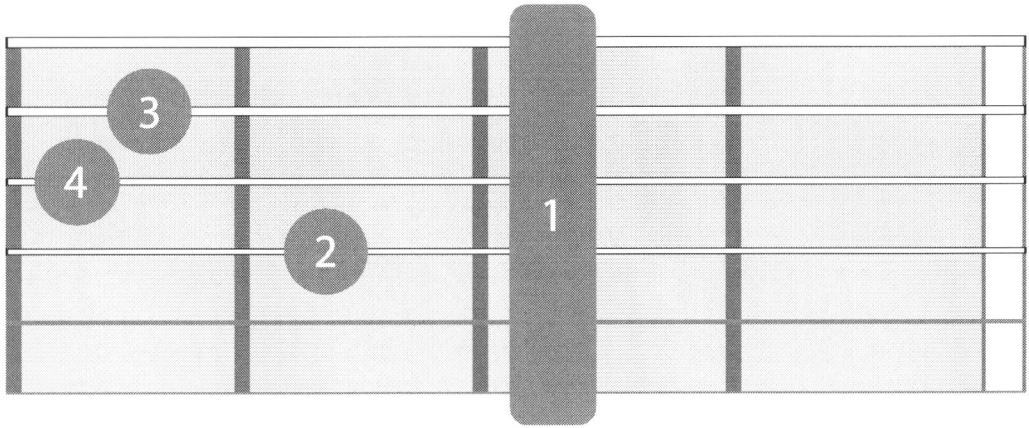

- Stretch your hand
- Thumb low and centred
- All 6 strings sound

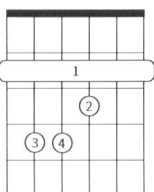

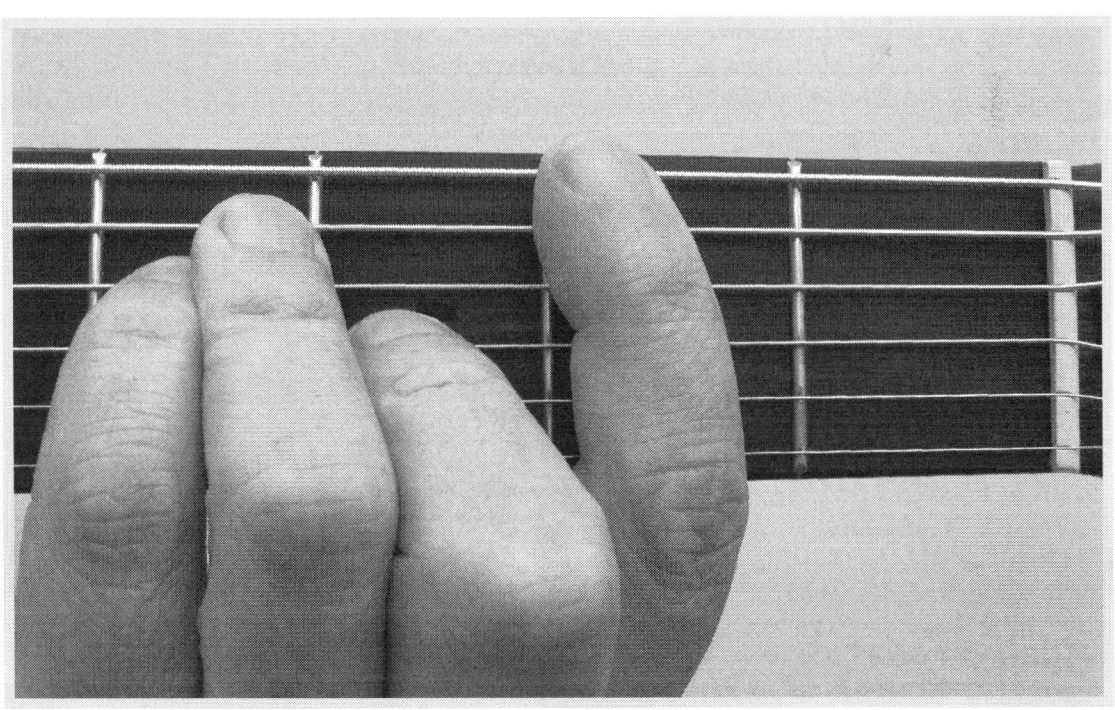

F#m

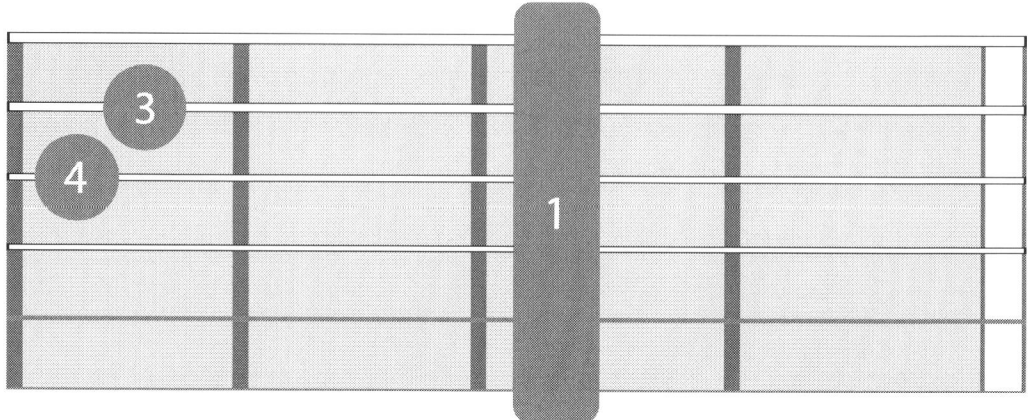

- Stretch your hand
- Thumb low and centred
- All 6 strings sound

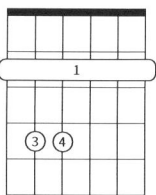

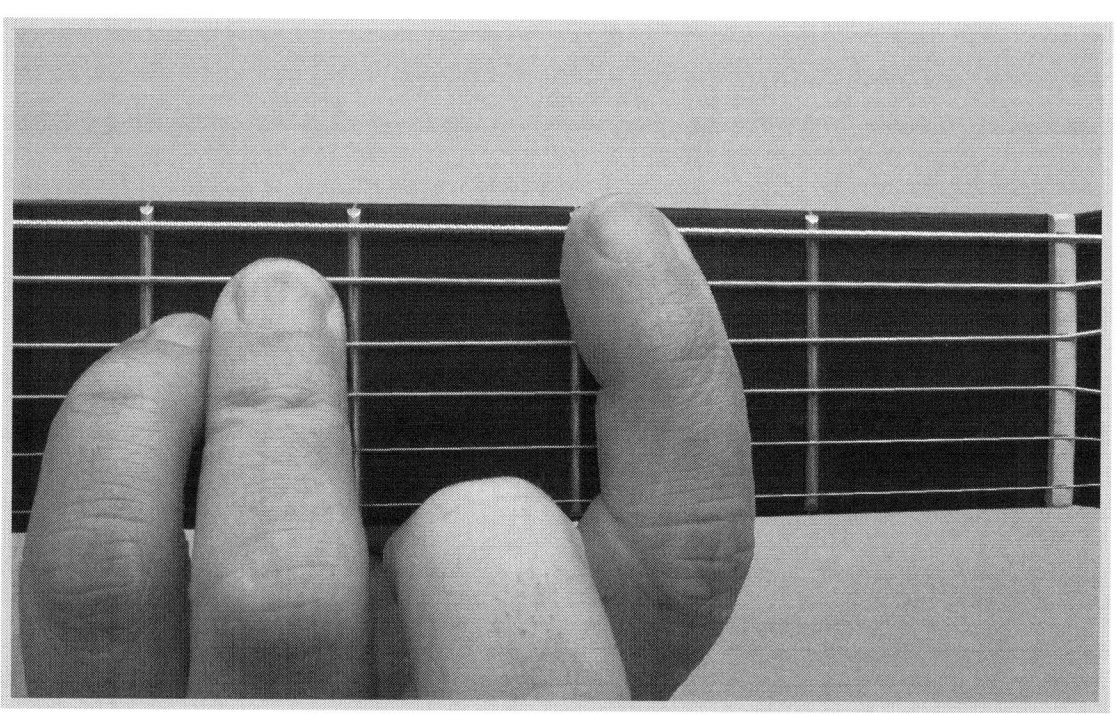

F#m EASIER

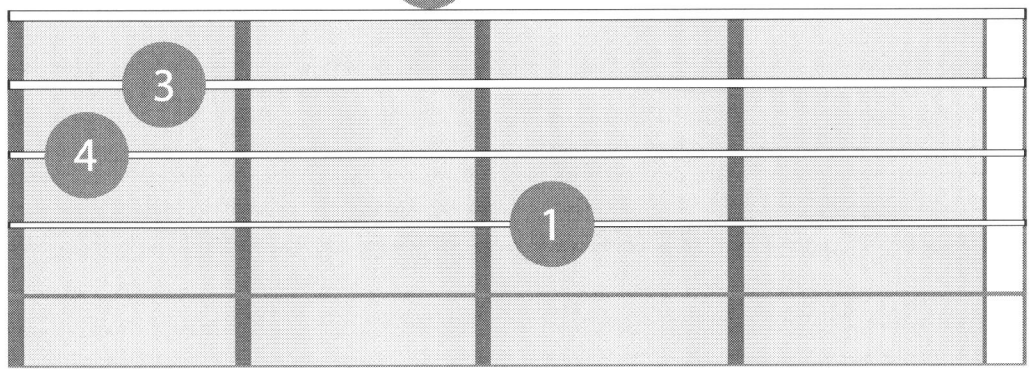

- Grab the guitar neck
- Thumb touching 6th string
- Strum 6 strings - Only 5 sound

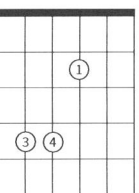

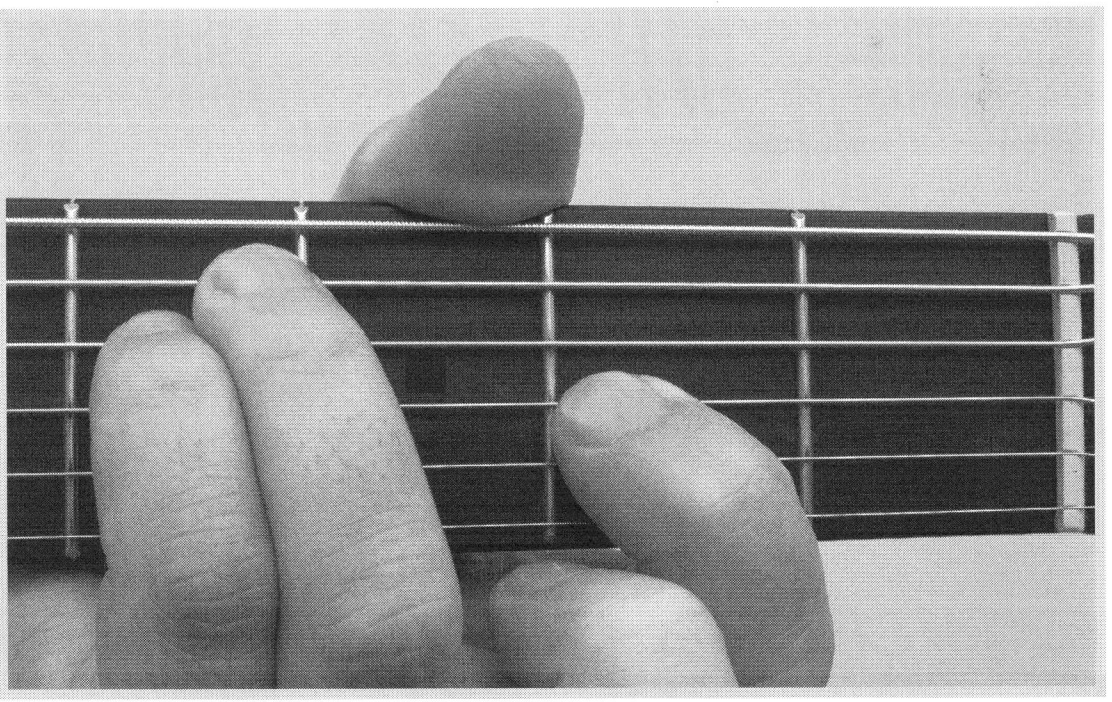

F#m7

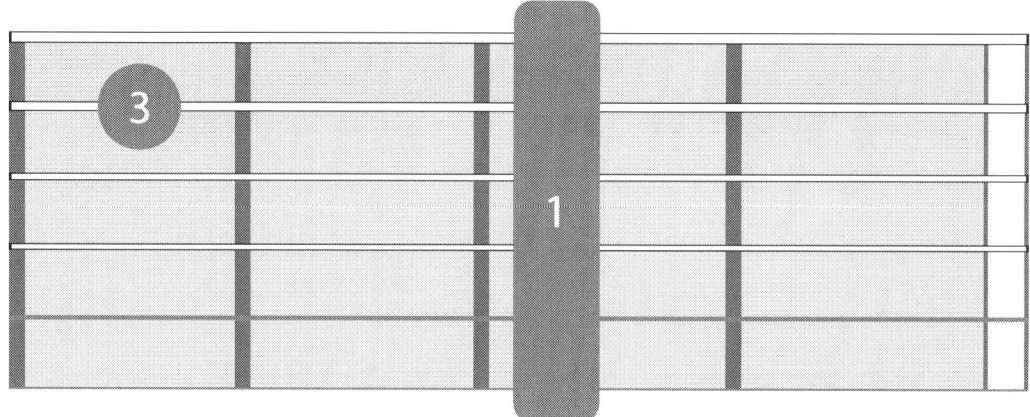

- Stretch your hand
- Thumb low and centred
- All 6 strings sound

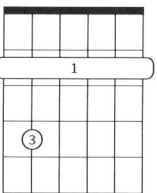

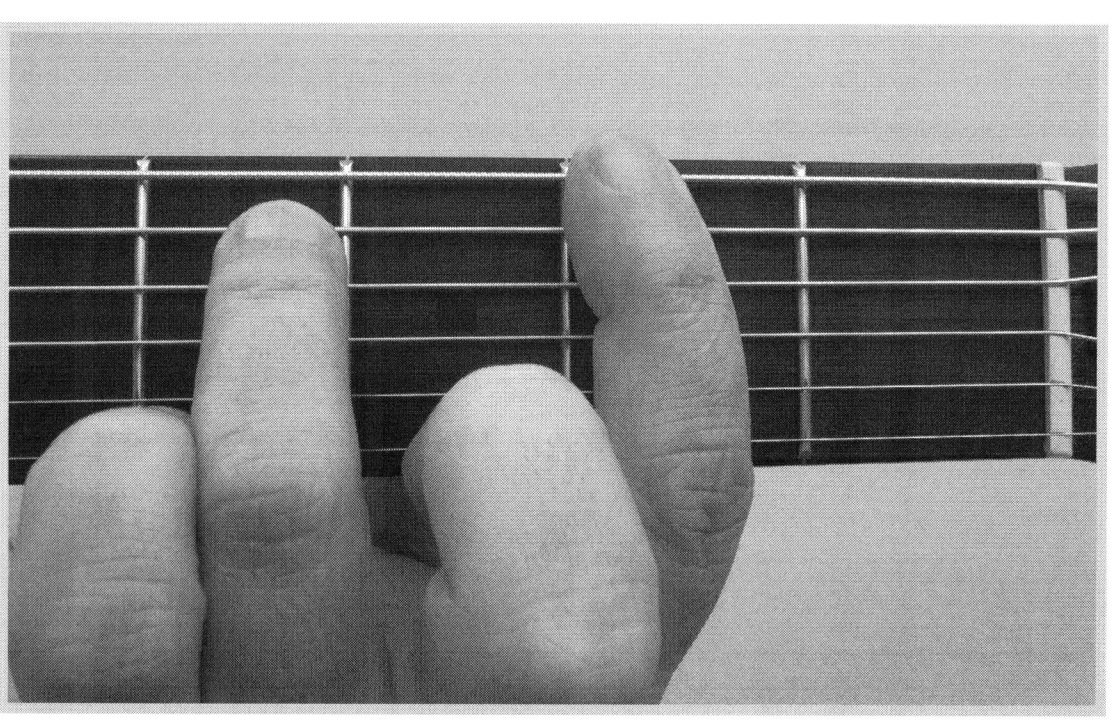

F#m7 EASIER

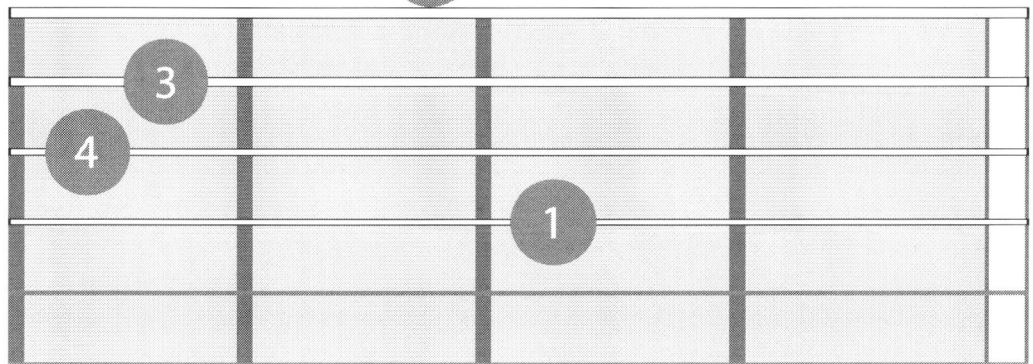

- Grab the guitar neck
- Thumb touching 6th string
- Strum 6 strings - Only 5 sound

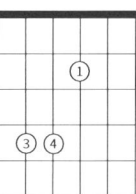

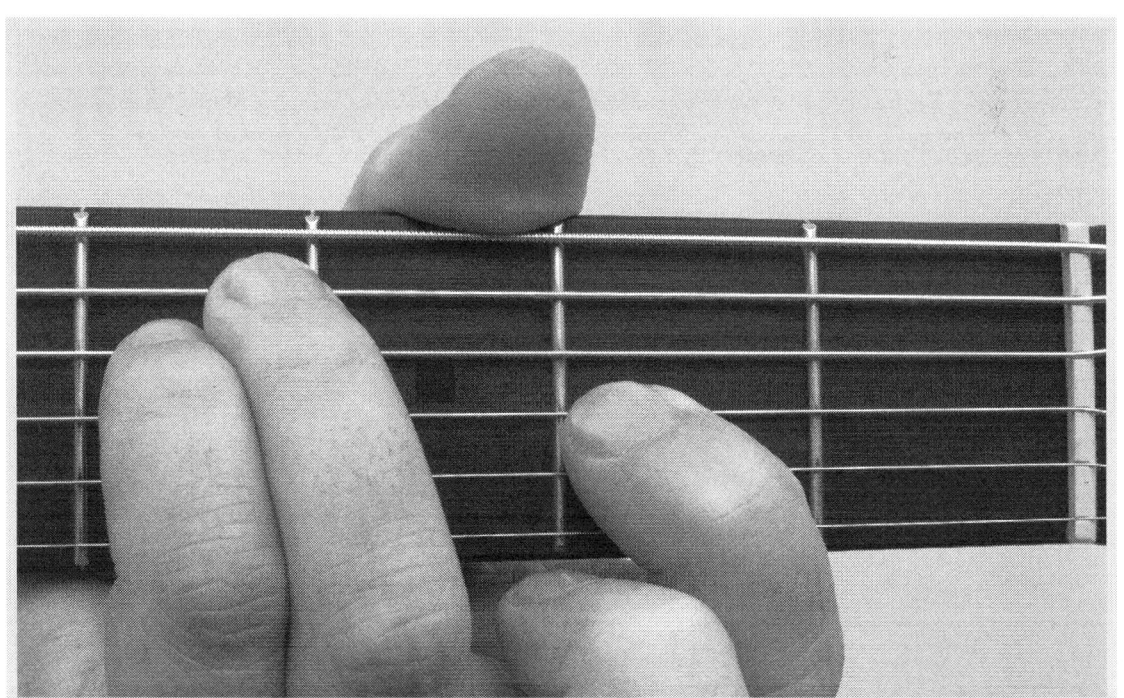

F#7

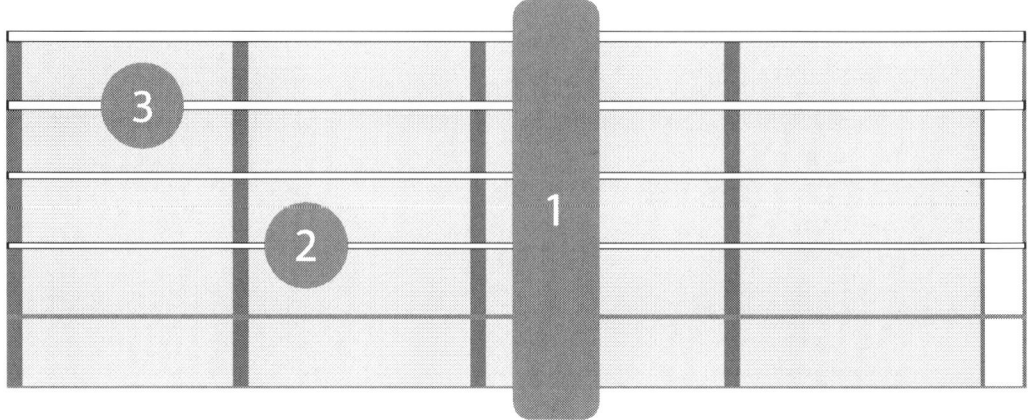

- Stretch your hand
- Thumb low and centred
- All 6 strings sound

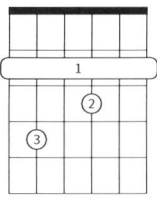

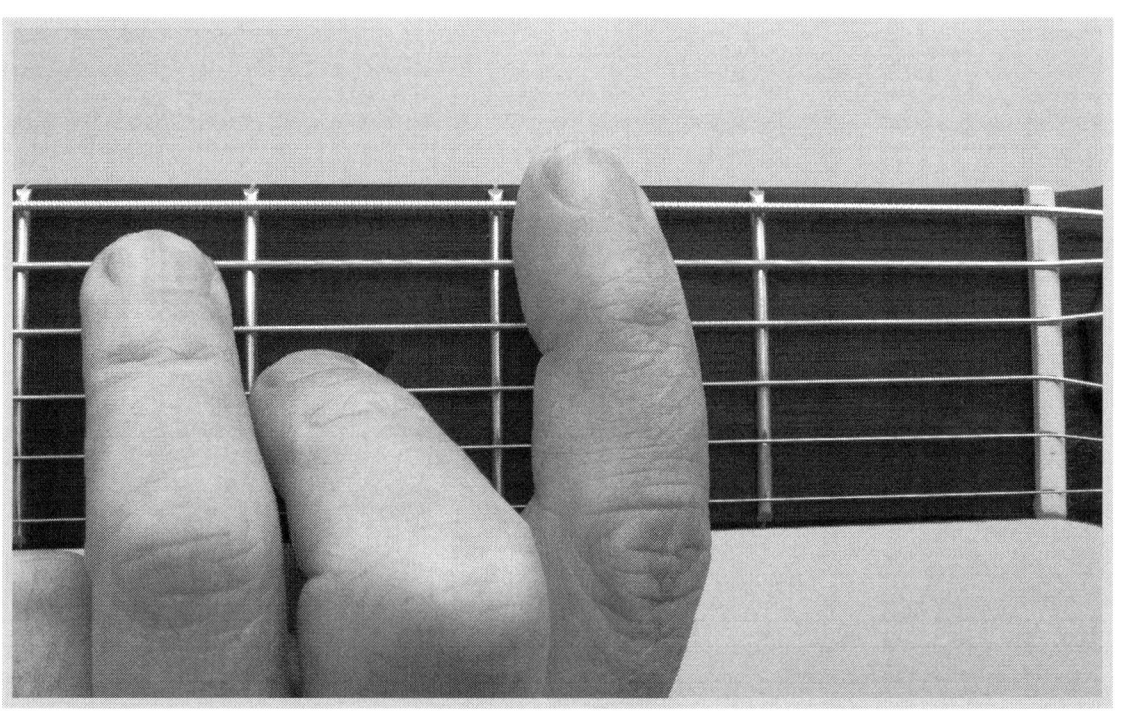

G

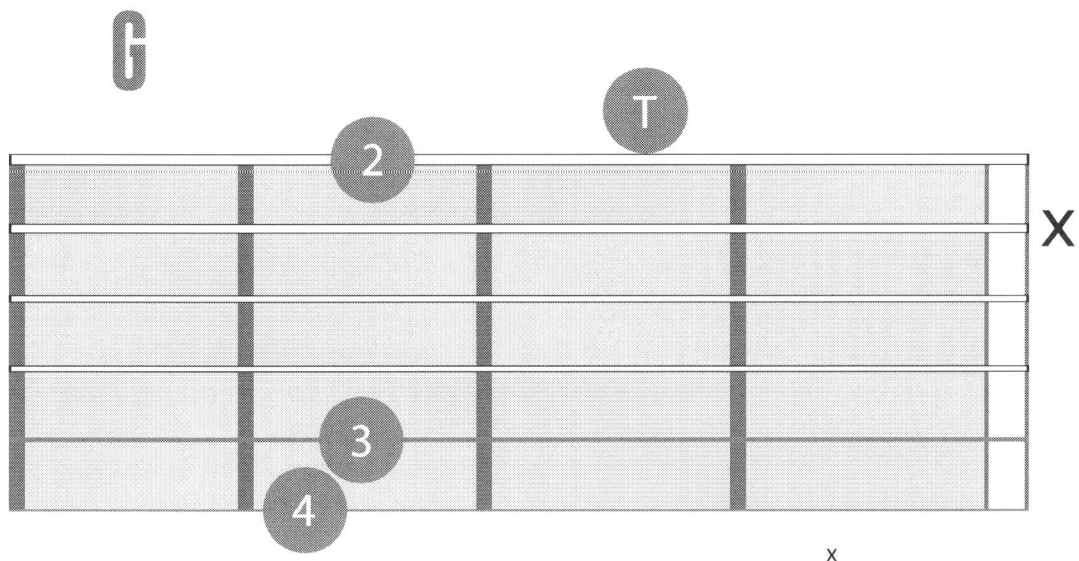

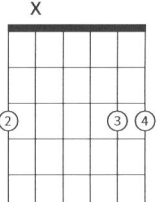

- Thumb may or may not touch 6th string
- 5th string muted by inside of 2nd finger
- Strum 6 strings - Only 5 sound

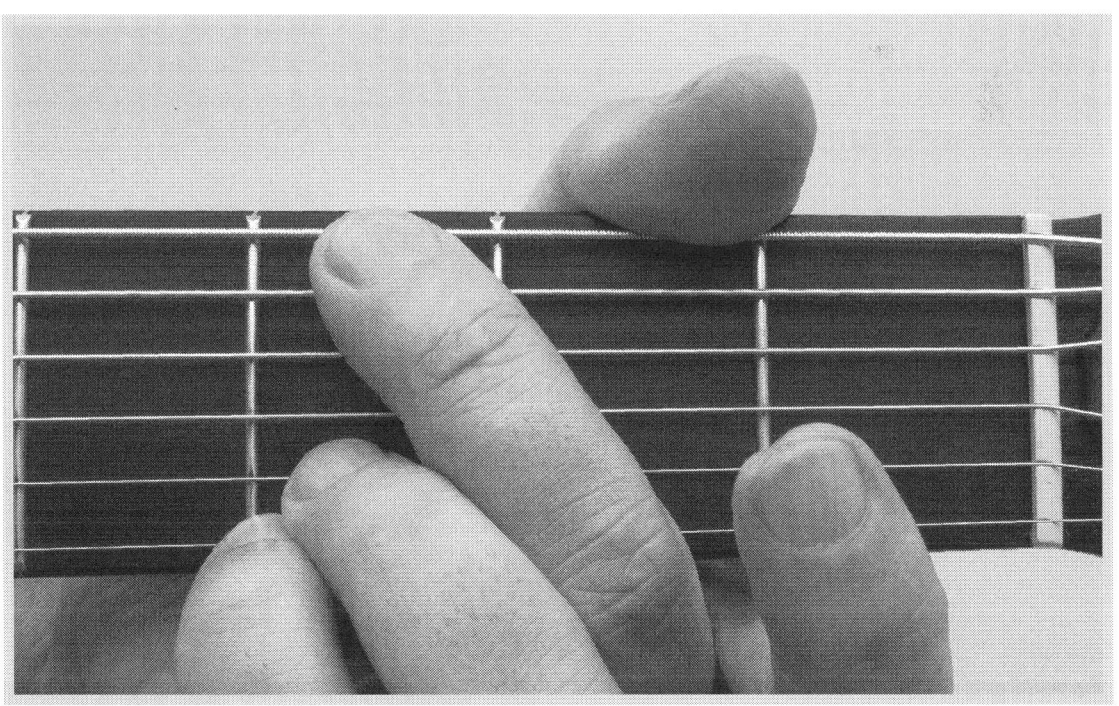

G EASIER

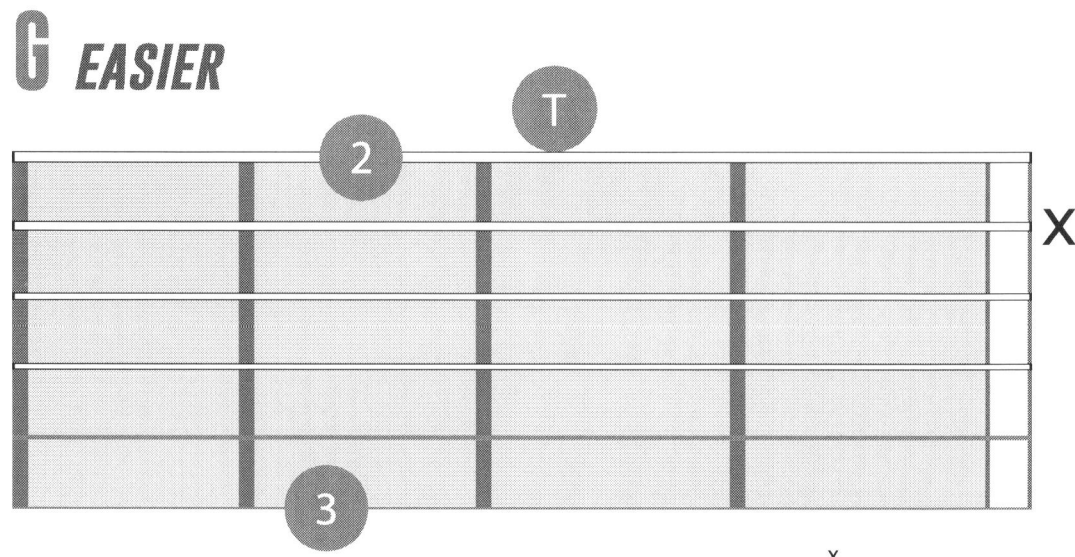

- Thumb can touch 6th string
- 5th string muted by inside of 2nd finger
- Strum 6 strings - Only 5 sound

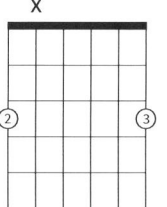

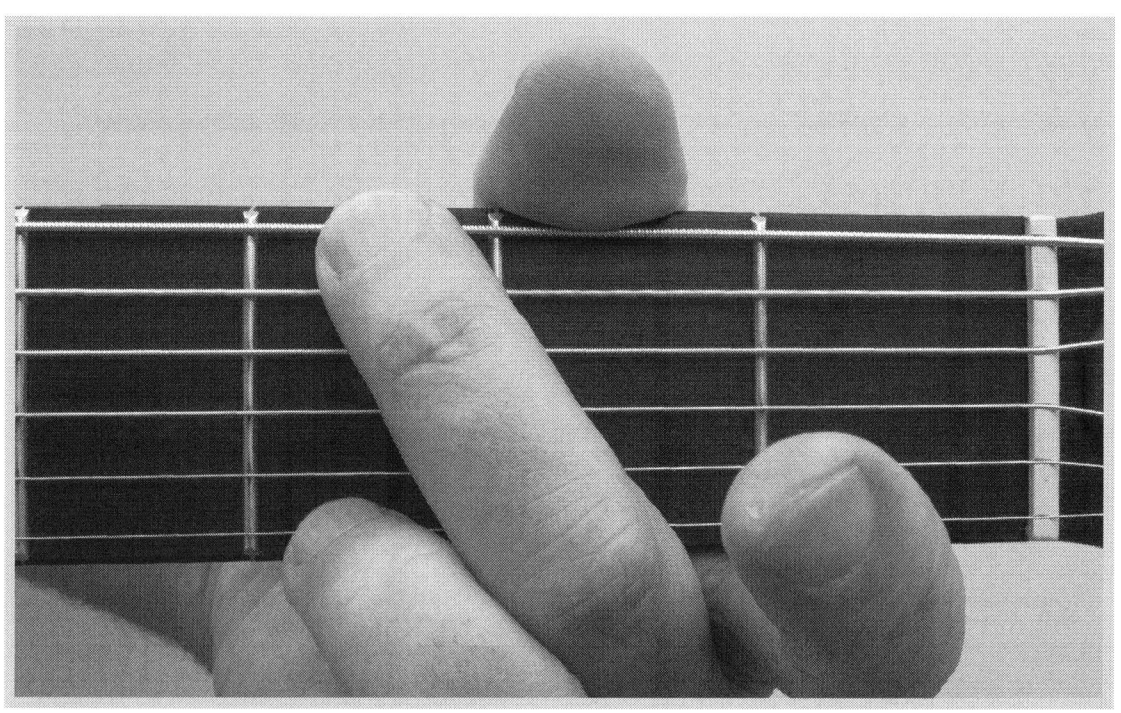

G ANOTHER WAY

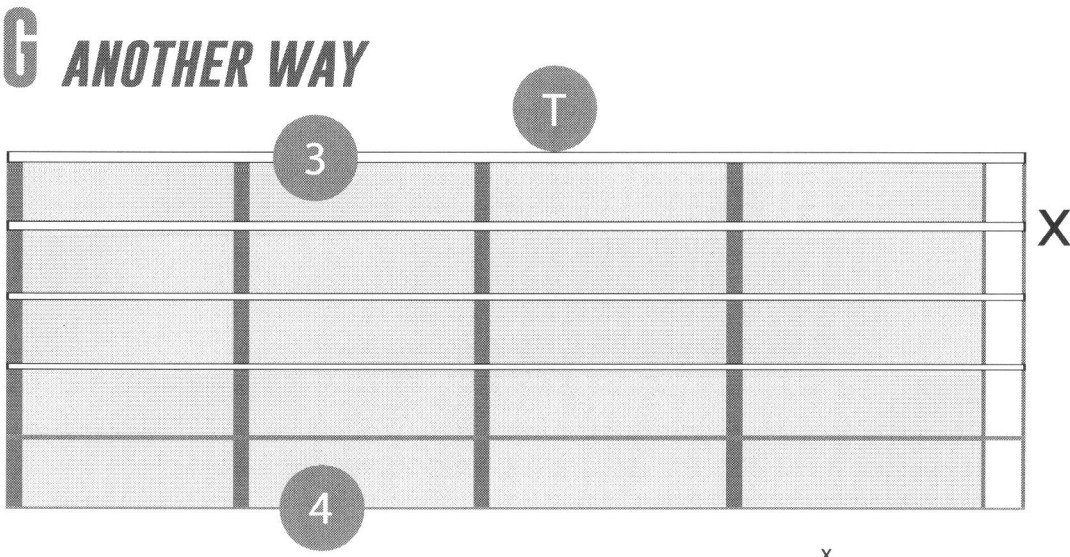

- Thumb may or may not touch 6th string
- 5th string muted by inside of 3rd finger
- Strum 6 strings - Only 5 sound

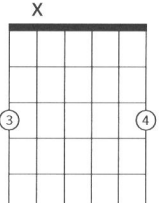

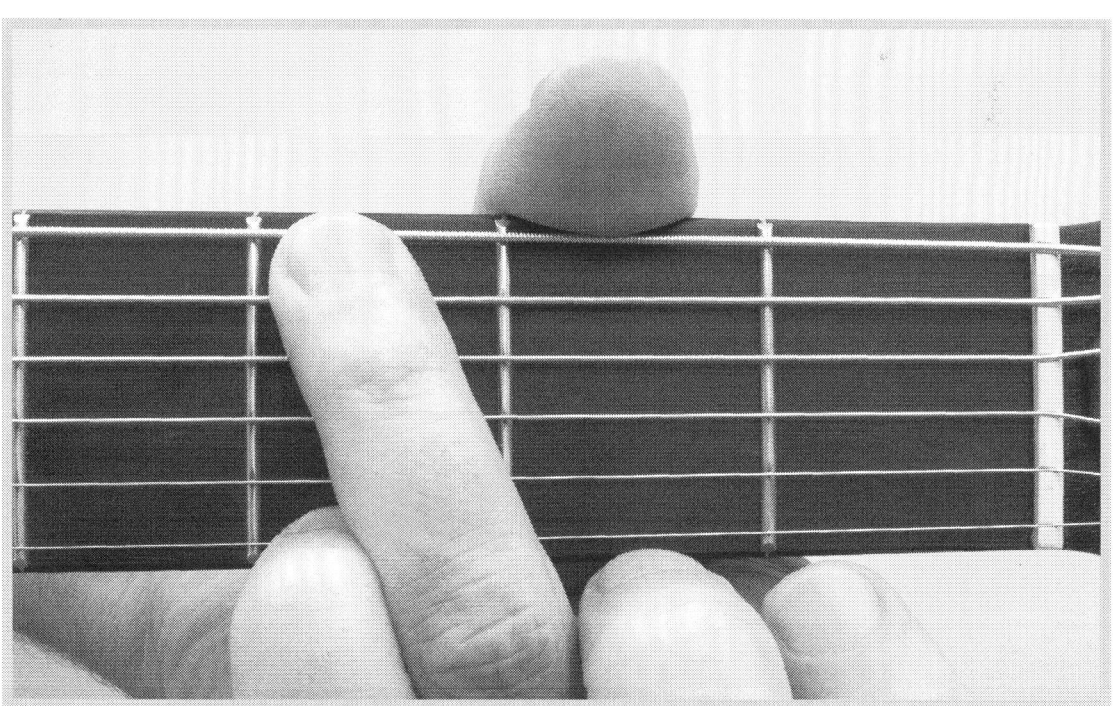

Gm

2ND FRET

- Stretch your hand
- Thumb low and centred
- All 6 strings sound

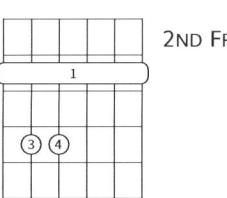

G/F#

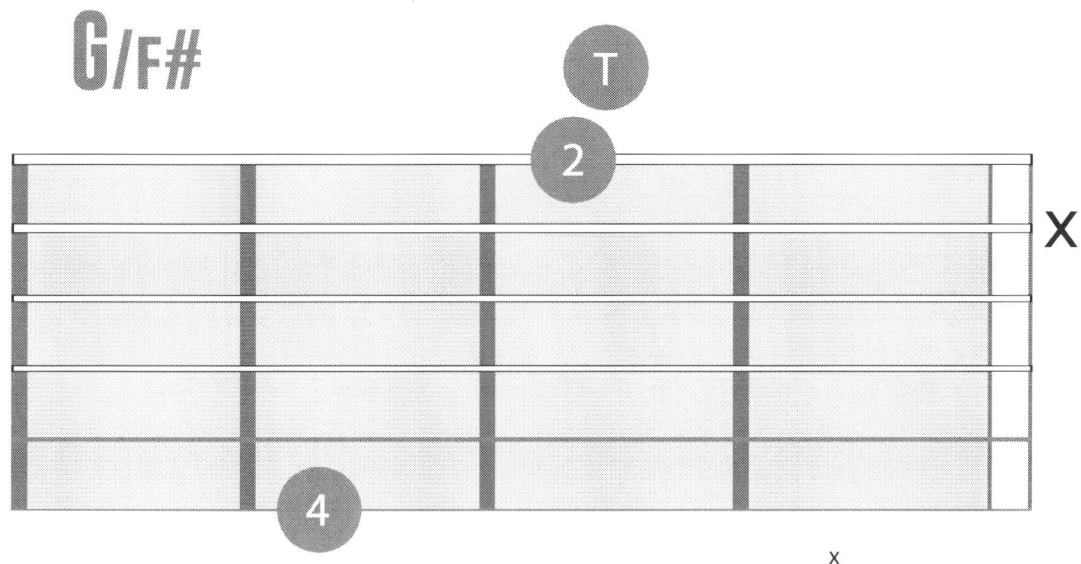

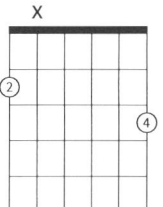

- Thumb may or may not touch 6th string
- 5th string muted by inside of 2nd finger
- Strum 6 strings - Only 5 sound

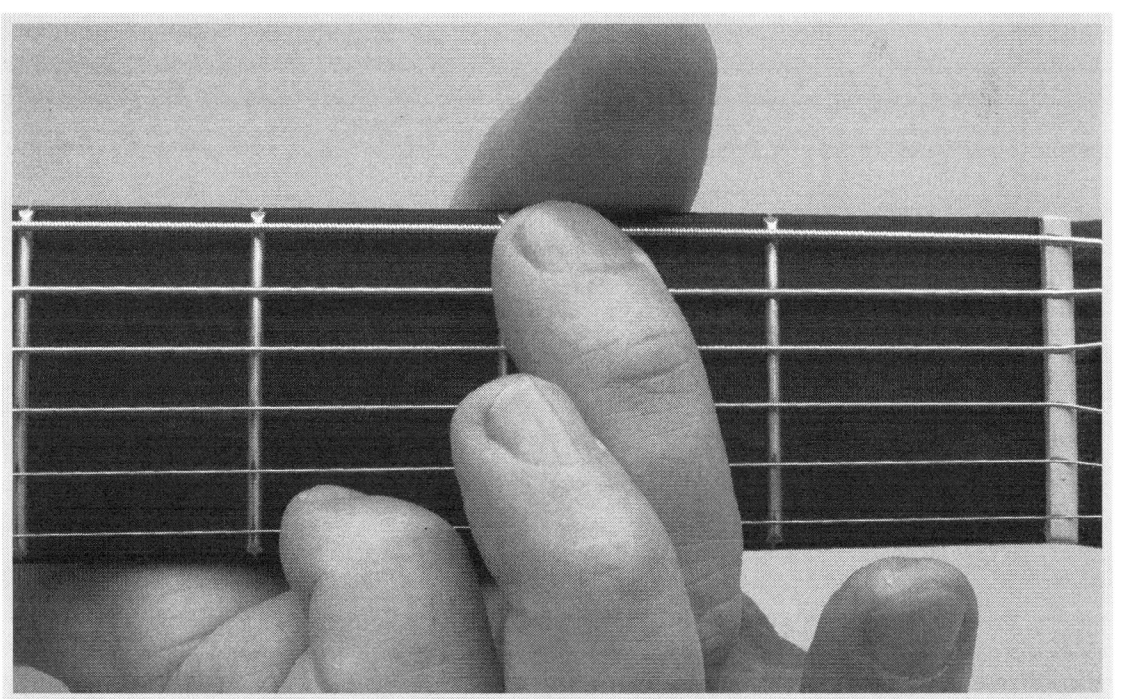

G/B

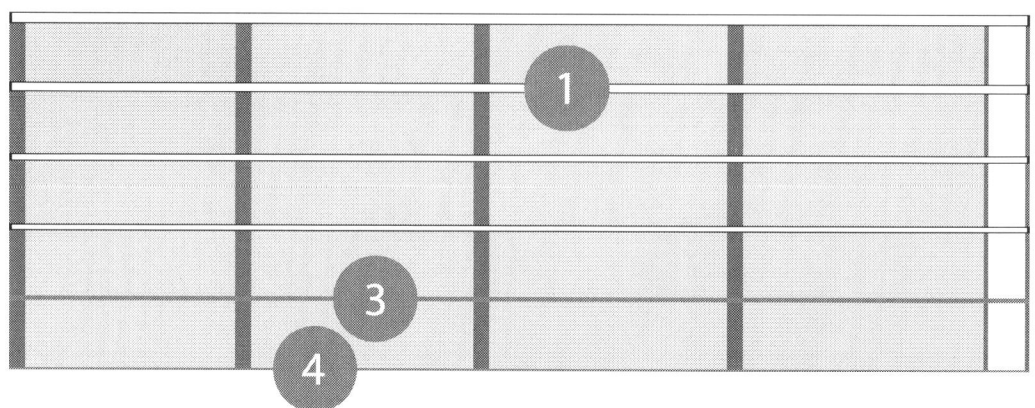

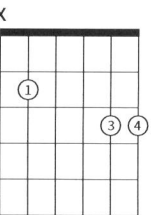

- Thumb may or may not touch 6th string
- 5th string muted by inside of 3rd finger
- Strum 6 strings - Only 5 sound

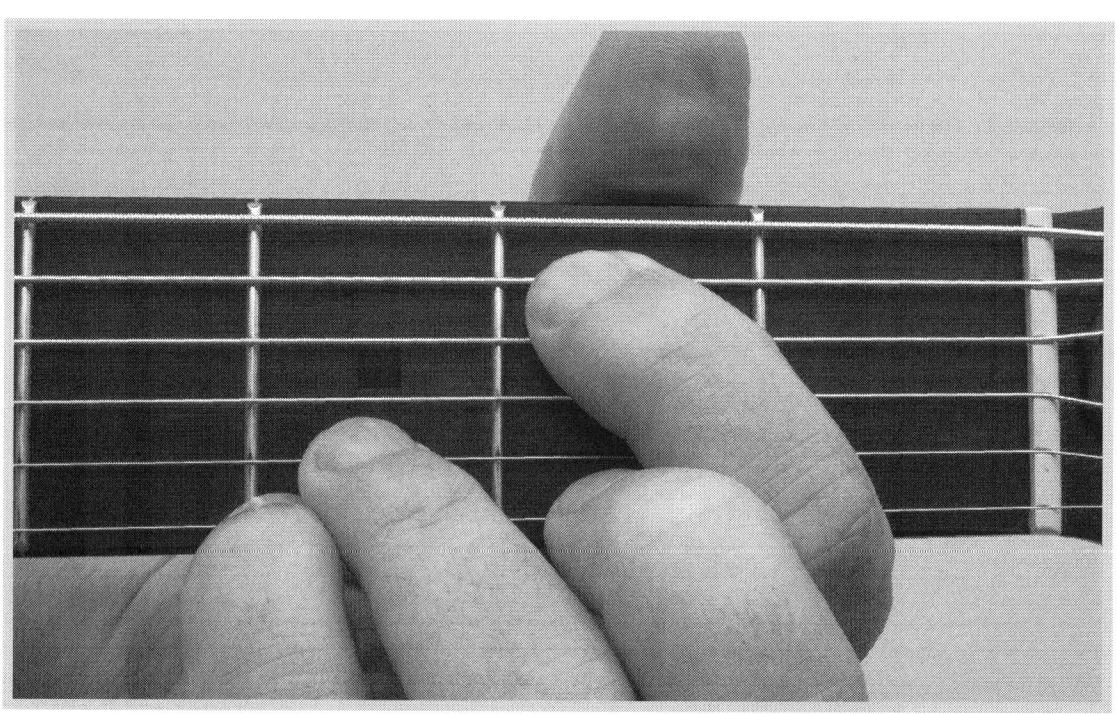

G/C

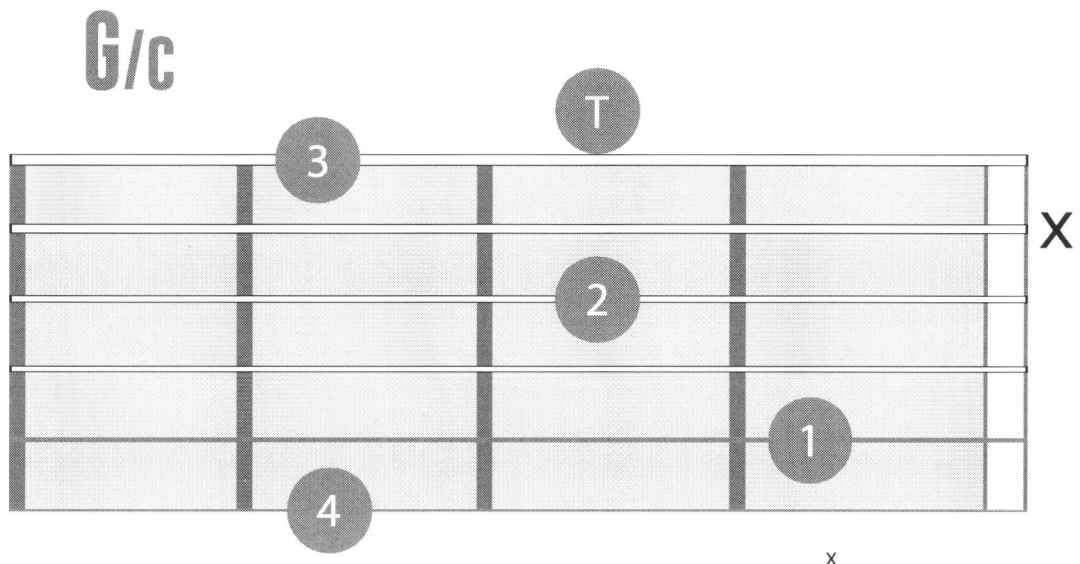

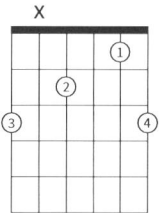

- Thumb may or may not touch 6th string
- 5th string muted by inside of 3rd finger
- Strum 6 strings - Only 5 sound

Gsus4

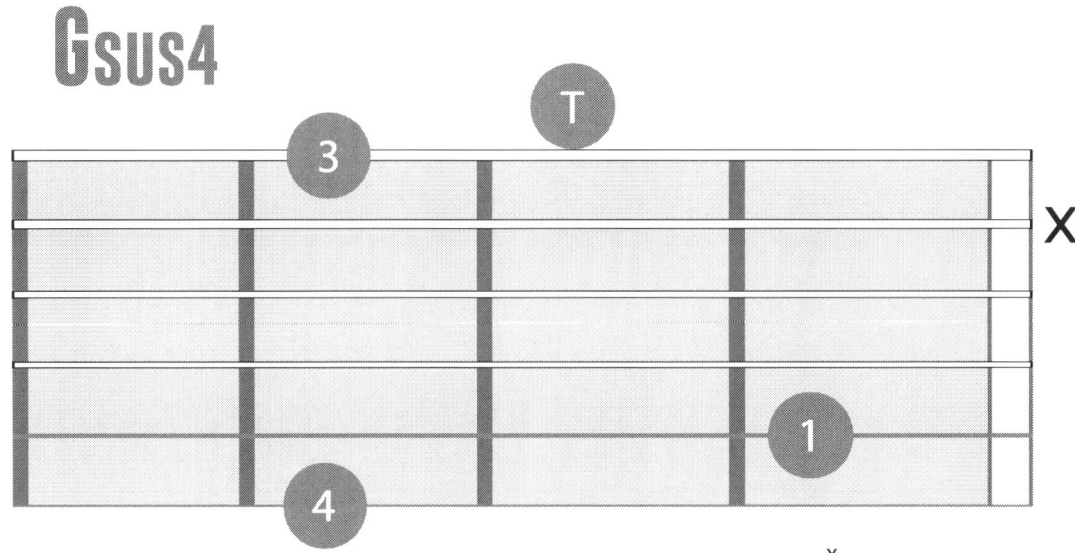

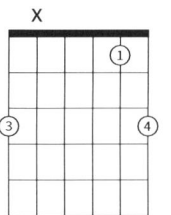

- Thumb may or may not touch 6th string
- 5th string muted by inside of 3rd finger
- Strum 6 strings - Only 5 sound

G5

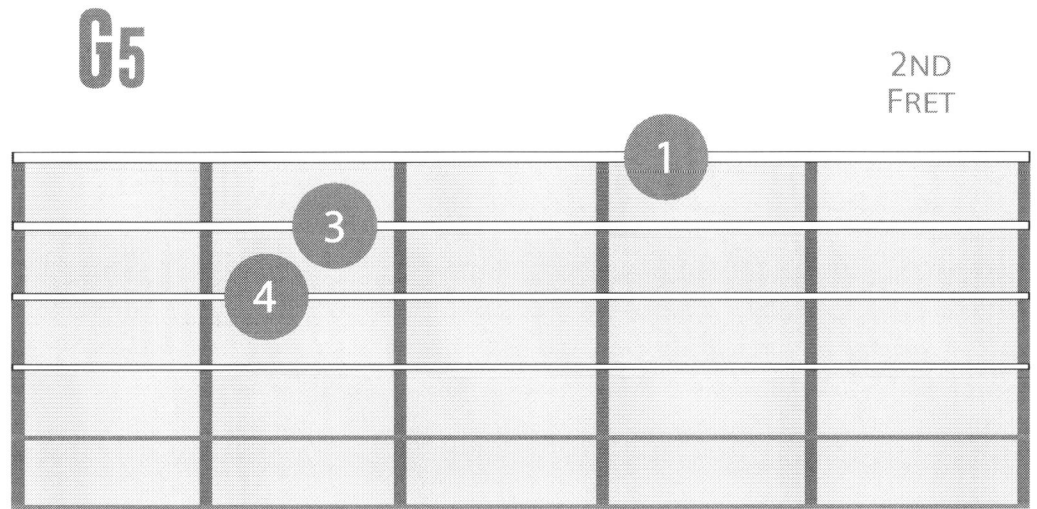

2ND FRET

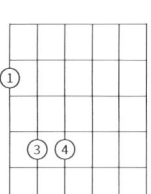

2ND FRET

- Stretch your hand
- Thumb low and centred
- Strum 6th 5th and 4th strings

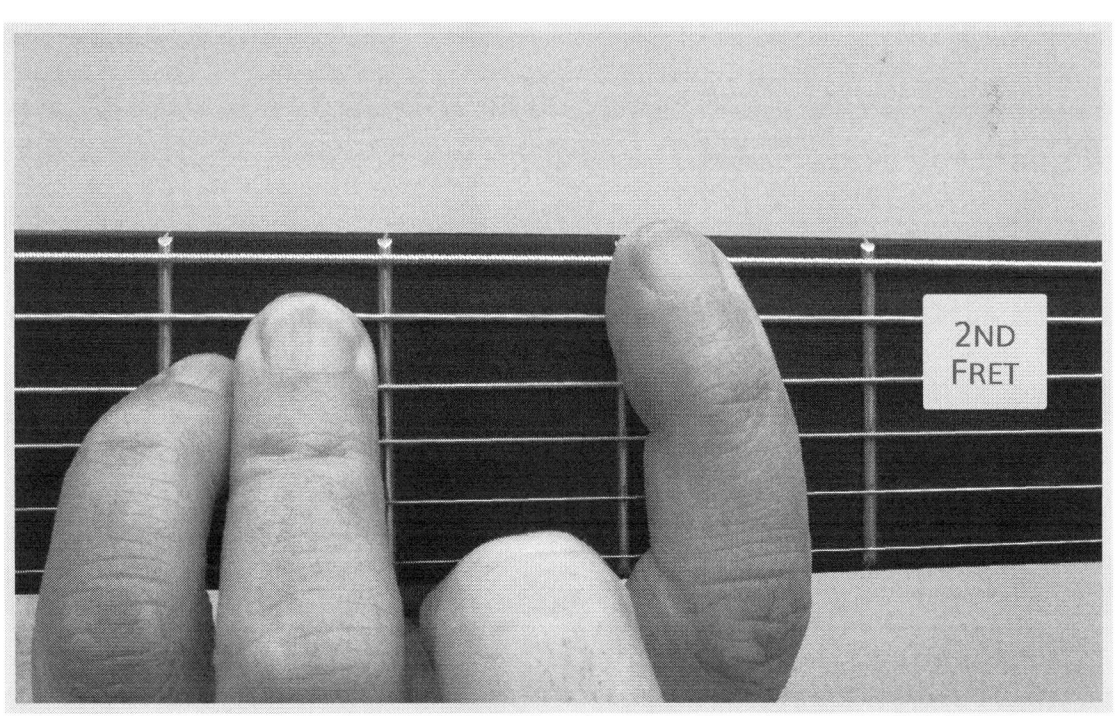

G6

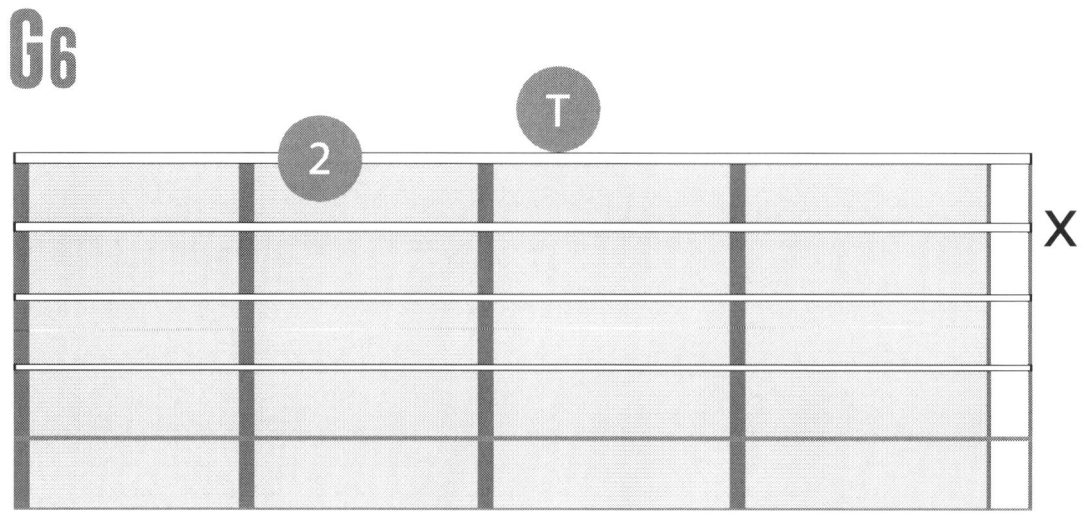

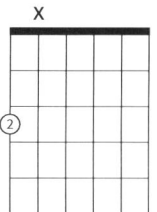

- Thumb may or may not touch 6th string
- 5th string muted by inside of 2nd finger
- Strum 6 strings - Only 5 sound

G7

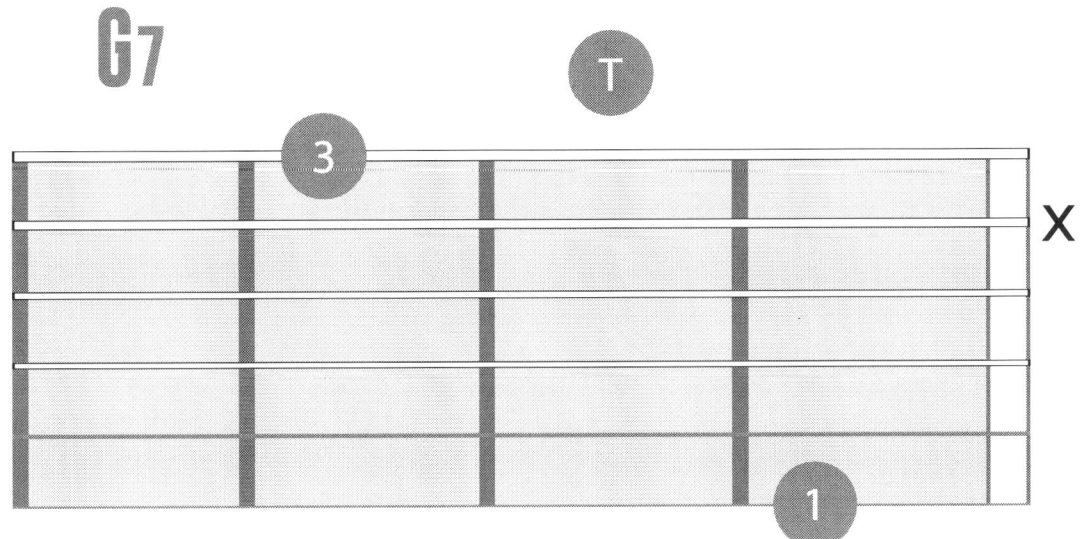

- Thumb may or may not touch 6th string
- 5th string muted by inside of 3rd finger
- Strum 6 strings - Only 5 sound

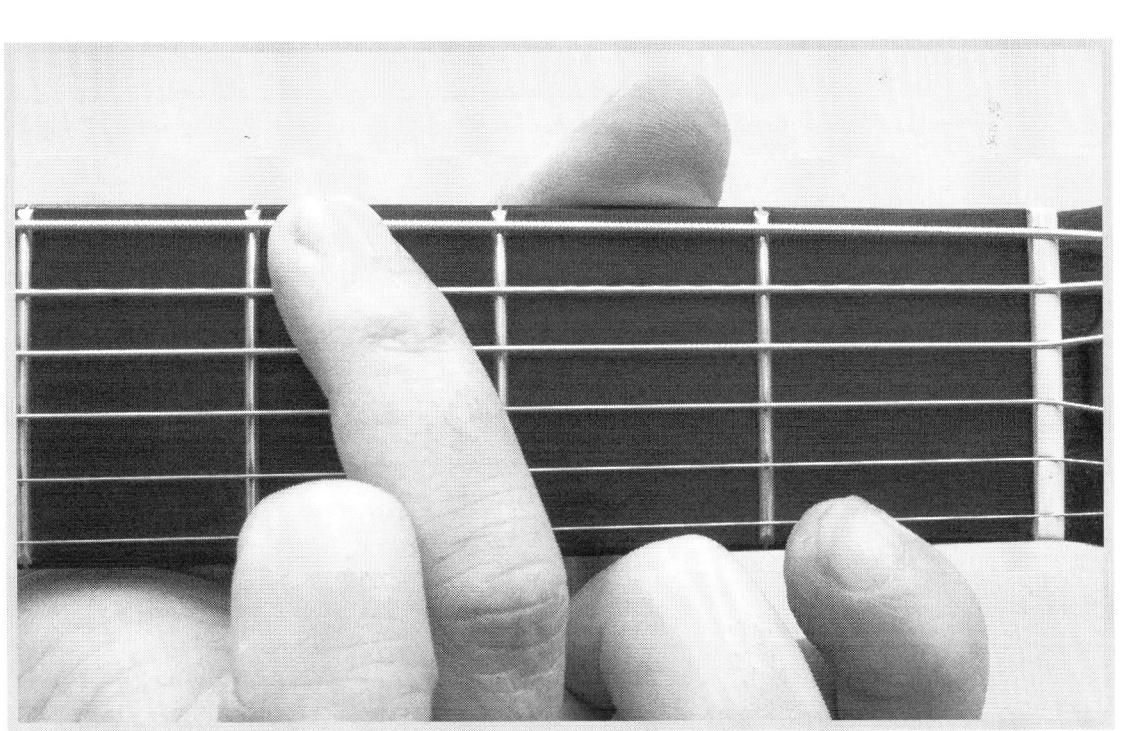

Gmaj7

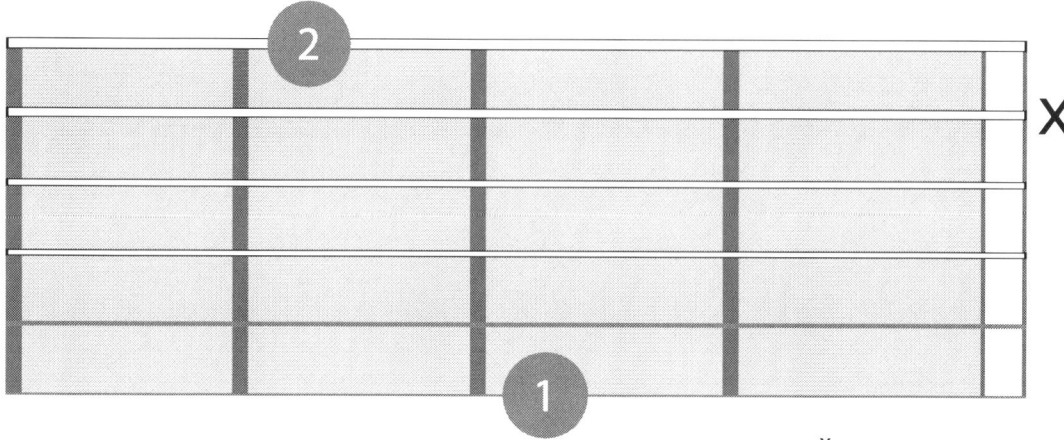

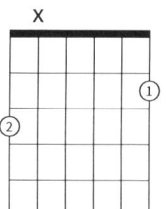

- 5th string muted by inside of 2nd finger
- Can also be played with 2nd and 3rd finger
- Strum 6 strings - Only 5 sound

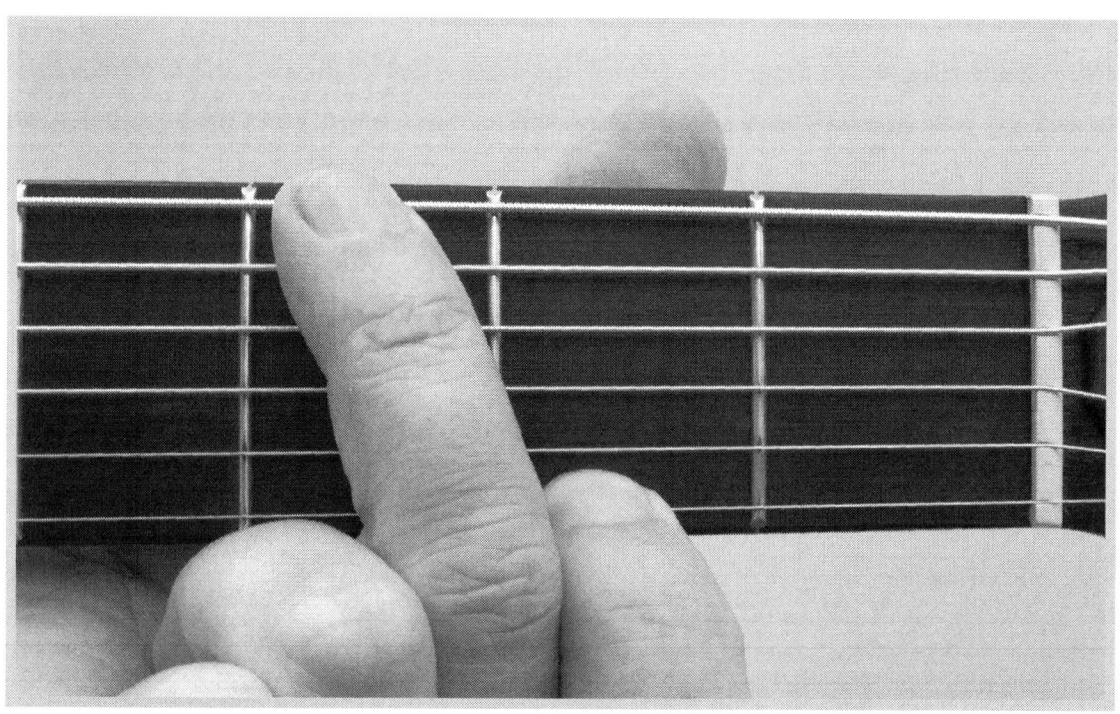

Gmaj7 *easier*

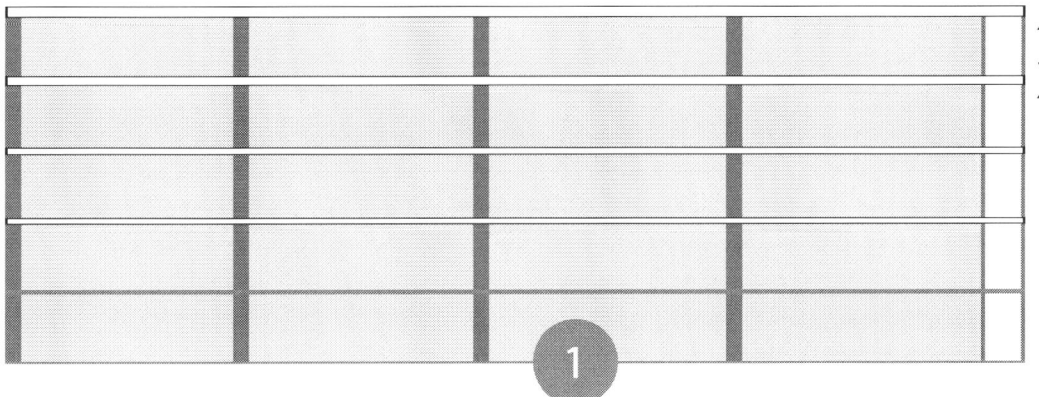

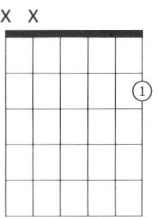

- Thumb may or may not touch 6th string
- Can also be played with 2nd finger
- Strum bottom 4 strings

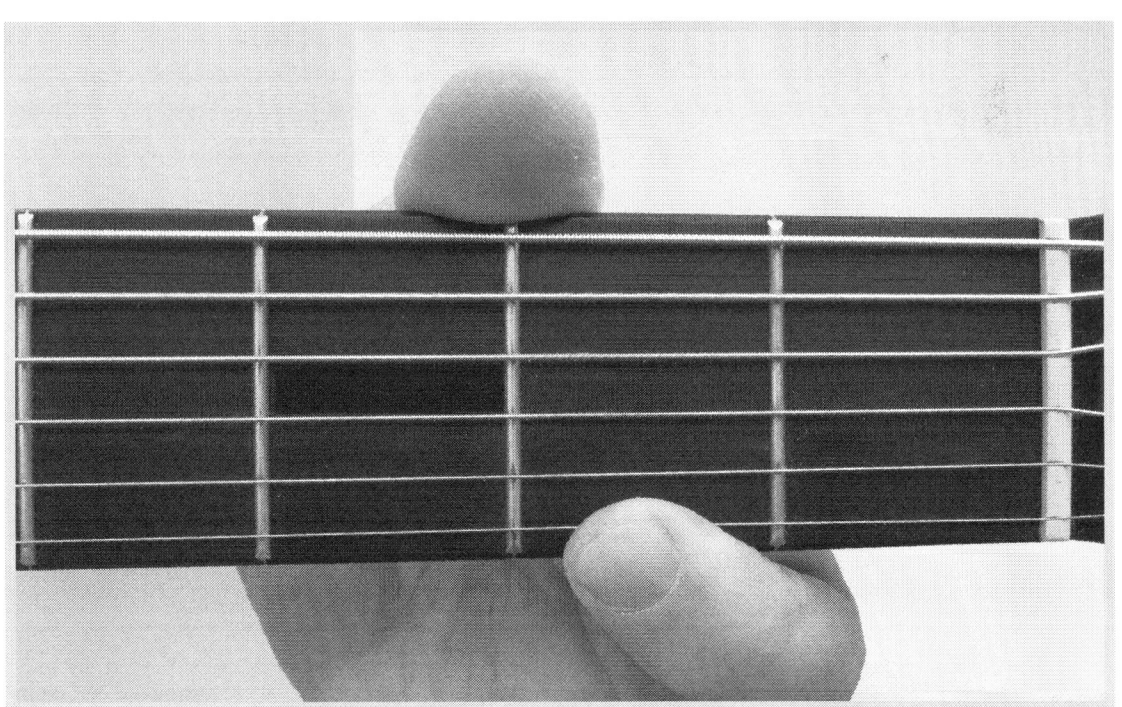

Gmaj7 ANOTHER WAY

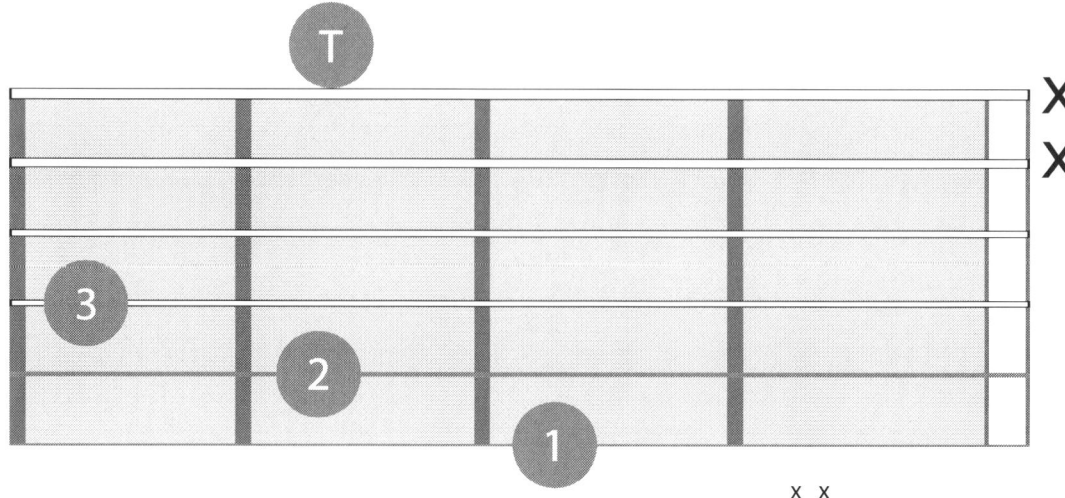

- Sometimes played instead of G
- Thumb touching 6th string
- Strum bottom 4 strings

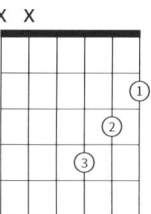

GM7

2ND FRET

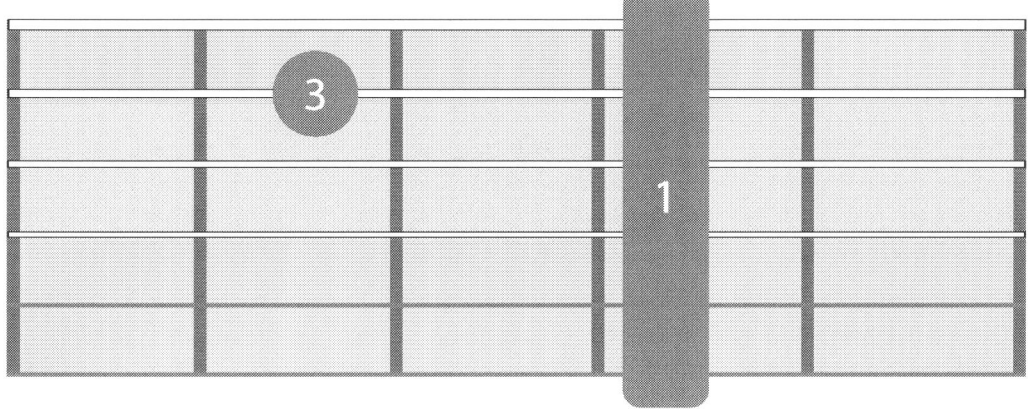

- Stretch your hand
- Thumb low and centred
- All 6 strings sound

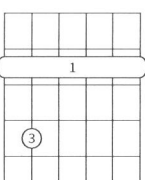

2ND FRET

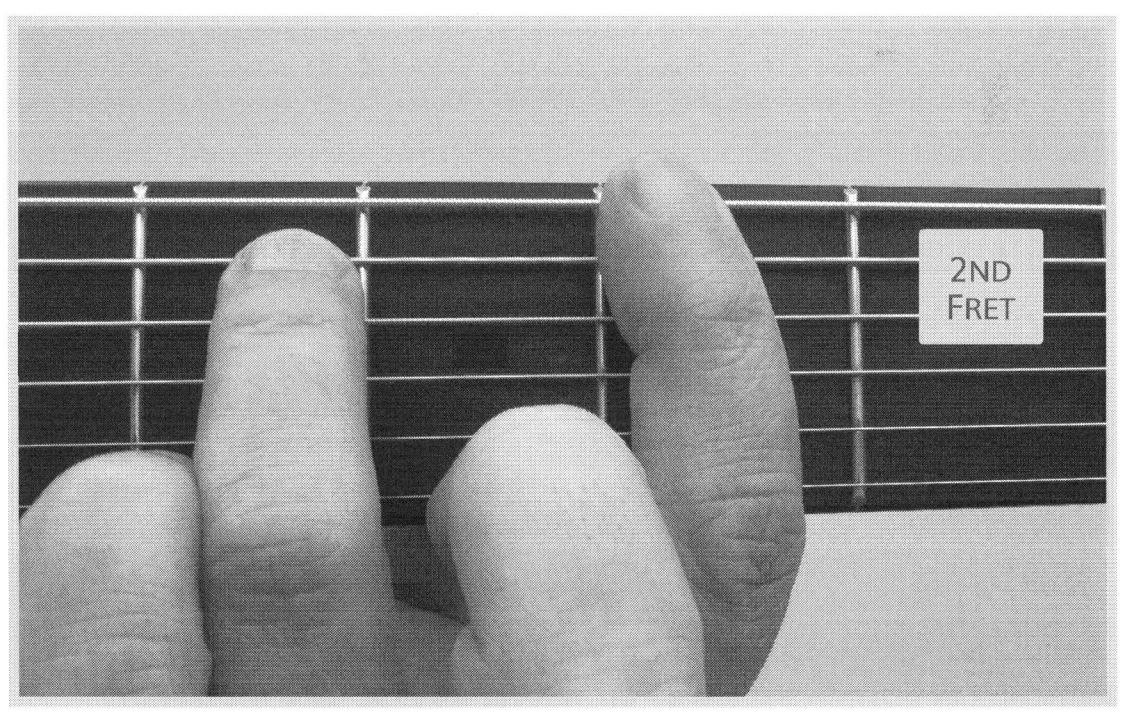

G/D7

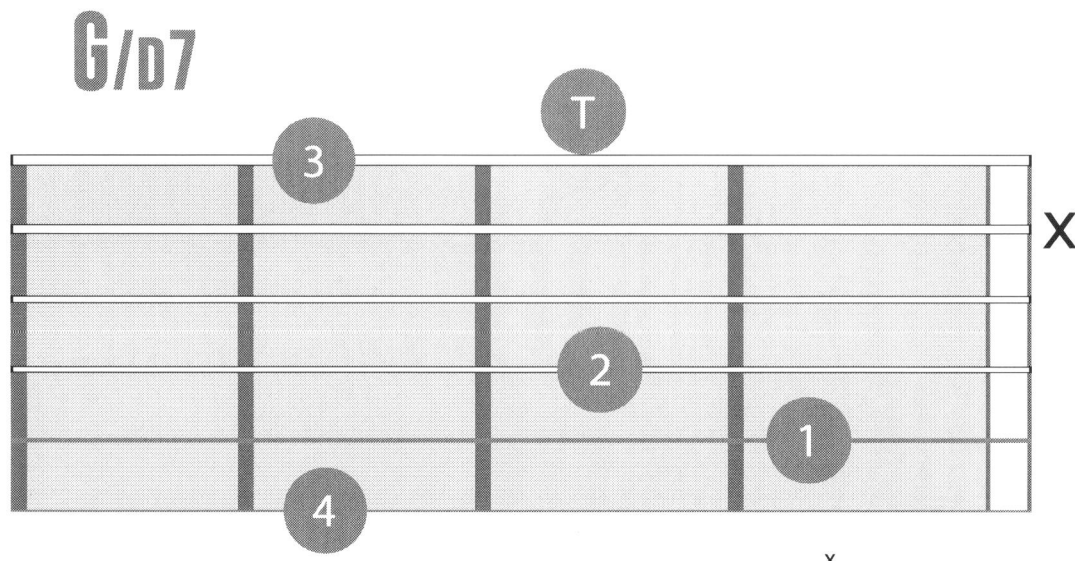

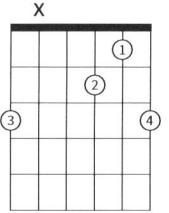

- Thumb may or may not touch 6th string
- 5th string muted by inside of 3rd finger
- Strum 6 strings - Only 5 sound

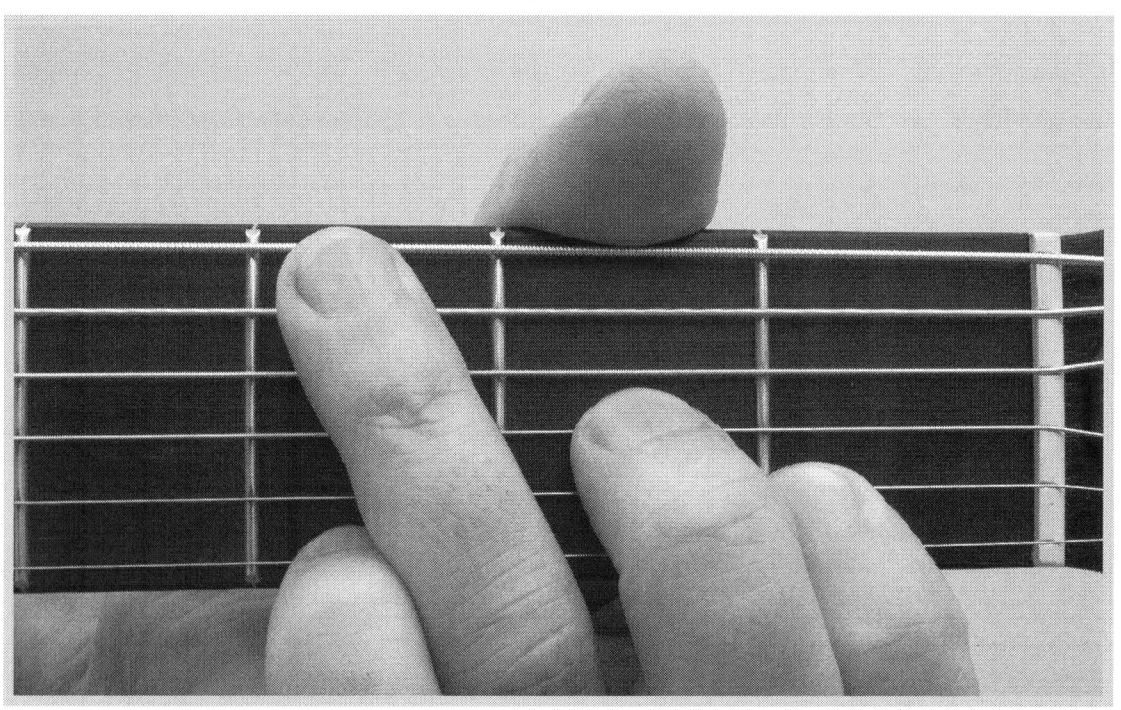

G/A

2ND FRET

- Sometimes played instead of G
- Thumb touching 6th string
- Strum 6 strings - Only 5 sound

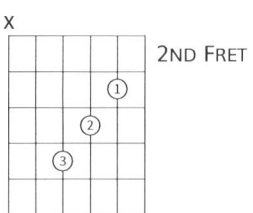

Gadd9

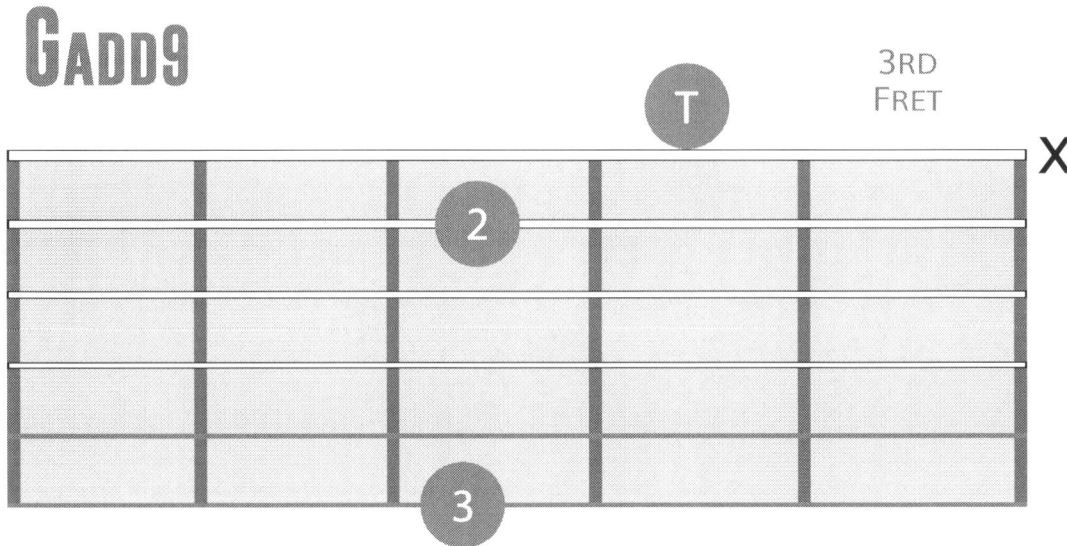

3RD FRET

- Sometimes played instead of G
- Thumb touching 6th string
- Strum bottom 4 strings only

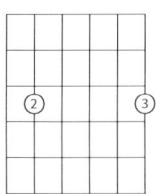

3RD FRET

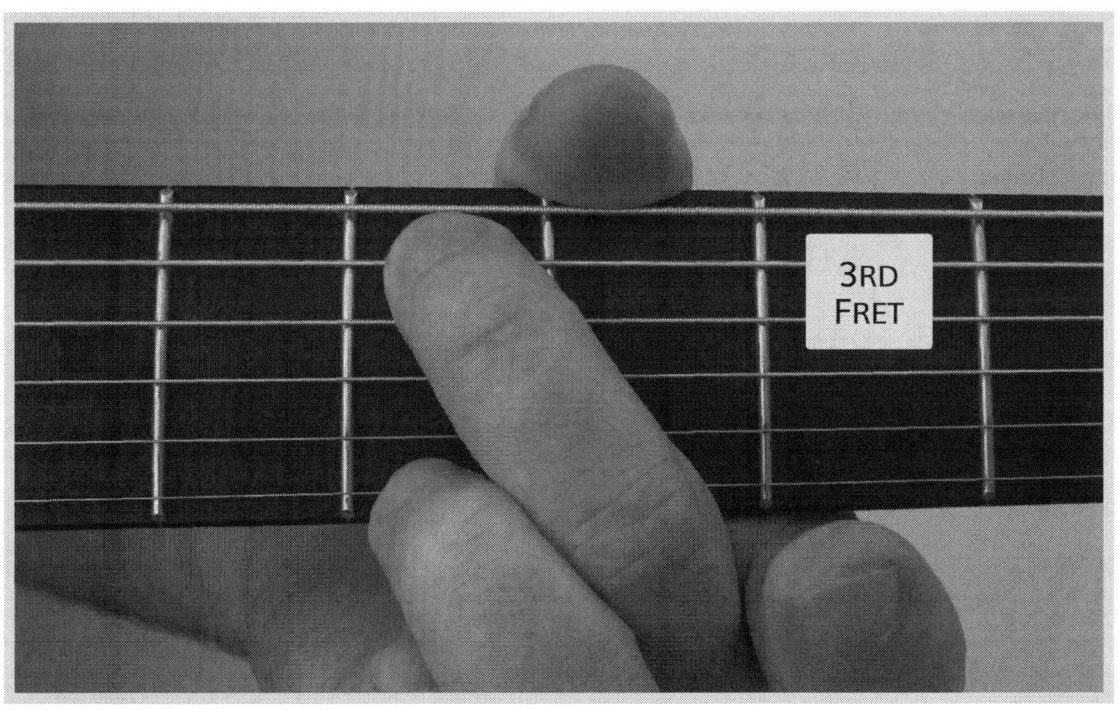

G#

3RD FRET

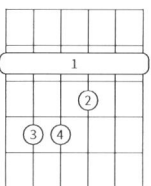

- Stretch your hand
- Thumb low and centred
- All 6 strings sound

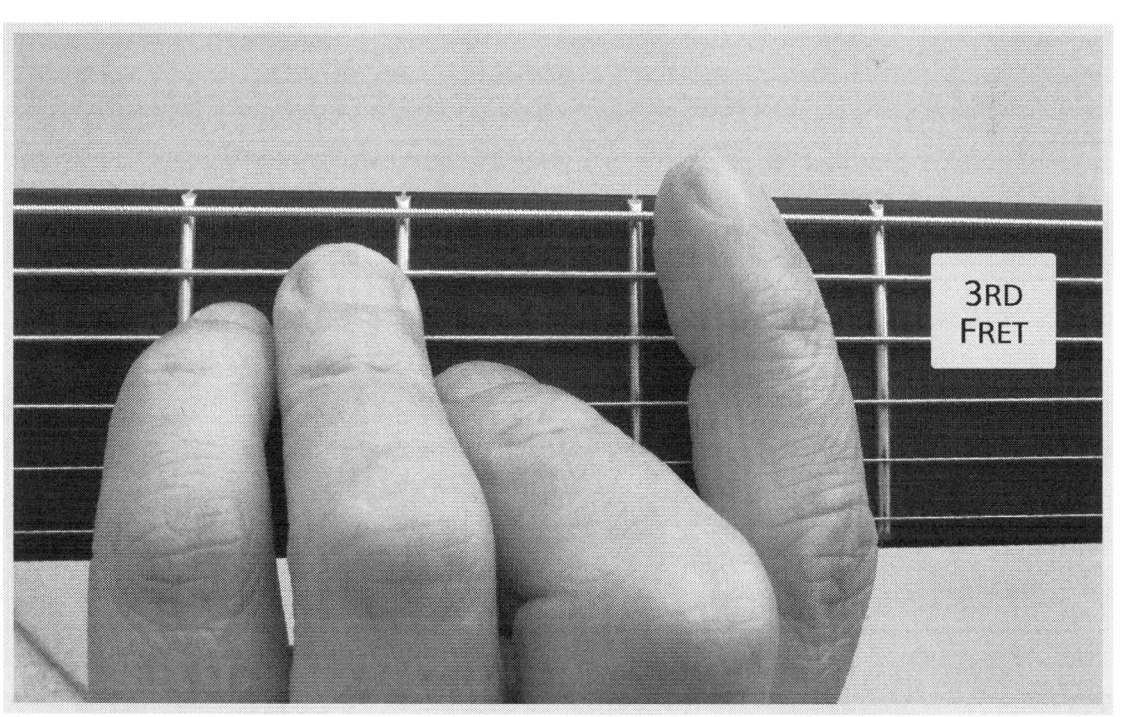

NOTES

MEET THE AUTHOR

Pauric Mather's ground breaking guitar books and lessons are truly unique. Easily the most individual and personalised you will ever find. They have helped thousands of people to learn guitar. What's even more remarkable is that you need no knowledge of music to learn from his teaching style.

As well as being an expert guitar teacher, Pauric Mather is the author of 4 #1 best sellers.

From Dublin, Ireland, he's been a professional guitarist since 1987, and has worked with many successful artists.

Pauric Mather is now the most translated guitar author in the world. His books and teaching methods are available in more than 10 languages.

Meet the author live online - And **SAVE 33%**

Just type "SAVE33" when booking at

PauricsGuitarSchool.com

Also By The Author

Printed in Great Britain
by Amazon